RENOVATING THE
Vietnamese Communist Party

The Institute of Southeast Asian Studies (ISEAS) was established as an autonomous organization in 1968. It is a regional research centre for scholars and other specialists concerned with modern Southeast Asia, particularly the many-faceted problems of stability and security, economic development, and political and social change.

The Institute is governed by a twenty-two-member Board of Trustees comprising nominees from the Singapore Government, the National University of Singapore, the various Chambers of Commerce, and professional and civic organizations. A ten-man Executive Committee oversees day-to-day operations; it is chaired by the Director, the Institute's chief academic and administrative officer.

The Indochina Unit (IU) of the Institute was formed in late 1991 to meet the increasing need for information and scholastic assessment on the fast-changing situation in Indochina in general and in Vietnam in particular. Research in the Unit is development-based, with a focus on contemporary issues of political economy. This is done by resident and visiting fellows of various nationalities, and to understand the Vietnamese perspective better, the Unit also has a regular programme whereby scholars from Vietnam are invited to do research on issues of topical interest.

RENOVATING THE
Vietnamese Communist Party

Nguyen Van Linh and
the Programme for
Organizational
Reform, 1987–91

Lewis M. Stern

ISEAS Indochina Unit
INSTITUTE OF SOUTHEAST ASIAN STUDIES

Published by
Institute of Southeast Asian Studies
Heng Mui Keng Terrace
Pasir Panjang
Singapore 0511

All rights reserved. No part of this publication may be reproduced, stored in a retrieval system, or transmitted in any form or by any means, electronic, mechanical, photocopying, recording or otherwise, without the prior permission of the Institute of Southeast Asian Studies.

© 1993 Institute of Southeast Asian Studies

The responsibility for facts and opinions expressed in this publication rests exclusively with the author and his interpretations do not necessarily reflect the views or the policy of the U.S. Department of Defense, the United States Government, the Institute of Southeast Asian Studies or its supporters.

Cataloguing-in-Publication Data

Stern, Lewis M.
  Renovating the Vietnamese Communist Party: Nguyen Van Linh and the programme for organizational reform, 1987–91.
  1. Vietnamese Communist Party—Reorganization.
  2. Vietnam—Politics and government—1975–
  3. Vietnam—Economic policy.
  4. Nguyễn Văn Linh
  I. Title.
DS559.912 S83   1993   sls93-33724

ISBN 981-3016-558 (soft cover, ISEAS, Singapore)
ISBN 981-3016-566 (hard cover, ISEAS, Singapore)
ISSN 0218-608X

For the USA and Canada, a hard cover edition (ISBN 0-312-12037-0) is published by St. Martin's Press, New York.

Typeset by The Fototype Business, Singapore
Printed in Singapore by Singapore National Printers

*Dedicated to the memory of
Professor K.S. Sandhu
Director of ISEAS, 1972–92*

Contents

Acknowledgements ix

Introduction 1

one
1987: Consolidating the Programme for Party Renovation 5

two
1988: Staying the Reformist Course 27

three
1989: Turning Back to Orthodoxies: Conservative Backlash and the Impact on Reform 55

four
1990: Economic Crisis, Organizational Failure and the Conflict over Reformist Goals 91

five
1991: Fashioning Consensus: Towards the National Party Congress 135

six
Conclusion:
Nguyen Van Linh and the "New Way of Thinking"   177

Notes   181

Note on Terminology   207

Acknowledgements

This project began as an essay for *Vietnam Commentary*, published by the Information Resource Centre of Singapore. I thank them for their encouragement. I initially developed some of the themes in this study in *Conflict and Transition in the Vietnamese Economic Reform Program*, published in 1988 by the Institute of Security and International Studies of Chulalongkorn University in Bangkok, Thailand. I gratefully acknowledge their assistance in preparing this early version of my views.

I profited from astute comments on the reforms in Vietnam by Sukhumbhand Boripatra, and Vo Nhan Tri's expert observations on Vietnam's economy. I thank William Turley for his trenchant commentary and encouragement, and Nayan Chanda for his succinct evaluation of my early drafts on Nguyen Van Linh. Jacques Bekaert, Elizabeth Becker, Robert Destatte, Bill Herod, Nguyen Manh Hung, Karl Jackson, Chau Kim Nhan, Douglas Pike, and Joseph Zasloff provided important criticism and advice, and opportunities for long discussions about Vietnam. General John W. Vessey, Jr., (ret), very kindly took me with him on several of his trips to Hanoi between October 1989 and April 1993.

I derived the energy it took to write this work from my wife, Mary, who prodded me to turn an odd-sized manuscript into a book-length study, and from my children, Eva and Anna, who thought that writing a book was a nice thing for their father to do, and volunteered many hand-drawn illustrations.

My father passed away before he could take this manuscript in hand and give it the close, discriminating examination all my work, from grade school on, received. I miss his loving assistance.

The views expressed in this publication are those of the author alone, and do not necessarily represent the positions of the Department of Defense or any part of the United States Government.

Introduction

The Vietnamese Communist Party (VNCP) has been preoccupied with renewal and reorganization for over a decade. Its regimen of self-reform has included efforts to eliminate inefficient, ineffective and corrupt cadre; recruit younger, skilled and better educated members; improve basic party chapter-level leadership and organization; and select and train a generation of party secretaries at all levels. These reform efforts have limped along since the late 1970s with an inconsistent momentum and have taken several forms, including the sustained attempts to reclassify party chapters and organized efforts to expel dead wood from the rank and file. During 1987–90, under the leadership of Nguyen Van Linh, party reform gained a new lease on life. The political consequences of economic transformation prompted the Vietnamese leadership to shape a parallel reform within the interiors of the party.

Linh's approach to party reform was unique in several respects. Linh relied less on mobilizational instruments — campaigns, exhortations, symbols — and more on bureaucratically co-ordinated programmes. Linh also utilized unique combinations of resources to attack specific party-related problems, often relying on media and selected mass organizations to propel his reformist agenda.

During 1987 and 1988 Linh fashioned a comprehensive package of party reforms that was more ambitious than the reformist goals of his predecessors. That package included efforts to empower local organizations to take on more responsibilities, parallel with the increasing economic autonomy gradually granted to enterprises. Under Linh the party also sought to introduce a more flexible style of management, rely increasingly on modern organizational skills and management techniques, and improve the training of party managers. The reforms also focused on confining the party to a more limited role as the conscience of the revolution responsible for fashioning social and political direction and maintaining the integrity of the revolutionary inheritance, while allowing responsibilities for daily governance to pass to a body of elected and appointed officials. The reforms attempted to guide the party towards quality control in operational matters and membership policy in a manner that emphasized responsiveness to direct, critical complaints against party personnel and organizations.

Under Linh, the party sought to instrument these goals through a variety of organizations, committees and local and provincial party committee meetings. Expanded sessions of provincial party committees were convened to facilitate the writing of Action Programmes intended to emphasize the pre-eminence of the economic reforms. Provincial and subordinate party organizations were empowered to orchestrate local Purification Campaigns at the branch, district and provincial party committee levels based on guidelines that governed the 1986 Criticism/Self-Criticism Campaign. Internal party and economic inspection teams were deployed at grass-root levels during the first quarter of 1987. Those teams were charged with closely monitoring and supervising the personal lives and individual morality of party members. Linh relied on visits to subordinate chapters by higher echelon party officials to supervise local party chapter self-inspection. He supported efforts by the party's secretariat to implement the revision of the party statutes put forth at the December 1986 Party Congress that shortened the length of the probationary period for candidates and allowed only minimal leeway for members found guilty of violations of the party's code of conduct. In addition, Linh sought to improve control department mechanisms at all levels by elucidating their role as ombudsmen-like structures to process the complaints and accusations triggered by his policy of opening the party to some public scrutiny.

Linh's actions emphasized the need for sharing power between members of the polity. He strongly argued that party building should properly include non-party entities: "We should not leave party-building work entirely to party committees at various levels. . . . We should overcome the tendency to separate administrative and specialized work from party work". Linh stressed the division of state and party labour in a manner intended to prohibit the party from tampering with governance. At the same time as Linh continued to seek means to broaden political participation by non-party entities and to maximize the independence of action of mass organizations, he took pains to stress the extent to which the party would remain central to the process, and would continue to exert a strategic, guiding influence. At the Sixth Congress of the Vietnamese Federation of Trade Unions in October 1988 Linh stated:

> It is true that, at present the working class and labourers are still dissatisfied with the party leadership and state management, but it is also true that they have never contended that there is any other political force that can replace the historical role of our party and state. . . [1]

Under Nguyen Van Linh, plenary sessions of the Central Committee took on increasing importance in the decision process as a forum where competing views on policies and fundamental political issues were articulated and actively discussed. In large part, this was a result of Linh's flexible, inventive and somewhat unconventional mode of operating in the context of the Vietnamese bureaucracy.

At critical junctures between National Congresses of the Vietnamese Communist Party, Central Committee plenary sessions addressed pressing strategic issues and defined policy direction for the party organization, often in highly charged environments.[2] However, the plenum had never been a highly structured format. The statutes of the VNCP disposed of the plenum in one brief, uncomplicated article which decreed that Central Committee plenary sessions are held to elect a Politburo, a Secretariat, and a General Secretary. The size of the Politburo and the Secretariat are decided by the plenary sessions. The Central Committee meets once every six months, and once every six months reports to the lower echelons (*cap duoi*) on the general situation and the work performed.[3] The meaning and impact of the plenary session have been more dependent on the operating style of the General Secretary and the chemistry of the Central Committee than on the party's formal rules.

At first, Linh used plenary sessions as a showcase for his policies and his skills as a spokesman for the new policies. He made strong speeches and took a highly visible, active role in representing his views on key issues at plenary meetings. Linh preferred a regular, predictable and more frequent schedule of plenary meetings in order to maximize his opportunities to lobby for his policies. However, by 1988 Linh was increasingly stymied by the closing of ranks of party conservatives, the glacial speed with which the party organization responded to pokes and prods intended to start the job of reshaping the organization, and the extent to which ineffective leadership, poor organizing habits and venality had saturated the core of the party. Though he was able to shift the balance of ministerial power more towards the advantage of non-Central Committee specialists, change provincial party leadership to a significant degree, and modify monopolies and regional policy cliques in at least small ways, by 1988 his ability to dominate the process of central party decision-making had slipped. In 1988 the schedule for plenary sessions reverted to the irregular calendar for meetings that was typical of Le Duan's stewardship over the VNCP. The decreased number of plenary meetings in 1988 suggested that the party required additional time to discuss sensitive issues before public statements representing consensus could be presented, and in some instances could not come to agreement on the pressing issues, all of which points to Linh's diminished ability to maintain strong control over the organization and its policy processes in the second year of his rule.

This book traces the evolution of the reforms of the party organization under Nguyen Van Linh.

one
1987: Consolidating the Programme for Party Renovation

Introduction
In 1987 the VNCP encouraged the streamlining of organizations, sought to improve the personnel assignment process, and to devise more orderly training programmes for party officials. The party sustained province-wide campaigns to reclassify party chapters, recruit new membership, and expel unreformable elements.[4] The party also focused on teaching party chapters to run orderly meetings, and clarifying the roles and responsibilities of party officers.[5] Finally, the party continued efforts to create regular training cycles for committee and chapter secretaries, the party's workhorses.[6]

Critical Introspection: Writing the Party's Report Card
From late January to late February, expanded sessions of the provincial party committees convened to examine the documents of the Sixth Party Congress and to write Action Programmes to familiarize the provinces with the Three Economic Programmes — food production, consumer goods production, and production for export.[7] Beginning in early February, on the occasion of the anniversary of

the founding of the party, the provincial and subordinate party organizations instituted local Purification Campaigns, systematic efforts to re-evaluate party members, and upgrade recruits.[8] The original schedules for the local campaigns, as defined in a VNCP Directive, stipulated that provincial party committees would receive district party accounts of a drive to improve party militancy and membership quality by 20 January. In addition, by that date the provincial party committees were to have received reports from district and provincial officers who had participated in the Meetings With The Masses in January. Those sessions were essentially town meetings at branch and district party committee levels that disseminated the results of the Sixth National Party Congress and discussed the criticisms levelled against the documents and resolutions drafted for the Congress. Proposed amendments to the Political and the Economic Reports to the Sixth Congress, and the Action Plans for putting that critical spirit to work, were to be recorded by participating cadre and dispatched to the provincial party committee standing bodies.

The party had committed itself to another period of critical introspection, on the model of the Criticism/Self-Criticism Campaigns of late 1986. It empowered the organizational machinery established for that purpose to process local complaints against party chapters and local government machinery. The result was a careful weeding-out of the membership's dead wood, the initiation of a sustained recruitment drive, and a concentrated attack on inefficiency and corruption in the newly-elected party committees.[9]

Provinces deployed internal and economic inspection teams to grass-root party chapters for a period of "membership surveillance", an exercise involving the close monitoring and supervision of the personal lives, individual morality, and the organizational capabilities of party cadres and members.[10] Local party chapters became more programmatic about enforcing self-inspection and undertaking chapter level evaluations. Higher echelon party officials paid visits to subordinate chapters to take the measure of chapter officials and the abilities of chapter cadre to deliver services and perform party functions.[11] In the February campaign, for example, ward committees in Ho Chi Minh City established standing committees for investigation, which were responsible for hearing cases involving alleged malfeasance of ward and basic level party members, and making decisions regarding reprimanding, warning, suspending or expelling from the party members judged to be culpable by those committees.[12]

Provincial party committees carefully reviewed reports on party personnel management and enforced the programme of intensified disciplinary work during the 3 February–19 May Political Activity Drive (*Phong Trao Hoat Dong Chinh Tri*). The drive emphasized educational and training tasks, and publicized the new Party Statutes.[13] The Secretariat issued a circular on the implementation of the Party Statutes that focused the attention of party committee echelons and basic party organizations on the amendments to and revisions of the statutes decided upon by the December 1986 Congress. Those revisions implemented a shorter probationary period for candidate members, reducing the 18-month term to 12 months; eliminated the disciplinary measure of returning a member accused of wrongdoing to probationary status; retained only four modes of punishment ranging from reprimand to expulsion; and allowed only a minimum of leeway for members found guilty of violations of the party's code of conduct.[14]

The party also focused on reinvigorating its control department mechanisms at all levels (*cac to chuc dang uy ban kiem tra cac cap*). A late May conference of the Central Committee's Central Control Committee in Hanoi, over which Politburo member Do Muoi presided, stressed the requirement of control work at the basic party organization level. The conference focused on the investigative roles of control departments as the keeper of party discipline, the arbiter of conflicts over the application of party statutes, and the point of control for local party financial matters.[15] Local control departments and mass organizations were urged to co-operate in these efforts. The formula describing co-operation between party and non-party entities was something of a compromise version of the "experimental" role for non-party instruments in the process of party reform that was prescribed during the June 1985 eighth plenary session. The compromise clearly sought to remove the intrusions into hallowed internal party business by non-party organizations appointed to monitor the party.[16]

The programme of reform for the party's apparatus at all levels provided for the broadening of control committee duties.[17] The programme paid continued attention to the question of refining the division of labour between the party and the state in precise terms, in a way that would rule out duplication of effort and preserve the party's guiding role and the state's administrative responsibilities.[18] The programme also focused on revising party membership criteria in a manner acknowledging the need for modern managerial abilities and technical economic and administrative knowledge,[19] and devising a more systematic and regularized public dissemination of the results of disciplinary measures taken at party meetings.[20]

While these were by no means radical departures from standard operating procedures, they were an indication that the long-standing Vietnamese practice of creating more organizations to solve organizational weaknesses, and the habit of multiplying levels of bureaucracy to cope with institutional breakdowns, had been at least partially replaced by real intentions to refrain from burdening the system with yet another complex of decision-making centres. The party, however, remained a rigidly formal conglomeration of rules and relationships whose activities and authority were conditioned by the mechanisms invented to ensure Democratic Centralism. Control work, inspection procedures, and some of the other organizational reforms were essentially a way to cut across those systems, without departing from the system itself.

Sharing Power:
The Calculus of Party-State Relations

During the early months of 1987 newspapers and radio broadcasts focused on the party's failures, stressed the need to eject corrupt and ineffectual members who had managed to linger in the party's ranks, and highlighted the new calculus of party-state relations. In February, Ho Chi Minh City Party Committee Chairman Vo Tran Chi spoke of the limited "consultative" role that the party should play in the enterprise of economic and managerial reform.[21]

Considerable media attention was devoted to the separation of party and state power through the middle of the year. In articles published in *Saigon Giai Phong* in advance of the National Assembly elections, a good deal of attention was paid to the importance of minimizing the role of the party in determining election lists, and the need to eliminate the set percentage of party members who must be elected to representative positions.[22] During March and early April, newspaper articles focused on the weaknesses of an incestuous candidate selection process whereby local organizations had relinquished control over the selection of applicants to party entities at higher levels, resulting in consistent election of low quality cadre.[23] Additionally, the media discussed the need to allow individuals without party credentials to attain leadership roles in government. The party was taken to task in newspaper articles for making party membership the determining criterion for all positions of authority, which effectively precluded the candidacy of qualified people outside of the party with unique technical backgrounds, experience and specialized training.[24]

By mid-year the party was bracing itself for a full-scale internal war against organizational inadequacies and personnel weaknesses. In late June, the media began to refer in elliptical terms to a cleansing campaign that the Politburo was poised to initiate, with the aim of purifying party ranks, stiffening the party organization, and strengthening the machinery of governance.[25] The campaign had its origins in late May meetings of chapter level party organizations, orchestrated by provincial party organizations, which were convened to consider the methods of membership candidacy, evaluation and selection.[26] Provincial party organizations and subordinate party entities reviewed the cases of party card holders who had declined in quality, neglected their duties, and freely violated party and state laws. By late July, party organizations had begun to dispense judgments, reassign cadres, dismiss unredeemable characters, and dismantle party organizations that were too thoroughly penetrated by inefficient members and ineffective leadership to warrant recycling. Ha Bac reported the expulsion of members of party organizations subordinate to the provincial establishment, and the prosecution and subsequent dismissal of members of the provincial foreign trade organization.[27] Cuu Long dissolved a subordinate party committee attached to a corporation.[28] Kien Giang

Province reviewed cases involving 2,290 members, and took undisclosed action against 184 members, including five party organization chiefs and deputies.[29] In an August interview, Nguyen Van Linh noted the party's plans to run a massive review of membership by the end of the year.[30]

The Second Plenum, April 1987: Setting Bottom Lines

The VNCP's second plenary session for 1987, from 1–9 April, provided General Secretary Nguyen Van Linh with the opportunity to demonstrate the strength of his convictions, reiterate the urgency of the issues, and argue in support of his special approach to remedial economic policies.[31] Linh spoke strongly on the need to address weaknesses in the area of pricing, finance, banking and wage, budget, and goods circulation policies. The General Secretary addressed the pressing problems caused by inflation through reductions of state expenditure, especially on capital construction projects; control of price increases on consumer items and essential supplies for production; and concerted efforts to confine the negative impact of inflation on state employees, workers and members of the armed forces.

Linh emphasized the need to set the party's sights on manageable and achievable undertakings. He spoke of efforts to untangle the country's most immediately consequential problems by the end of 1987 as a "first step", deferring major systemic reforms until after the urgent issues underlying the "current chaotic situation" were addressed. Linh reaffirmed the basic reform programme, forbidding reversions to the habit of "bureaucratic centralism" and the practices of state subsidies to enterprises. He also set an outside limit on the extent of the reforms, describing the plunge toward an unbridled contract economy as similarly anathema.

In his opening speech to the plenum, Linh outlined the several fundamental questions that were to occupy the attention of the policy-makers for the near-term future. To Linh, the central debate was over the role of the party and government in an economy consisting of increasingly autonomous components and sectors. A second issue was the process of economic planning, including the conflict over the balance between organized markets and "spontaneously developed markets", and the need for a more orderly division of labour between the central authorities and sectors on strategic and tactical economic decisions. Finally, Linh noted the party's focus on the debate over the choice between taking the means of production (the sum total of economic relationships that constitute the system of economic life) or the process of productivity (the more mechanical application of energy and input to produce an item) as the economic starting point. In his opening and closing speeches at the plenary session, Linh noted the prominence that this issue received in the months leading up to the Central Committee session, and the extent to which the issue was a major sticking point during the proceedings of the plenum itself.

Linh's speeches and the plenary session communiqué demonstrated that though the need for reform was a widely accepted premise, the direction and intent of the economic reform package defined during 1984 and 1985 continued to be the subject of a Politburo level debate. The party continued to debate its role and organizational capabilities in the context of a complex and changing economic structure, and the efficacy of granting autonomy to economic production units. The party had not reached agreement on the means of balancing increasing local decision-making power in economic affairs with the maintenance of a centrally-run and state-controlled market. Finally, the party continued to disagree on the new patterns of authority for existing political instruments, new practices of management and power-sharing, and new instruments to run new economic forms born of the regime's flexibility on the rules governing joint state-private businesses and independent enterprises.

Finally, Linh suggested that though slow and ponderous, the system had begun to demonstrate an ability to heal itself. The party had empowered new and specialized components to undertake sensitive tasks in the context of the reformist process. The party had invigorated moribund or hitherto low level, little-known or clandestine organizations within the party's executive structure, and charged those elements with new mandates in support of the reforms. The party had also encouraged working styles for those party organizations that were less capricious and more easily monitored, including basic habits of discussing and communicating decisions to lower levels through the "transmission belt" connecting higher echelons to their wards.

The plenum, as evidenced by the Central Committee communiqué, was ultimately little more than an organized attempt to equivocate on hard questions over the role of free markets, the conditions for granting enterprises full managerial responsibility for profits and losses, the reduction of mandatory planning, and the increasing scope of "guidance planning" and market regulation. Linh, however, demonstrated his ability to speak firmly, to take on the tough issues in straightforward language, and to challenge and chide the Central Committee to take controversial steps along the reformist road.

Post-Plenary Developments

In the aftermath of the second plenary meeting, the regime sought to devise the enabling legislation to implement Linh's specific programmes, and to define the operative economic units and market forms that had been authorized by the party.

Among the central instruments for propelling the reforms were the pilot projects, islands of experimentation empowered to stay one or two steps ahead of the programme.[32] The regime was to keep its bargain by stabilizing contractual norms and readjusting taxation; allowing certain market forces to prevail, for example in enterprise purchases of raw materials; and authorizing the inventive use of banking resources, business revenues, and capital depreciation funds, among other commitments.[33] In return, the pilot projects were to feel their way along, attempting solutions to economic quandaries with newly available tools.

There was not much order or energy behind the organization and management of such pilot projects. The most inventive uses of the new rules of socialist economics seemed, from journalistic accounts, to have been little more than local enterprises that forcefully and cleverly organized marketing efforts based on astute readings of consumer demands and opportunities presented by local economic disarray.[34]

Before the flirtation with market forms could proceed too far, the regime became embroiled in a slight backlash of second thoughts that had simmered from the period prior to the Second Plenum. Strongly stated articles in the party's daily newspaper spoke of the need to recall the importance of state control over new forms of business, including private enterprise.[35] Vigorous jabs at the reforms, phrased as reminders to submit non-socialist economic components to the "guidance" of the socialist economy, appeared in the press from the days immediately following the Second Plenum through July.[36]

Throughout, the regime continued to criticize party and state mechanisms. Some provincial party committees and municipalities established specialized groups directly subordinate to the standing committee of the party organization, which facilitated the investigation of cadre corruption.[37] The party emphasized a more global co-ordination of ministerial level control and inspection work.[38] Following the National Assembly elections in July, the regime focused attention on the weaknesses of people's councils and sought to (1) synchronize the work of "specialized agencies" of local inspection and control with the existing judicial apparatus, (2) upgrade the status of people's councils and committees, and (3) turn disorderly local government into systematic administration.[39]

The Vietnamese, however, seemed to have reached the limits of reformist possibilities between June and July. Merchants began to note the constraints on their maneuverability. The media began to highlight lapses in the system, including failures to register private businesses, fragmented supply distribution, and ineffectively co-ordinated plans. The government began to point out significant revenue losses and its dissatisfaction with the pace of the implementation of new economic laws.[40]

Consolidating the Reform Programme: The Third Plenum, August 1987

The third plenary session of the VNCP Central Committee, which ran from 20–28 August, provided an opportunity for the leadership to collect their thoughts and consider alternatives. Earlier signs had suggested that while the Second Plenum had addressed policy questions in areas of pricing, finance, banking, wages, budget and goods circulation, the Third Plenum was to focus all its energies on nailing down the character and details of the new economic management mechanism.[41] The sum and substance of the Third Plenum, however, was less fixed on the business of defining the new economic mechanisms than on the cumulative effects of the reforms and the need for a consolidation of gains prior to the next step of the programme.

The plenary communiqué emphasized the impact of renovated planning practices, including a reduction of centrally articulated norms and other regulatory pronouncements. The communiqué called for an "intensification" of the role of the party leadership in the renovation of the state's role in economic management, and restated the need to establish a "clear" definition of the "limits" of the decision-making power of primary economic installations. The plenum endorsed the cessation of "managerial control" of production and business by administrative agencies, and supported attempts to confine state economic management to decision-making areas having less to do with the allocation of materials and delivery of product, and more to do with overall strategic planning.

General Secretary Linh's speech to the session was a frank catalogue of the areas of disagreement over the reforms. There seems to have been disagreement as to whether the starting point for the reorganization of management practices was to be the grass-root level, or the state management mechanism itself. Linh, who saw these two alternatives as being "organically related", recommended that the changes be undertaken in the local economic units and the state economic structure simultaneously. He argued against those taking the view that the grass-root level mechanisms should be the first subjects of the management experiments, leaving the state mechanisms intact and untouched. Linh viewed those levels as the "starting point for renovating economic management at the higher state level instead of the other way around", suggesting that he rejected using the central government's apparatus as the test case while allowing local units to function without modification. Linh's point was that the version of the reforms which saw change proceeding in two stages negated the integrity of the system, cutting natural links and violating relationships that themselves suggested the need for a tandem approach. He noted that substantial disagreement surrounded the issue, and encouraged continued discussion but was firm about maintaining a centralized structure and agenda for the reform programme, and full control over the local manifestations of the programme.

Another point of contention was the definition of the first stage of the programme. One view was that Politburo Draft Resolution Number 306 on economic autonomy should focus on grass-root level state-run economic units (industrial and agricultural) and collective economic units (agricultural, artisan, and handicraft industries), *in addition to* individual private enterprises, joint state-private enterprises, and family-run enterprises. The basis for this viewpoint was that the urgency of the economic issues required a more global plan, encompassing all the incarnations of local economic structures, if only because of the need to rapidly establish a "management mechanism" for economic units in agriculture in support of the primary programme of grain and food production.

A second view was that the Draft Resolution need not, at the outset, address the problems of the entire panoply of "models of grass-root economic units" cited in Resolution Number 306. This viewpoint was based on the assumption that the larger menu of target units risked trivializing the reform plans by requiring massive and general aims rather than more tailored changes. In this instance, Linh accorded legitimacy to the argument that speed was essential, but added another angle to the difference of views by taking the position that the core issue was not the pressing nature of the problems to be addressed, but the time required to prepare comprehensive reforms to address all forms of grass-root economic structures.

Linh, then, accepted the necessity of a global approach to reforms that would address "all models" of economic enterprise, but he placed emphasis on a slow and careful planning stage, encouraging deliberate but measured speed in the programme rather than headlong progress. Linh noted that the third plenary session would focus on grass-root level units and state-run industry, since several years of experimentation with business methods and management practices had provided a good starting point, along with the preparatory work addressing those economic forms accomplished in the course of drafting the Politburo resolution on economic autonomy. Importantly, Linh allowed slightly more than a year to fiddle with alternative structures enroute to establishing the basic forms of decision making and management for those categories of economic enterprise.[42]

Linh also challenged those who argued that there was a need to establish a basic set of regulations for the new managerial devices. He rejected the need for strict guidelines for the reform of the management mechanisms, and supported an approach to reforms that allowed local variations in form and substance, considerable room for interpretation at the local and sectoral economic decision centres, and minimum central interference in the daily business of at least the individual and private capitalist economies. In his speech to the plenum, Linh stated that,

> Grasping the general absolutely requires a generalization of the specific through research. Otherwise, the general could very easily become a premise that has little concrete effect on practical guidance.[43]

Official recognition of the private and individual economies had authorized a host of unknown forces which would act on the overall economic structure in unanticipated ways. Linh acknowledged that autonomy would take different forms in the state-run economy, and that the private and individual economies already presumed the existence of a certain amount of autonomous decision-making power. He acknowledged that the consequences of authorized private and individual enterprise remained unexplored, that the regime had little knowledge of the likely impact of those sectors on the overall economic structure, and that the country was at present ill-equipped to test propositions regarding those variables. Linh stated that at this critical juncture the regime had put itself in the position of having to integrate new organizational entities, of which it had only the most basic understanding, into an unstable economic system,

> If what we want is to deal with general issues more fully, more deeply, and in a manner closer to [the] reality of economic development, to provide concrete guidance for the building of management

models for various economic forms, I do not think we can do it at this time because we have not yet accumulated sufficient experience, as well as a theoretical basis.[44]

Finally, Linh acknowledged the system's severe internal imbalances, the ill-defined economic strategy, the only partially articulated vision of the structural reforms, the continuing influence of the old habits of state subsidization and the lingering impact of centralist economic management. He took note of the ill-equipped body of state functionaries who would run the new economy, and concluded that, in view of all this, the country "lacked the premises and conditions for the establishment of an economic system that is new in nature, perfect, and uniform".

Linh resolved the central issues for himself by stating that to get by in the near term the system and the reform programme should not seek to comply with general laws, and should not attempt to measure success by a fixed gauge of accomplishments meant to demonstrate progress along a continuum towards an advanced stage of socialist construction,

> In these circumstances, what is most important to us at this time is a strategy of management geared to the existing economic state. This is a highly unstable economic state in which old economic forms remain firmly rooted, and the new ones are in an embryonic state. In other words, this transitional economic state requires a transitional mechanism of management that simultaneously employs both old and new factors.[45]

Linh also contended with several other positions that clashed with his own view of the reform process. For example, Linh challenged the view that the regime should "immediately abolish a number of necessary legal norms", characterizing that demand as impossible. He noted that the number of norms had been drastically reduced, but rejected the need to replace state norms with "indirect economic instruments" which would prematurely place the regime at the mercy of contractual economic relations and market forces. Linh also stated that the demand for "immediate" commercialization of trading among various economic components was an unrealistic suggestion, and noted that serious material shortages that impacted heavily on state enterprises necessitated the continued distribution of strategic production materials "in accordance with the state plan's priority objectives". Finally, Linh described the demand for the immediate and widespread application of a one-price system as similarly unrealistic. He noted that the proposed policy of decontrolled prices, which apparently had substantial backing, was theoretically correct but too "idealistic" for application in Vietnam, where serious imbalances in supply and demand and high inflation reigned, necessitating continued quotas and controlled prices.

Linh's solutions to the problems were tentative, based on the assumption that a certain amount of experimentation must take place before authoritative decisions about the form of management mechanisms could be made. He was very inclined to accept local innovation and tinkering with basic prescriptions for economic organization, but was firm in retaining the primacy of state control and unequivocal about the party's role in providing "comprehensive leadership". To Linh, the entire process was taking place in a transitional context where none of the old rules of operation and measures of success made sense. The process required deliberate and careful study; pilot investigations of the impact of new managerial forms on production; close observation of the efficacy of enterprise level experiments, including the use of joint enterprise forms and "enterprise alliances"; and attentiveness to the question of the role of party organizations in the new enterprise structures.

Linh's careful outline of the disputes over strategy and tactics in the area of economic reforms, and his own assessments of the competing views, suggest that he was attempting to serve as a conciliator, brokering compromises between contending policy positions. He evinced flexibility, while making a firm commitment to the programmatic ends of the reformist campaign. Yet, there was a sense that he was not in a position to speak as the ultimate and authoritative arbiter, and that he may have only represented the opinions of a narrow band of the leadership. On several occasions in his plenary speech, Linh noted what amounted to a virtual third position, not a compromise view but a completely different tack on a problem. Linh hinted that there were limits to his strength and influence, and that he was possibly incapable of swinging the vote towards his side.

The Purification Campaign

On 12 September the party Central Committee issued a resolution on the Campaign to Purify Party Organizations and State Bureaucracies.[46] The document defined the campaign as an effort that would continue through the end of the tenure of the Central Committee elected at the Sixth Congress. The backbone of the campaign was to be the Criticism/Self-Criticism (C/SC) Campaign. The C/SC Campaign consisted of locally-sponsored efforts to encourage cadre introspection and centrally-orchestrated investigations by control and inspection organs. The critical journalism activated by Nguyen Van Linh's commentaries was intended to play a role in moving the process along.[47]

The media-publicized text of the resolution confirmed that the campaign was to continue to the end of the term of the Sixth Congress, but the resolution defined operational goals for a much more limited period of time. From September 1987 through late 1988, according to the document, the campaign would focus the attention of party and state cadre on completing the adjudication of unfinished disciplinary cases and maintaining a pace that would prevent new cases from clogging the system. The campaign would also scrutinize the regime's managerial personnel resources and the sectors involved in running the economic reform programmes, along with examining party membership and judging the fitness of current card-holders. Finally, the campaign would be fine-tuned into a system of periodic inspections. As such, the September resolution did not go far beyond the initial formulations of the Purification Campaigns defined by provincial party organizations during late January and February.

The resolution did, however, detail a command structure for the campaign. The Standing Committee of the Office of the Council of Ministers and the party's Secretariat were to run the campaign. The party's Secretariat was charged with developing a team of "specially designated cadre" who would oversee the daily operation of the campaign, suggesting that the VNCP had reserved control over tactical matters and local organization for itself, and had written itself a wide-open mandate to establish an implementing mechanism for the campaign.[48] The Secretariat, according to the resolution, could call upon a range of party and state organs to run the campaign, including party control, organization, propaganda and training organs, and civilian proselytizing entities; state control, inspection, public security services, and people's tribunals; and mass organizations, including youth and women's organizations, trade union and peasant associations. The machinery that was to run the campaign focused authority on the line-level Central Committee departments and their chain of command descending through local party organizations, and deposited fundamental responsibility over provincial, municipal, special zone, precinct, district and grass-root level programmes with the party echelon. Heads of public organs and sectoral chiefs were to run their own individual campaigns, sharing the responsibility for guiding the operations with the specific party committee chairmen within those organizations.[49]

By late September provincial party committees had been instructed to take stock of what had been accomplished to date. They did so in an uneven manner that demonstrated major local variations in the organized response to central directives. For example, a 21 September account of the Kien Giang Provincial Party Committee's actions regarding the Purification Campaign noted that throughout the year the committee had issued instructions and resolutions intended to guide local implementation of the centrally-decreed review of party work, but by late in the year local chapters had, in general, failed to put any of the disseminated instructions into action. In late September, the provincial party committee organized a series of working sessions to review the problem and evaluate the implementation of instructions. As a result of those sessions, a body drawn from the provincial party standing committee and the party committee was entrusted with monitoring implementation of provincial committee instructions by subordinate party blocs, groups and committees under their normal jurisdiction. In addition, the provincial party committee also assigned cadres to districts to oversee the implementation of "specialized tasks" by party branches. The party Control Committee, the Organizational Committee, and the Propaganda and Training Committee were organized to serve as an advisory board for the provincial party committees on matters pertaining to the Purification Campaign. These committees were to be represented at the provincial party committee review sessions that were to be convened to take up the business of province-wide actions regarding the campaign. Finally, the Kien Giang Provincial Party Committee organized a parallel monthly "political day", under the supervision of the Standing Committee, for party committee echelons and cadres from every organization to meet with mass organization counterparts in discussion sessions, replicating an earlier nationwide effort to institutionalize provincial party committee-run criticism sessions.[50] By late September it appeared that other provinces had fashioned similar ad hoc committees of department level party committee entities, and had made provisions for regularly-convened, executive level working sessions to facilitate the campaign within the provinces. By mid-November, provincial and municipal party organizations and central level party entities had convened study and planning meetings in response to the Politburo's resolution. Some provincial committees — the Hanoi party organization and the Economic, Industrial and the Mass Motivation Party Blocs, for example — held enlarged party committee conferences to define operating parameters for the implementation of the resolution.[51]

In late October and early November, the central party mechanism encouraged another round of guidance meetings on the model of the 3 November Hanoi Executive Committee meeting to plan the Purification Campaign.[52] Those meetings were apparently intended to discuss the reduction of the size of party and state organizations, the trimming of subordinate offices and sections, the elimination of unnecessary deputy positions, and the redefinition of standards and qualifications for cadre and civil servant positions.[53]

The changes in structure, leadership and organizational habits were described in Vietnamese press accounts as dramatic renovations. The centrally-orchestrated nature of the Campaign to Purify Party and State Organizations seemed to mark a reversion to grand, sweeping political movements with sprawling programmes and pronounced ideological underpinnings.[54] Importantly, the entire enterprise was under the stewardship of party secretaries Do Muoi and Tran Xuan Bach, both Politburo members. Muoi seemed to have been charged with reviewing the accomplishments and organization of various General Departments in 1985, and was therefore experienced in oversight activities and singularly well-equipped to contribute to an exercise focused on mending organizational weaknesses in governmental machinery.[55] Bach, a party Secretariat member since 1982, had held sensitive positions since the Fifth Party Congress, including the responsibility for overseeing Vietnamese experts attached to Cambodian ministries. His rapid promotions from relative obscurity in the 1960s as a mass organization religious proselytizing cadre and provincial party secretary during the 1970s, to limelight positions in the 1980s, suggest high level sponsorship, perhaps by a combination of party elders including Le Duc Tho and Le Duc Anh.[56] Additionally, Politburo member and Hanoi Party Committee Secretary Nguyen Thanh Binh played a spokesman's role and was a key figure in prodding the municipalities, especially the capital city, towards active participation in the campaign. Binh, who headed the Central Committee Department for Distribution and Circulation from at least mid-1981 to 1986, had been an active supporter of the economic reforms. As an experienced observer of the intractable problems plaguing Vietnam's distribution system, he was particularly qualified to comment on party and state bureaucracy and the steps necessary to put the reformist strategies to work through that bureaucracy.[57] The combination of top talent called upon to run the centre's role in the campaign underscored the party's commitment to remaking the party organization and the parallel government structures.

The End-Of-Year Retrospectives:
The Fourth Party Plenum, Council of State,
Council of Ministers, and
National Assembly Sessions, December 1987

The customary end-of-year retrospectives by the Central Committee's fourth plenary session (8–17 December), the Council of State (18–19 December), the Council of Ministers (19–20 December), and the National Assembly (23–29 December) were highly critical of the regime's performance in economic affairs, offered a bleak picture of sectoral accomplishments, and made massive demands of the system's organizational resources in the context of the 1988 plan.[58]

Consolidating the Programme for Party Renovation

The Central Committee's plenary session, which led the train of year-end recapitulations, began with a strong indictment of the leadership of the topmost party apparatus and the Council of Ministers for the laggard pace of change in the country's economy. The fourth plenary session's catalogue of economic policy failures, billed as a "unanimous assessment" of the regime's performance from the time of the December 1986 National Party Congress, was an extremely critical look at the party's post-Second Plenum record. The plenum noted production slumps, major inadequacies in tax policies, inflated market prices, enduring structural unemployment, and an unsettled programme of state investment in capital construction. The programme of action proposed by the plenum was confined to stabilizing the market situation and encouraging hikes in commodity production.

According to the plenary session communiqué, Nguyen Van Linh delivered both the opening and the closing speeches, though he shared the podium on the final day of the plenum with Council of Ministers Chairman Pham Hung, whose address to the closing session was highlighted in the media.[59] Linh's opening remarks focused entirely on the economic record and the rules guiding the developmental plans for the period through 1990, and they closely paralleled the thrust of the plenary resolution and the plenary communiqué. The plenary communiqué detailed the major leadership failings and the resulting accumulation of "acute" economic difficulties, a rather familiar litany. The plenum singled out the inner circle's inability to limit damages as earlier economic reform policies and implementing strategies faltered, and the government's lumbering and confused efforts to turn policy intentions into practices. The communiqué also referred to the problem of bloated, executive level offices and ingrained habits of centralized rule, plus the weakness of untalented and uninventive though ideologically proper cadre.

In his opening remarks, Linh recited the basic structural and organizational shortcomings of the economy,

> There is a big gap between income and spending and export and import and no accumulation in [the] economy. The production and business transactions, in general, suffer losses. Productivity, equality,

and economic effectiveness are reduced. The distribution of national income is irrational and unequal, and the circulation of goods faces many obstacles. The mechanism of bureaucratic centralism based on state subsidies remains in force. The new socialist economic accounting and business transactions have been institutionalized strongly. The li[ves] of workers, public employees, and armed forces, and people in general [are] facing many difficulties and [instabilities]. Meanwhile, we have great potentials which have not yet been [tapped] to develop the economy, including those at home and abroad.[60]

He dealt with the same rash of failings and inadequacies in the areas of circulation, distribution, personnel work, and economic management that were treated in the communiqué, and offered the same basic support for future improvements in productivity, organization, and leadership.

Linh's plenary performance was somewhat understated, compared to his stronger speeches and more dominating presence at the second and third Central Committee plenary sessions. His statements took a back seat to the communiqué, which expressed consensus views of the Central Committee on the practical effects of the reforms. Importantly, the communiqué included a prioritization of goals that provided a hint of the relative strength of these competing policy interests. The more conservative advocates of a measured and cautious economic reform were able to reassert the importance of public security issues, though apparently agreeing to accord a lesser level of importance to those issues against fundamental issues of economic recovery. The fourth and fifth order of policy imperatives of six enumerated priorities focused on public order and national defence, and were clearly sandwiched between more strictly economic imperatives — addressing the issue of unemployment and long-range economic planning. The conservative reformists had also negotiated the reassertion of the agenda of socialist transformation, shorthand for efforts to ensure a firm government role in determining the structure of enterprise ownership and market participation through statutory limits on the size of businesses, taxation strategies, and stringent rules on participation in specific commodity markets. The conservatives were able to bargain such modified strategies into the programme, at relatively respectable levels of priority.[61]

The plenary session itself was intentionally given equal time alongside the meetings of the Council of State and the Council of Ministers, and the National Assembly, to emphasize the importance Linh accorded to expanding the role of the government implementing agencies and bureaucracies in the reformist process. The scripts for these year-end meetings offered sound thrashings for the new leadership team's policies and the capacity of the governing bodies to turn legislation into action. The Council of State session, chaired by Vo Chi Cong, concluded with an admonition to upgrade ministerial and sectoral co-ordination, to improve control work within the state legislative and executive offices at all levels, and to reinforce the rule of law.[62] The Council of Ministers plenary session took the Council to task for a dismaying performance, and called for a massive revamping of state management machinery with the aim of confining state functions to "socio-economic management", or strategic planning issues, and limiting state intervention in issues of production and business management.[63] A Council of Ministers cadre conference in mid-December strongly endorsed reforms in planning within state enterprises, and underscored the need for immediate action to convince enterprises to cease relying on the state for inputs.[64] The National Assembly session in late December featured a major speech by Vo Van Kiet, Vice Chairman of the Council of Ministers and Chairman of the State Planning Committee, which catalogued Vietnam's economic failures. Kiet, widely known as one of the key proponents of the reform programme, gave prominence to sagging production levels, galloping inflation, daunting capital shortages, high levels of structural unemployment and shrinking resources available to tide over a population that continued to grow at an unchecked pace.[65]

The December Central Committee plenary session represented the culmination of a year of consolidation for Linh during which he sought to assure his political position and guarantee longevity for his reformist programmes. In 1987 Linh presided over a clean sweep of the Cabinet, a restructuring of ministries, and a major house-cleaning of subordinate government and party bureaucracies. The majority of provincial and district party committee secretaries and administrative teams were quietly replaced, and the aggressive campaign against corruption, malfeasance and general incompetence was prosecuted with intensity. Linh demonstrated his ability to shape priorities and articulate manageable programmes, to cope with crises without losing sight of ultimate policy ends, and to remain focused and committed to "renovation" in the midst of reversals caused by uncontrolled inflation and persistent foreign exchange deficits, plus cyclical agricultural problems, food shortages, and a weakening of the ability of the central government to command necessary resources through taxation. In three important plenary sessions during the year, Linh spoke of efforts to untangle the country's most immediately consequential problems by the end of 1987 as a "first step", deferring major systemic reforms until after the urgent issues underlying the "current chaotic situation" were addressed. Linh reaffirmed the basic overarching and structural context of the reform programme, forbidding a reversion to the habit of "bureaucratic centralism" and the practices of state subsidization of enterprises.

By the end of 1987, however, Linh's performance in the economic realm suggested that he had endured some slippage in his general standing. In late 1987, at the end-of-year sessions of the party Central Committee, the Council of State and the National Assembly, Linh encountered resistance to portions of his programme of reform. The December plenary session was highly critical of the regime's economic performance and offered a bleak picture of sectoral accomplishments. The plenary communiqué was a strong indictment of the top party and government leaders for their inability to limit the amount of damage as the earlier economic reform policies began to falter, and the confused efforts to deal with the acute economic problems. Linh's ability to salvage the programme of reforms, while directly confronting dwindling food supplies and declining grain production levels, suffered after the Fourth Plenum. His two critical capacities were noticeably weakened after the December session of the Central Committee: his ability to act as the conciliator, drawing divergent policy positions together through inventive compromises, and his ability to authoritatively make judgments about policy alternatives posed by competing interests.

two
1988: Staying the Reformist Course

Introduction
The party approached organizational reform in 1988 with urgency and a sense that the lethargy and disorder that had marked nationwide efforts to clean house had done irreparable harm to the party's standing. Throughout the year the central leadership sought to re-energize the faltering Campaign to Purify the Party and State Organization, reinvigorate the party membership recruitment drives, and reconstitute party committee leadership at provincial and subordinate echelons throughout the country.

Purification and Self-Criticism: Rejuvenating the Campaign
The Campaign to Purify the Party and State Organization proceeded unevenly through the first months of 1988, to the frustration of the central party leadership.[66] By early February central level organs and sectors, various central party blocs and some provinces had taken the first steps towards advertising the objectives and rules of the Campaign to their subordinate organizations. Some provincial party committees and some "pilot projects" in provinces and cities

had begun to expand the process beyond participation of party officials to include the involvement of the membership at large. An unstated but clearly small number of party echelons were able to orchestrate a connection between the Purification Campaign and the Criticism/Self-Criticism (C/SC) Campaign initiated in 1987.

By early February the regime had outlined a three-step plan for the C/SC Campaign in 1989. The first step involved an inventory of the standards and qualifications of grass-root level party membership; the reorganization of sectoral and unit level party organizations, especially in major municipalities; and the preparation for grass-root level party organization congresses. That stage was to run from February to June, a serious miscalculation of the time required to organize local party meetings. During the second step, a six-month period from June to November 1988, the party was to supervise the organization of precinct, district and sub-district party congresses; review key cadre assignments at those levels; and evaluate key cadre assignments at the sectoral level and in municipal mass organizations. During the third step in the C/SC Campaign, which was to run throughout 1989, the party was to focus on efforts to improve the quality of party members, consolidate grass-root level party organization, and strengthen bloc and sector party committees in preparation for the National Party Congress in 1990.[67]

At the outset, the entire schedule was thrown off by two or three months. Between April and May provincial party committees began public scrutiny of their membership review process. The provinces reported that they had only achieved partial results in basic efforts to educate the membership about the aims and organization of the Purification Campaign, especially the efforts to undertake formal membership qualification reviews, and attempts to dispose of pending cases of membership and committee level leadership misconduct and dereliction of duty.[68]

By early June, however, provinces had begun reporting the virtual completion of the first step in the Purification Campaign. For example, in early June Vinh Phu Province indicated that disciplinary cases involving transgressions by party leaders and members had been reviewed by provincial level echelons. Basic units had received advice on proceeding with the adjudication of such cases, and the provincial party committee had started designating model units. Further, the majority of basic party units had conducted the appropriate C/SC exercises. Additionally, the provincial party committee had organized district and municipal level conferences to discuss plans for coping with economic problems, and for accomplishing the economic actions necessary to buoy productivity and survive diminishing food supplies, scarcity of money and commodity shortfalls. In some provinces the process took much longer. In Thanh Hoa Province the process took the better part of a year because the provincial party committee leadership was accused of heavy-handed administrative practices, major acts of corruption and violations of rules governing internal investigation and control work. Ultimately, the party committee secretary and several close associates were relieved of their positions. That case set an example for co-operative policing of the party's leadership by people's committees, local party organizations and the central level.[69] By the middle of the year basic party organizations were focused more closely on personality assessments of party members, and on reviewing and categorizing all card-holders. Disciplinary actions initiated during the first months of 1988 had, by mid-year, been concluded and tabulated, and were being prominently displayed in the media as measures of the surgical success of the campaign to eliminate corrupt and inefficient members who had cluttered the party's membership rolls.

The task of reducing organizational proportions took centre stage in mid-year, in part as an austerity measure, but also as an attempt to collapse portions of two stages of the Purification Campaign — step one, involving the internal reorganization of governing bodies and basic party organizations at the sectoral and unit level, and the portion of step two calling for a massive review of cadre assignments.

In early June, office, branch and sectoral level party entities had initiated co-ordinated efforts to reduce the number of sub-office chiefs and deputies as part of a general reduction in administrative personnel and managers. The emphasis of district level organizational reform had shifted to reducing office heads, deputy slots and line personnel. In June, provincial committees convened conferences to plan the reorganization of party offices and production establishments by eliminating unnecessary "intermediate links" and redundant cadre. The party also endorsed, and may very well have begun to act upon, the demand for more effective vertical organizational communication through the conduct of opinion polls, organizational studies, and efforts to canvas lower level entities on problems and policy questions. Several party organizations joined with parallel state agencies to form consolidated committees responsible for hearing complaints about the system and accusations against officials and cadre.[70]

In June and July the media highlighted the importance of formulating cadre training plans for the period from 1989 to 1990 and for the years 1990 to 1995, in anticipation of serious shortages of cadre.[71] The tone of the purification drive had begun to shift from immediate problem solving – the elimination of corrupt and inefficient cadre – to long-term planning for cadre replacement.

In the third quarter of 1988 the party sought to exert slightly more centralized influence on the Purification Campaign. In late August the Secretariat convened to hear a preliminary report on the implementation of Politburo Resolution Number 4, which defined and activated the machinery for the Purification Campaign. In early September the Secretariat issued guidance on implementing the resolution that was apparently intended to accelerate and intensify national efforts. The Secretariat focused on the role of the Central Committee's Internal Affairs Department as the key instrument in the "anti-negativism struggle", and spoke of the responsibilities of bloc secretaries in monitoring and guiding Central Committee blocs. Finally, the Secretariat noted that sectors and localities would begin to file reports on Purification Campaign accomplishments directly with the Secretariat according to a schedule that would be defined at a later, unspecified date. In June, Ho Chi Minh City introduced a more streamlined system of local administrative meetings involving party, state and economic decision-makers. The "unified steering committee" consisted of party secretaries and administrative committee chairmen, central and provincial agencies assigned to subordinate levels, security and military units, and market management entities at the ward and village level.[72]

Membership and Recruitment

A major part of the Purification Campaign was a thorough review of personnel assets by party committees and the rapid discharge of members who had become liabilities in accordance with the due process established by the revised party statutes approved by the Sixth National Congress. To that end, in early February sectoral and district level party organizations undertook systematic assessments of their recruitment efforts, the status of disciplinary cases against party officers and members, and the relative strengths and weaknesses of subordinate chapters. By the end of March provincial party committees had begun to report the results of efforts to take stock of provincial level party organizations and grass-root level party committees.

Slightly more than a third of the districts featured in media coverage at the time reported basically successful efforts to enhance advancement of membership skills and performance. However, the major portion of district party organization membership remained rather average, judging from the partial statistics and impressions communicated in media reports. For example, 10 per cent of the members affiliated with district party components were categorized as "weak". However, far more dismaying to the party was the level of backsliding. According to media reports, a third of all grass-root party organizations subordinate to district party committees had failed to retain the level of efficiency that had entitled those organizations to recognition as "strong" party components in the recent past. The party was also troubled by the increase to 20 per cent in the number of alternate members whose eligibility for full party membership had lapsed, or whose initial recruitment had been shown to have been based on an inflated, inaccurate evaluation of the ability to satisfy the minimum membership standards.[73] These figures on membership weaknesses and chapter organization inadequacies were replicated in assessments of recruiting in the small industry, handicraft and trade sectors.[74] Reporting on the provincial committees yielded a picture of similarly weakened membership, and a measure of ineffective lower level party organizations. Twenty per cent of subordinate basic party organizations were rated as ineffective. Of approximately 2,000 disciplinary cases derived from the C/SC process in Ha Bac Province, about 100 were focused on the provincial party committee, about 60 involved district or municipal level officials or members, and the remainder were concerned with the most fundamental, basic level organizations under the provincial party committee. A quarter of those cases were concerned exclusively with the behaviour or capabilities of cadres and party members, and were apparently settled by removing individuals from office or from the party membership rolls.[75] Minh Hai, Dac Lac and Song Be Provinces reported similar percentages of cadre and party members unable to satisfy the most fundamental tests of effectiveness. About a quarter of the total number of prosecuted cases against party members resulted in dismissals from office, expulsions from the party, and further legal actions in these provinces.[76]

The party devised several strategies to cope with the problem of rapidly diminishing personnel assets and the disintegration of membership standards. The regime intensified its focus on retaining the membership of suitable students, developing candidates for party memberships, and activating the Youth Federation as an adjunct of the Communist Youth Union. Linh was a strong advocate for applying to the Youth Union the methods of the campaign used to upgrade party organizations and of closer organizational contact between the party and its major recruiting pool. The party repeated its longstanding call for institutionalized rotational assignments that would place individuals from central and superior party committee levels in grass-root level organizations in order to ensure that lower level organizations could make use of talented and tested personnel.

In May, provincial party organizations began to publicly declare the results of several convergent efforts to inventory the quality of party membership. Those efforts included the process of "settling letters of complaint" initiated as part of the C/SC Campaign, organized attempts to verify and investigate violations of party discipline and state law, and the nationwide "quality check" of grass-root level organizations launched in 1987.[77] In what amounted to a mass confessional, provincial party organizations listed the results of basic party unit disciplinary investigations; tallied the resultant expulsions, dismissals, censures and legal proceedings initiated as a result of the actions; and produced a measure of party efficiency and membership quality. In follow-up actions, provinces helped reduce the size of district level offices, branches and sectors. Provinces named trial districts as showcases for efforts to streamline party entities through cadre reassignment and organizational realignment. Provinces also organized district, city and township conferences to disseminate the basic lessons of party reform and membership discipline.[78]

The announced results of the inventory of district level membership assets portrayed a solid body of qualified and law-abiding cadre (80–90 per cent), a miniscule percentage of unqualified members whose lapses mandated expulsion (1–4 per cent), and a slightly larger group of party card-holders who broke rules but were salvageable (8–20 per cent).[79] From July to September basic level party organizations implemented disciplinary actions against local party leaders as well as village people's committee chairmen and directors of cooperatives.[80] By November village party organization congresses were reporting the replacement of significant numbers of party committee secretaries (30 per cent in some instances). From September to November, local party conferences, centrally organized meetings of provincial secretaries, party executive committee sessions and preliminary grass-root and municipal conferences on the Party Congress cycle stressed the election of competent and young party executives and rank and file to replace the significant numbers of party members who were dropped in the mid-year purges.[81] Linh and close supporters, including Vo Tran Tri, emphasized the need for congresses of basic party organizations to focus on technical expertise as a central requirement for party leadership positions.[82]

Grass-root Congresses: Tentative Steps towards a 1990 National Congress

Beginning in early February the media highlighted the goal of convening Party Congresses at the grass-root level and at the district and precinct level by the end of 1988.[83] The party statutes, revised by the Sixth National Congress in December 1986, provided for the possibility of convening conferences of delegates (*hoi nghi dai bieu*) between two National Party Congresses (*dai hoi dai bieu toan quoc*), in the event of "special cases" (*truong hop dac biet*) involving the need to make decisions concerning important problems or to add members to an executive committee.[84] District and precinct party organization congresses, which continued through the middle of the year, discussed the need to convene special congresses of delegates at their level, and focused on the establishment of "norms" for party personnel policies and plans for facilitating the process of organizational purification.

In late July and early August the party's daily paper began to editorialize about the "immediate objective" of organizing grass-root and district party organization congresses. The congresses were to implement the fifth plenary resolutions on cadre quality and training by facilitating investigations of party members and redefining selection criteria for party officials. The congresses were also to concern themselves with personnel planning and cadre management, and the regulations governing cadre participation in economic activity.[85] According to a 30 July *Saigon Giai Phong* article, the Ho Chi Minh City Party Committee issued "guidelines" on 23 July that called for the convening of grass-root congresses in selected wards, villages, enterprises, state stores, administrative organs, hospitals and schools beginning in August. The full cycle of grass-root and district party congresses was to run from September through November. District level party organization congresses were to be in full swing by January 1989, and would continue through March. The meetings would also review Programmes of Action, agree upon new programmes for the coming term, elect party organization executive committees and delegates to the congresses of the immediately superior levels, and replace at least one-third of the incumbent party committee members with young and qualified cadre.[86]

Between August and November several key meetings moved the process of convening congresses forward. In early September, the party Central Committee's Organization Department convened a conference in Hai Hung Province that focused on rural congresses. The conference defined three themes that were to be central to the meetings: the clarification of the relationship between the authority of the party, the government and the mass organizations; the problem of weak grass-root level party organizations; and the integration of youthful, female and ethnic minority cadre into executive committees at the level of the fundamental party organization.[87] In mid-September the standing committee of the Hanoi Party held a conference of secretaries from district, ward, and township organizations to discuss plans for local congresses. The meeting stressed rejuvenation of party committee membership; the election of competent, qualified executive committees; and the careful definition of economic and political tasks in the 1989–90 action programmes. The meeting also slightly adjusted the calendar for the congresses. Grass-root level meetings were to be conducted from September to December, and district, ward and township meetings were to be scheduled during the first quarter of 1989.[88] A mid-October conference chaired by the party Central Committee's Organization Department in Ho Chi Minh City, and attended by deputy party secretaries and organization department heads from southern provinces, focused on the new and reputedly "democratic means" of compiling, evaluating and screening candidates for party committee slots. The conference underscored the higher-echelon guidance that had facilitated the convening of pilot precinct and district level meetings in two southern provinces – Ben Tre and Long An.[89]

The Fifth Plenum, June 1988

The fifth plenary session ran from 14–20 June, a total of seven working days, making it one of the two shorter plenums in the first two years of the Sixth Congress cycle. The Fifth Plenum took up the "urgent" issue of "party building" – the question of leadership, personnel policies, training, and organizational roles in the reformist programme.

The plenary communiqué condemned the party's approach to social problems, the inadequacy of its internal regimen of self-examination and structural reform, and the overall shape of party leadership at every level.[90] The communiqué proposed a programme of improvements that focused on the reorganization and strengthening of the party's "ideological task", the development of the cadre selection and training system and the reorganization of the cadre career structure, and the overall enhancement of the quality of party members.

According to the communiqué, the first portion of this self-improvement programme was to consist of incremental efforts to reorganize party attitudes and practices about the flow of information, the habits of co-operation between party echelons, the sharing of resources, and the essential attitudes towards responsibilities, performance of assigned tasks, and chains of command. The communiqué urged that the party inculcate reformed attitudes towards the practice of joint studies and fact-finding efforts. This was one of the means by which Linh had attempted to invigorate the role of the state: by requiring organized measurements of the progress of policy implementation and the efficacy of new economic rules through ministerially-supervised long-term studies and reports.

The proposed application of this practice to the party reflected Linh's preoccupation with reapportioning responsibilities to operational levels, driving the party towards a practical habit of self-inspection, and creating a systemic imperative for receiving and processing new information to sustain programmes and keep policies informed, current and vigorous. At the same time, the communiqué reiterated the need to guard national secrets and heighten responsibilities for the protection of the party, reflecting Central Committee concern over the possible consequences of the critical use of information.

Alongside this summons to reorganize information services, the communiqué urged the party to exert more control over the press, publishing, and cultural and artistic matters in order to direct those realms towards a more active support of the reforms. Linh was unarguably committed to a freer, critical press and an unfettered, expressive community of artists and writers, a commitment he made in late 1986 and again in early 1987 promises to the professional associations of writers, artists and journalists. The process of reform served to strengthen his view of the ombudsmen-like role for journalists. The fifth plenary communiqué, however, tempered the vision of an activist press and a freely critical literati, placing a primacy on the party's need to control and shape the roles of media, artists, and writers when those roles affect policy. The communiqué also emphasized the party's need to subordinate some of the reformist processes to normal chains of command that might have loosened as the system sought to accommodate new additions to the economic decision-making *apparat*. The plenary communiqué's point about normal chains of command was a direct jab at some of the unique entities out of the mainstream of policy implementation – the press, the professionally organized writers and cultural workers – called by Linh to play a role in the renovation process, and appealed to by him when the party was most resistant to his initiatives.

The second portion of the programme – the development of cadre selection and reform of the training system – reiterated the long-standing positions on the need to separate party and state functions and constrain the party from assuming roles more properly reserved for governing bodies. The plenary communiqué also mandated fixed terms of 10 years for party secretaries, and supported a concerted reduction of party committee membership at all levels. The communiqué endorsed more systematic cadre promotions based on tested abilities and the planned rotation of cadre, including the assignment of central level cadre to localities and primary installations for mandatory, fixed periods of service.

The third portion of the programme emphasized the need to improve the overall quality of party members through education and "rejuvenation", and through orderly efforts to upgrade the level of performance of basic party organizations. The communiqué re-emphasized the importance of maintaining membership standards and purging unqualified members, a familiar litany on sustaining organizational development tasks.

Nguyen Van Linh's plenary address suggested that while there was broad agreement on the need to vigorously address the basic problems in the realm of ideological work, cadre selection, organizational reform and party membership standards, there was also nuanced disagreement over the nature and content of reform strategies offered as a means of redressing these lapses in policy, personnel and organizational matters.[91] Linh echoed the contents of the communiqué, though he seemed to place more emphasis on the extent to which weaknesses in the "decisive factors" for the party – leadership, and an aggressive and close relationship with the "people" — caused the systemic breakdown and massive economic failures. The communiqué acknowledged that leadership over political, ideological and organizational domains had not succeeded in fulfilling the "revolutionary tasks", and that the party had been slow to change its viewpoint and its policies on cadre-related matters. Linh spoke in stronger terms of paralysing disunity and party organs capable of nothing more than the perfunctory discharge of ideological and organizational responsibilities. He stated that those weaknesses had deterred the party from its fundamental role of defining the political line and reacting quickly to changing situations. Linh spoke of an overall confusion about the kinds of policies necessary during the "transitional period". He noted the manner in which incorrect assumptions about collective abilities and the basic economics of development had affected planning decisions, the creation of an economic managerial system, and the pursuit of policies that neglected the realities of the multi-sectoral economy. The communiqué did not devote any significant attention to the economic issues, noting simply that the "poor situation" stemmed primarily from mistakes in formulating socio-economic guidelines and policies, and weak control over ideological, organizational and cadre-related tasks.

In his speech, Linh stated that there were still "many issues" in the plenary session's draft resolution on party building that required "discussion and debate" before unanimity could be achieved by the Central Committee. Linh emphasized that two prior efforts to draft resolutions on party building, at the third (1960) and the fifth (1982) National Party Congresses, had failed to devise a means of implementing the proposed programmes. He appealed to the Central Committee members for suggestions and viewpoints, and offered three points for consideration to the plenary session.

First, he noted the importance of a more explicit link between the enterprise of internal party reform and the agenda of economic renovation. The implementation of the resolution on party building must be "closely linked to and aimed at supporting the implementation of other resolutions of the party, especially those on economic affairs".

Second, he argued that party-building projects should properly include non-party entities, since mass organizations and governing bodies had a range of equities in such reforms. "We should not leave party building work entirely to party organization committees at various levels," Linh argued. In his words,

> This is the duty of all party committee echelons as well as of key party administrative and specialized organs and of mass organizations at all levels. We must overcome the tendency to separate administrative and specialized work from party building work. Whatever the field of work, it will be impossible for key leading cadres to successfully realize the viewpoints and policies devised for the sectors and areas of activities under their charge unless they pay attention to the work of the party, the Community Youth Union, and various mass organizations. Therefore, leaders of all sectors must at the same time take care of their special line of work and pay attention to party building work.

Third, Linh urged a more localized authority for defining individual, sector and echelon level Action Programmes for the implementation of the party building resolution. Linh stated that,

> In implementing the resolution on party building, each sector, each echelon and each grass-root unit must come up with a specific programme of action, taking into account its own specific situation. No one can do this job for it. Higher echelons can only provide correct guidelines. As for the contents of specific measures of cadre planning, they must be figured out by each sector, each echelon and each grass-root unit. Leaders of various sectors and echelons must personally anticipate their potential successors as well as candidates for any positions within their given areas of responsibility and then, through the mechanism of democratic selection, reach a final decision.

Linh's appeal for a wider use of extra-party entities, and his support for increased responsibility for local level party bodies in setting their individual reformist agendas, were singularly unpopular with a Central Committee that was intent upon strengthening tried and true chains of command. Linh acknowledged that his perspectives were not widely shared, and vaguely indicated that his position on the matter of party building had not been incorporated into the draft version of the resolution. He concluded his points on the quality of party membership and cadre work, and prefaced his three suggestions by saying that he did not intend to talk about other issues already fully addressed in the draft resolution, the implication being that the views he expressed in his speech had not been integrated into the resolution itself. The last position of his speech acknowledged the comprehensive manner in which the resolution dealt with party reform, and clearly characterized Linh's remaining points as items that had not been treated in the resolution.

Linh's performance during the fifth plenary session demonstrated his unwillingness to give up his frontline position on the reformist process, and his awareness that he could not press beyond the consensus of his colleagues. He acknowledged disagreements over certain of his reformist strategies and conceded some ground, though not without restating his positions and defending his approach to reforming the party.

The fifth plenary session was an exercise in accommodation: between the intention to reform and the instinct to salvage basic organization, enduring principles, leadership practices; between the innovative introduction of new party members from a wider recruitment pool, and a quietly revived consciousness of security issues and concern over the sanctity of vaunted institutions and traditional recruiting pools; and between the perception of a need for a heightened political role for the press, non-party entities, along with a vibrant and independent state mechanism, and the reflexive consolidation of party predominance over key decision processes and the media.

Post-Plenary Issues and Developments

The third session of the Eighth National Assembly convened two days after the closing of the fifth plenary session of the Central Committee, and ran for a total of seven working days.[92] Before the closing day of business on 28 June the National Assembly had elected Do Muoi as new Chairman of the Council of Ministers; approved the resolution of the state budget estimate for 1988, including major austerity features intended to reduce the annual budget shortfall; and charged the Council of Ministers with operational control of the budget, and with increasing revenues and decreasing expenses to compensate for the cessation of subsidies, and implementing the new tax laws. The session also approved a resolution amending the preamble of the Constitution to reflect the "current revolutionary situation" — including the excision of disparaging references to China and the United States — and entrusted the Council of State with the preparation of the mandated changes for submission to the next National Assembly session. The National Assembly endorsed the draft law on nationality and approved the draft law on criminal procedures, and placed its imprimatur on the past year's foreign relations activities undertaken with the authority of the Council of Ministers.

Importantly, the National Assembly criticized the governance of the country in the same terms applied to the party by the Fifth Plenum: the system had failed to foresee the most consequential crises that befell the economy in 1987, and especially failed to anticipate the major grain shortage in late 1987 and early 1988. Once the problems had manifested themselves, the system demonstrated its basic inability to act decisively to minimize further damage. Vo Van Kiet noted the government's failure to co-ordinate important policies on prices, import-export rules, foreign currency exchange rates, and management according to the new rules of operation in a timely manner. Leadership indecisiveness, Kiet stated, had left major problems unresolved and forced the reliance on temporary plans. Production and business activity suffered from delays in signing contracts and the slow adoption of official plans. The most costly failures were in the handling of the grain shortages, openly admitted to have led to "social problems" by the middle of the year — a euphemism for popular demonstrations of dissatisfaction over the unavailability of affordable rice.[93]

The selection of Do Muoi over Vo Van Kiet as Pham Hung's successor in a secret ballot on the second day of the National Assembly proceedings was a vote for experience, balance and caution, rather than a censure aimed against the reforms. Muoi's election represented a gentle backlash by conservatives who had come to subscribe to the basic imperatives of the programme but who wished to exert a modifying influence on the pace and intensity of the reformist attacks on the party's hand in economics and the assault against the party-state balance of power. Those conservatives were central to the election of Muoi, a northerner with long ministerial experience who would speak for the interests of those urging a slower, more deliberately incremental process of reform that would be less costly to the party's pre-eminent role. At that time Muoi appeared to be a natural ally for those interests, having taken an early, narrow and conservative position on the economic reform package. As early as 1984, he cast his lot with a group inclined to conceive of the programme of reform as a series of tentative problem-solving devices including instruments to facilitate the abolition of state subsidization and the implementation of new wage and price policies. Muoi's position stood in contrast to the group that saw the reforms as part of a strategic chain of processes dating from the late 1970s that sought to address more fundamental and systemic matters, including planning problems and the distribution of economic decision-making power.[94]

Three areas of concern, given initial expression in Linh's speech to the Fifth Plenum, endured as the party's central preoccupations in the months after the fifth plenary session: (1) the importance of drawing a more explicit link between the internal party reforms and the agenda of economic renovation, (2) the need to grant more profound responsibility to local level party entities in the process of defining action programmes for implementing the Central Committee's party-building resolution, and (3) the need to integrate non-party entities into the enterprise of party reform. The appeal for a wider use of extra-party organizations was of particular importance to Linh. To the General Secretary, mass organizations and governing bodies had a distinct role to play in the party reform programme.

In the second half of the year the party continued to seek the means to broaden political participation by non-party entities and to maximize the independence of action of mass organizations and party affiliates. Throughout the year the regime fixed a critical eye on youth union membership levels, the deficiencies of youth union organizations, and the waning attractiveness of the unions to youths. General Secretary Linh urged the integration of youth unions into provincial and subordinate level administrative structures, and supported granting the unions a heightened role in educational and economic matters at the various levels of governance, and a more complete involvement in relevant economic management mechanisms. The regime supported roles for the youth union in the organization of assault youth groups, the establishment of service co-operative teams, and the process of selecting and organizing the "international co-operation" labour for dispatch to foreign countries for on-the-job training.[95]

The draft report to the Sixth Congress of the Vietnamese Trade Unions announced that the unions were to be reorganized into a central council which was to function as a "converging point" for occupational trade union representatives elected by occupational unions, not the hitherto unified national congress of unions.[96] In his address to the 17 October session of the conference, Linh argued that the trade unions required an independence of opinion so that they could pursue activism on behalf of their clientele without undue dependence on party committees and management organs. In Linh's words,

> The trade unions must fully reflect their independent character in terms of organization. This is the condition for the trade unions to further develop their role and work efficiency in the system of proletarian dictatorship. Trade union activities, by their nature, are not independent of other organizations in the system of proletarian dictatorship. But as far as their functions and operational methods are concerned, trade unions do not entirely resemble the other organizations. By clearly defining and fully putting into practice their functions and operational methods, the trade unions will surely be able to ensure their organizational independence. This requires not only efforts on the part of the trade unions themselves but also the responsibility of party and state organs. Efforts must come from both sides. The trade unions themselves must be more active and dynamic in their work, especially in discharging their functions of protecting the working people's interests and participating in the management, control and supervision of the activities of state management organs. To do this we need not only correct political awareness, the requisite capability, and pure virtues and ethics which are very important criteria — but also, as required in many cases, courage, perseverance, and determination in the

struggle against the negative forces of management. The trade union's role as a gainsayer is called for in many necessary relations. However, as this has not been observed, people sometimes ridicule the trade unions, saying that they are an organization which eats and speaks in the wake of others or which serves as the fifth wheel. We demand that the trade unions have their own independent opinions rather than leaning on party committee echelons and tying themselves to management organs. Naturally, organizational independence is far different from the concept of organizational opposition. The trade unions cannot be a detached organization of the trade unionism type or an organization which follows the backward masses.[97]

However, Linh prefaced his call for a new trade union activism and organizational reform by noting the extent to which the party would continue to exert a strategic influence on the trade union efforts to extend their activities to private and foreign-funded enterprises, streamline their bloated bureaucracies, jettison weak membership, and improve training of union cadre. In Linh's words,

It is true that, at present, the working class and labourers are still dissatisfied with the party leadership and state management. But, it is also true that they have never contended that there is any other political force that can replace the historical role of our party and state. They wish and demand that the party prove itself equal to the requirements of the revolution and quickly discover solutions to change the situation. They understand that if the party is to fulfil its historical responsibility, the labourers, especially the working class, must remain deeply attached to the party, actively participate in trade unions, and strive to stand in the party's rank to successfully carry out the tasks set forth by the party. They have shown their determination to join efforts with the party and state to overcome all trials.[98]

The Party and the Land Problem

Public demonstrations of discontent by irate farmers over land distribution, arbitrary appropriation of lands by cadre and their families, and the inequitable practices of settling land disputes reached a crescendo in August, prompting a series of emergency meetings of the central government *apparat* responsible for agricultural affairs.[99]

In April the party adopted a resolution downgrading the role of agricultural co-operatives. In August the party issued a directive which called for the return of illegally or arbitrarily appropriated land. During that period, the regime sought to protect state ownership of land while simultaneously guaranteeing farmers the uninterrupted long-term use of plots and more favourable terms under revised product contracts that entitled farmers to keep about half of their production, an increase over previous terms which authorized individual producers to retain one-quarter of their production.

The regime responded to the earliest cues of discontent over land issues by fashioning a broad Politburo directive that attempted to more assertively integrate reformist approaches — reliance on limited market forces, cleansing of local, decrepit administrative and party entities, devolution of decision-making authority to sectors and key production points — into the arena of agricultural production. The April Politburo resolution reorganized agricultural management, divided co-operatives and diminished their central role, and upheld the rights of private and individual companies to engage in legitimate business. The resolution noted broad, systemic failures and leadership lapses in planning overall development strategy, rational resource planning, and specific sectoral inadequacies including improper collectivization, coercive tactics in the transformation of agricultural production, and weak material supply policies. The Politburo resolution endorsed the basic strategic priorities for improving food production, and underwrote efforts to terminate state-owned installations that continually incurred losses, redistribute the work force, improve production levels for industrial crops and long-term agricultural investments (coffee, rubber), review sectoral management, and reorganize general corporations established by the Council of Ministers. The resolution reiterated the central importance of district level planning, and called for increased direct and indirect investment in agriculture, the establishment of an agricultural development investment bank, the rationalization of tax policies, and the strengthening of rural markets.[100]

The April directive was translated into an authorization for family and individual enterprises to bid for reclaimed land, for co-operatives to pool capital instead of labour, and for private individuals to bid for the purchase or hire of unprofitable state enterprises, primary economic installations and shops that were earmarked for dismantling.[101] Additionally, the April resolution resulted in a diminishing of the importance of state-defined norms as a means of exercising control. The fabric of the relationship between the state and agricultural co-operatives was altered, at least in principle, as co-operative and production collectives were freed to undertake their own planning, subject to the authorization of the co-operative members' congress.

Tinkering with managerial structures and rules of co-operative organization did not go far towards lessening the intensity of the problem. In April and May farmers escalated their activism. Some southern peasant protestors called for the occupation of collectivized paddy fields.[102] The regime's response was diffuse. In May, Politburo member Do Muoi attempted to describe the key land policy issues as a matter of levels of productivity influenced by application of inputs that varied regionally and local toleration of illicit or unproductive land use. Muoi proposed support for decentralized land management, reliance on detailed local planning for land use, regular land inspections and the prompt organization of land management organizations as a means of addressing wasteful land use, illegal sales and occupation of land, and inappropriate allocation and utilization of land.[103] He also noted the importance of the land law adopted by the National Assembly.

In July and August popular support in the southern provinces of Tay Ninh, An Giang, Cuu Long and Tien Giang for the reversal of land allocation decisions, and challenges by central highland ethnic groups claiming the land designated for New Economic Zones, galvanized the party to more responsive action.[104] During 17–19 August the party Secretariat and the Standing Committee of the Council of Ministers convened a meeting to redefine the process of adjusting land allocations and to confront the issue of the continued operation of weak co-operatives and production collectives. Vo Van Kiet presided over the meeting, attended by southern party committee secretaries, administrative committee chairmen, propaganda and training section chiefs, and peasant association chairmen. Kiet underscored the Politburo's high level of concern over the issue, and Party Secretary Le Phuoc Tho, Chairman of the Central Committee's Agricultural Department, articulated the party's draft response to the problem. The problem, according to the media's account of the meeting, was defined as essentially a local one. Provinces were to be responsible for solving the land problems that confronted their individual state farms. Local party organizations, in conjunction with district administrative and party structures, were to review the disposition of individual cases handled directly by state-run economic organs and units. The policy articulated at the meeting held the line of redistributing allocated land to two criteria. Only land initially distributed to recipients lacking good prior records of production would be reallocated. The party was not prepared to entertain claims by organized owners. The only other instance in which the party and state were prepared to reverse land use decisions involved cases where unclaimed lands were taken from farmers who had fallow plots under cultivation. The party sought to protect land utilized by co-operatives and production collectives, and land that had been put to "stabilized production" use for a long time on the basis of "voluntary mutual aid" or production partnerships not organized by the state.

Public demonstrations of peasant discontent continued unabated through early September. Late August press reports mentioned farmers squatting in fields to reclaim lands confiscated without compensation. By late August provincial authorities in An Giang, Cuu Long and Tien Giang had completed the first steps necessary for the prosecution of individuals arrested for creating public disturbances.[105] A late August Politburo resolution promised that administrative measures or legal action would be taken against violators of the land law and those who undertook "ruthless land appropriations".[106] The resolution also noted that the Council of Ministers would supervise promulgation of legal implementing documents for the land law and Politburo Resolution Ten, in co-ordination with the Ministry of Agriculture and Food Industry, the General Land Management Department, the Central Committee's Agricultural Department, and the Peasant Association. By early September, on the basis of the authority of that resolution, the Council of Ministers had been charged with directing the sectors that were judged responsible for "irrational" land planning to co-ordinate with local governmental structures in reformulating land allocations.[107]

During the last quarter of 1988 the party sought to preserve the reform policies in the agricultural sphere and to confront intensifying local disputes over land allocations. The priority was achieving stability in production and confining the land problem to as narrow a band of legal issues as possible, including title, right of occupancy and appropriate legal use of lands. The party convened several sessions and sought to bring to bear the influence of increasingly higher levels of leadership in resolving the land problem, while simultaneously validating the party's agricultural development strategy.

In mid-September General Secretary Linh addressed a conference of party secretaries in Ho Chi Minh City that was convened by the Central Committee Secretariat. The conference brought together party secretaries, agricultural service heads and propaganda and training cadre from 21 southern provinces with the aim of focusing on Politburo Directive 47 of 31 August. Linh encouraged support for the party's agricultural policy, and urged that farmers intensify cultivation and engage in multicropping. He endorsed population redistribution programmes and the development of new land areas.[108]

In the last quarter of the year the party continued to emphasize the importance of local solutions and supported the strategy that empowered provincial authorities to adjudicate peasant complaints, with the aim of confining public demonstrations against agricultural and land use policy.[109] The Central Committee Secretariat and the Standing Committee of the Council of Ministers issued directives to the effect that all provinces should resolve farm land issues locally in a manner that would discourage peasants from taking their complaints to Ho Chi Minh City.[110]

Though the party urged local resolution of the conflict over land use decisions, it increasingly undertook to structure the process of local inspections in the last quarter of the year. The party gave its blessing to southern provincial key cadre conferences that convened in October to discuss local land disputes, and the subsequent dispatching of provincial cadre to select villages to hear local complaints about land policy. By mid-November there was some indication that efforts to solve land disputes had been linked to the convening of grass-root Party Congresses.[111]

In early November five teams of central level cadre led by four Central Committee members and one State Committee Chairman descended on five provinces — Tieng Giang, Hau Giang, Long An, Cuu Long and Dong Thap — to inspect the local process of resolving land issues.[112] The regime named Nguyen Thanh Binh, a standing member of the Secretariat, and Central Committee Secretary Le Phuoc Tho to head two of the teams, demonstrating the priority the Politburo accorded to the quick resolution of land conflicts.[113] During the first week of November the standing body of the Council of Ministers charged Chairman of the State Inspection Committee Huynh Chau So with the responsibility of representing the central government in the establishment of inspection teams, which were to join with people's committee chairmen, vice chairmen, and functional organs of the provinces in confronting the problem of land disputes.[114] On 10 November, Nguyen Thanh Binh and Le Phuoc Tho, and an assortment of Central Committee members and the Chairman of the State Inspection Committee convened a conference of nine Mekong Delta provinces in Ho Chi Minh City to review the record of efforts to implement Politburo Resolution Ten and Directive 47. Press coverage of the conference noted that the participants acknowledged the sluggishness of efforts to provide "concrete guidance" to localities seeking to put the party's pronouncements into effect, and suggested that the Politburo was poised to issue such guidelines.[115] On 24 and 25 November the Central Committee's Agricultural Department convened a meeting of heads of agricultural and economic committees from five northern provinces, in conjunction with the Ministry of Agriculture and Food Industry and the General Department of Land Management, to focus on inadequacies of Resolution Ten's effort to restructure economic management. The conference delved into local difficulties over the subdivision of co-operatives, and the definition of co-operative management board responsibilities.[116] In late November the Council of Ministers sought to clarify the regulations on individual economic holdings and privately operated enterprises, rearticulating the outer limits of permissible use of land and special considerations regarding the parcelling out of state lands to private enterprises.[117] On 5 and 6 December the Secretariat held a conference in Ho Chi Minh City to assess the results of Politburo Directive 47.[118]

The combination of the decision to devolve responsibility for adjudicating land disputes to local levels and the urge to retain a salient role for the central party apparatus yielded an awkward status for local decision-making structures and demonstrated the inability of the central authorities to react in decisive and effective ways in the face of difficult questions involving the allocation of diminishing economic resources. Administrative levels subordinate to the provinces were to make spot decisions and orchestrate rapid inspection work, while being required to pay close attention to the confusing directives of a surprised and stuttering central apparatus. The local structures involved in processing complaints were often dominated by party functionaries holding multiple roles who were capable of effectively protecting their distinct interests and nullifying or ignoring decisions by the provincial party committee.[119] The conflict over land policy caught the party ill-prepared to confront public demonstrations, unable to compromise in a rapid, effective manner that would have diffused the issue, and unprepared to try acting strongly for fear of jeopardizing the agricultural reforms.

Party and State End-of-Year Sessions

In December 1988 the National Assembly pre-empted the customary end-of-year plenary session that would have capped the year with a final, comprehensive report for the party. Instead, the Assembly session dominated the last month of 1988, and the plenum was postponed. The next Central Committee meeting was not convened until March 1989. The decision to rearrange the cycle of Central Committee meetings was meant to highlight the independence and strength of the Parliament, and underscore the regime's actual progress towards instrumenting a separation of government and party functions. Nguyen Van Linh did not attend the opening session of the National Assembly, breaking another customary practice that had served to remind the legislature of the ubiquitous power of the party.[120] A late December Vietnamese News Agency summary report of the ten-day legislative session emphasized the importance of this alteration in schedule,

> The most obvious renovation that can be seen in this session is the renovation on the leadership of the party towards the National Assembly's work. While in the past such problems as the state plan and budget were worked out and decided beforehand by the party, this time, the Politburo of the party Central Committee laid down only the general orientations and major tasks, leaving the concrete contents, targets and measures of implementation to the Council of Ministers which has the duty to report to the National Assembly for deliberation and adoption.[121]

Though the plenary meeting was postponed, the party did convene a special Politburo session in early December that focused on ideological work, and culminated in the establishment of a committee for ideological tasks (Uy Ban Cong Tac Tu Tuong) which was subordinate to the Politburo. That special session, presided over by Nguyen Van Linh, enumerated a set of requirements for "broadening democracy" that placed the burden of action on the government. The Politburo called for the enacting of a press law, a law governing publishing, a law controlling cultural and artistic activities, and new statutes enabling the National Assembly and people's councils to take a more activist hand in state affairs.[122]

The rearrangement of the schedule of party and government meetings, and the Politburo's acknowledgement of the importance of legislation to the implementation of reformist goals, marked a significant realignment of authority and a reorientation of institutional relations that had begun in earnest with the June National Assembly session. The stiff, formal and cosmetic parliamentary process had become more distinctively active, relevant and effective. A more free-wheeling approach to on-the-floor parliamentary debate, open nomination and election practices, and an activism on the part of younger, better educated and more serious-minded representatives who assertively used their positions to demand government accountability combined to yield a National Assembly with teeth. Elected representatives demonstrated an ability and will to closely question ministers and state committee chairmen on government policies and actions, and to call for the redress of specific grievances and appropriate disciplinary steps against government and party officials.[123] At the December session, National Assembly deputies were especially exacting in their analyses of internal economic and social problems and foreign policy issues. For example, deputies pointedly criticized Vo Van Kiet's report to the National Assembly on the state of the economic reforms, taking him and the system to task for the Council of Ministers' halting and ineffective responses to problems associated with foreign currency exchange rates, and tax and subsidy policies. Deputies spoke forcefully about the failure of the Council to correct the procedures and the cumbersome staff structures that continued to impede its functioning.[124] The National Assembly's standing committees were to convene more frequently and for longer periods to increase their responsiveness to the citizenry. National Assembly delegates had begun to establish offices in the provinces by mid-1988, in imitation of the activism of Ho Chi Minh City delegate members of the functional committees. A sharper sense of the role of laws and regulations emphasized the leverage available to members of the Assembly through the authority to reform standing law, make decisions on proposed bills, and formulate means for implementing party decisions and policies. The changes in the functioning and influence of the legislature continued the disciplined evolution in the role of the party, increasingly confined to the watchdog role of ensuring the strategic soundness of the policy, and the procedural and organizational changes decreed by the Sixth Party Congress. This reflected Linh's emphasis on the distinction between "line and policies" and "implementation".

The adjustments in the division of labour represented by the empowering of the National Assembly were not intended to alter the party's position as the fulcrum of the reformed system, but rather to rebalance the relationship so that a more thoroughly co-operative exercise of power at all levels would characterize the link between the governing apparatus and the party. In Linh's version of a reformed calculus of party-state relations, the party coexisted with: (1) a streamlined state machinery responsible for carrying out policies, (2) a system of elective organs and a National Assembly with a significantly enhanced legislative role, and (3) mass organizations developed to capably represent distinct sectoral interests and special groups. To Linh, the party would remain the centre of gravity for this system. At every level party committees would retain the leadership role, but as one element of the equation of power in tandem with local administrative committees. Administrative committees would yield a greater influence over decisions, but the process of decision-making would involve a closer co-ordination between all of the elements of the system.[125]

three
1989: Turning Back to Orthodoxies
Conservative Backlash and
the Impact on Reform

Introduction
In the first months of 1989 the party set the pace for the rapid completion of the grass-root organization congresses. District level pilot projects sought to integrate government and non-party representatives into the conventions of delegates that were held up as the models for the future provincial party congresses. The party attempted to widen participation and to change the rules governing party-state relations while guaranteeing the continuity of the party's ruling role. The reformist momentum was sustained, but a strong undercurrent of concern for old values, basic revolutionary precepts, and the consequences of organizational change for the party served as a partial brake on reform.

District Party Congresses and
the Continuing Grass-root Process
Basic party organization and district congresses proceeded in January, focusing on the economic steps necessary to confront pressing shortages. The congresses addressed critical organizational and leadership shortcomings and defined future plans and programmes in agricultural

production, cadre education and "socio-economic development".[126] Pilot project districts set the pace for the process of reviewing targets and evaluating shortcomings in local socio-economic programmes and economic plans. Some district party committees allowed non-party delegates representing privately-owned and family-operated enterprises to participate in congresses. Representatives of special sectors and interests including technical and scientific cadre were entitled to seek delegate status.[127]

The Vietnamese media advertised the efforts of the grass-root congresses to introduce "democracy and openness" in the discussions, replicating the free-wheeling approach to debate of the December 1988 National Assembly session.[128] In February provincial party committees began to exert more of a structuring influence on the grass-root process by articulating time-sensitive plans for the accomplishment of party and administrative reorganization, announcing a time limitation for the formulation of the 1990–95 cadre plans (the end of the first quarter of 1989), and setting recruitment quotas for 1989–90.[129] Following the plenum in March, provincial and municipal party committees convened party and government conferences, enlarged executive committee sessions, and special cadre meetings to study the Central Committee's plenary resolution and review efforts to implement the economic reforms. Politburo members and Central Committee secretaries chaired some of the conferences and emphasized the importance of the three economic programmes, the urgency of controlling inflation, the central importance of party renovation and continued efforts to "broaden democracy" and transform the relationship between the party, the government and the mass organizations.[130]

By mid-March, most precincts and districts had concluded their Congresses. Municipal and district party secretaries and deputies were assigned to monitor the progress of subordinate level party organizations in the drafting of reviews of achievements since the last local resolution and in defining the agenda for the next term of the local committee. "Key cadres", under the supervision of designated members of the local standing committee, were to receive the draft reports and action plans. Specialized seminars convened by district party organizations or enterprise party committees were to provide one additional level of review for the documents. The seminars were to draw on science and technology cadres, representatives of municipal-level party and administrative committees, and ordinary, unaffiliated citizens to complete these reviews.

The party advertised several distinctive changes in the organization and conduct of these local congresses. For example it presented supplementary reports on local economic performance to the congresses to support a more exacting review of local productivity and performance. The organization was measurably more attentive to administrative matters beyond the standard preoccupation with basic policy and programmes. The party was more systematic in its approach to elections based on the 1988 membership reviews, and more scrupulous in its approach to the conduct of elections to the point of experimenting with the use of secret ballots and candidacy lists that contained more names than the number of executive committee slots to be filled by election.[131]

Provincial party key cadre conferences were convened through May and September, and generated local discussion concerning the modalities of the reforms. The provincial meetings focused on local efforts to operationalize the sixth plenary resolution, economic productivity, the programme of agricultural reform according to Politburo Resolution Ten, and the means of granting provincial "economic units" a freer hand in import-export ventures.[132] Enlarged executive committee sessions also focused on the need to restore the party's central role through organizational reform and more effective leadership, and on the decline of "public order". Provinces committed themselves to house-cleaning efforts. For example, the Song Be Provincial Party Committee resolved to replace unqualified enterprise directors and to establish a management board to oversee budget planning down to the village level.[133] Party Congresses in Hau Giang focused on recommending candidates to the new provincial party executive committees.[134]

Staying the Reformist Course:
The Sixth Plenum, March 1989

The sixth plenary session of the Sixth Central Committee was held from 20 to 29 March 1989. Nguyen Van Linh's closing address of 29 March depicted a plenum marked by "frank and open discussion" that had focused on evaluating progress in the economic field and the process of "social democratization", and ended by claiming modest successes for the programme of reforms. According to Linh, under the regimen of economic and social reforms a wider range of consumer goods and foodstuff had been made available in greater quantities, the grain supply had increased slightly, the rate of price increases had slowed, and the people's confidence in the system's ability to provide minimal economic security had been "initially restored". In Linh's words,

> The policies on renovating the economic structure along the line of concentrating on the three economic programmes, on developing the potential of the various economic components, on renovating the mechanism of economic management, on reorienting foreign, national defence and security policies, on democratizing social life, and so forth have been more clearly reflected in life and brought about initial results. We cherish the fruits of labour created by the untold energy and the unwavering spirit of struggle of our cadre, party members and the people. Like a person who can now begin to get up, though unsteadily, after a long, serious illness, this is a welcome and encouraging sign.[135]

However, the "high level of unanimity" was limited to a broad agreement on the shape of the enduring problems, and a basic consensus on the instruments required to address those problems. Serious disagreements continued within the party Central Committee over the thrusts of programmes central to the reforms, and over approaches to particular issues. Linh crystallized several of the disagreements in his closing address to the plenary session on 29 March, focusing on the differences of opinion over the expansion of foreign trade, the role of market mechanisms, the importance of the mixed economic forms to the programme of renovation, the character of government control over the economy, and the role of the party.

Foreign Trade

Linh identified two opposite "tendencies" within the party over the strategic decision to expand foreign economic relations.[136] The first was reluctance to expand relations and excessive caution once the doors were opened. The second was the excessive emphasis on the positive, redeeming aspects of an open trade and investment environment that rejected "preventative measures" against "unfavourable possibilities". Linh advocated continued initiatives to expand foreign economic relations, and urged the party to take initiatives to cope with the dislocations and problems caused by this decision by applying reasoned, planned but dynamic means of implementing the strategy. Linh spoke of the need to revamp the State Committee for Investment and to train a substantial cadre to do business with foreign countries as two indispensable steps, suggesting that ministerial and personnel weaknesses continued to threaten the efforts to upgrade Vietnam's "active participation in the process of the international division of labour".

The Central Committee's plenary communiqué, however, was somewhat more terse and less prescriptive in formulating a position on the foreign trade issue. Linh may have represented a more optimistic, forward-leaning position than the Central Committee was prepared to take. He reported "unanimous agreement" on the need to "actively participate in international trade — particularly with the Soviet Union, Laos, Cambodia and other socialist countries as well as India while developing... foreign economic relations with all other countries". However, the communiqué did not acknowledge this formula as an article of faith, and offered a more agnostic expression of the role that dynamic foreign economic interaction would play in the process of renovation. The communiqué noted that the regime had indeed "shifted" guidelines for foreign relations strategy, and that this had "gradually opened up new possibilities and advantages to develop our relations of co-operation with our neighbouring countries and with other countries in the world". However, the communiqué was much less programmatic about actively pursuing this end, and called for more modest, incremental change, and acknowledged the trend towards expanded economic relations without the enthusiasm reflected in Linh's prescription for participation in an altered division of national economic labour. The plenary communiqué committed the party to gradually work out a socio-economic strategy to determine guidelines for the arrangement of the economic structure and investment structure in the 1991–95 five-year plan and the expansion of economic relations with foreign countries.

Moreover, the communiqué contained a terse reminder of Vietnam's obligations to the socialist community of nations as the context in which the expansion of foreign trade should be considered.

The Role of the Market and the Strategy of the Mixed Economy

According to the General Secretary, a significant number within the party continued to abhor the market, and consequently had failed to understand the necessity of the limited experiments with market forms that characterized the Soviet reforms.[137] Linh supported expanded reliance on market mechanisms and closer examination of the application of market structures to select sectors, especially the export programme.

Though Linh spoke of the "high level of identical views" on the "necessity and long-term strategic significance" of "economic democracy", he seemed to suggest that a strong lobby for extremely limited, closely controlled utilization of the private and household economies in the reform of the Vietnamese economy continued to exist in the party. Linh defended the introduction of mixed forms and unbridled private business, arguing that the contours of the socialist economy had been irrevocably altered by the introduction of the mixed economic forms, and that the non-socialist elements in the economy would continue to function uninterrupted for the foreseeable future.

Linh confronted those within the party who argued for a statute of limitations on the functioning of those capitalist forms on the assumption that they represented a quick means of fixing the state-controlled economy, and should be corralled and expunged as soon as the situation had stabilized. The General Secretary argued that the new rules would remain the governing guidelines for economic behaviour. In his words,

> Marx observed an economic form does not disappear when it still has its production force and when there is no higher and effective form to substitute for it. At present and for a long time to come the state economic sector and co-operatives will still be unable to satisfy the people's multifarous demands. The length of time [that the state and co-operative economy will have to coexist with the mixed and the individual economy] cannot be determined by a specific number of months and years. It can be settled only by the level of economic development and by the vigorous growth of the socialist economy to the point of meeting nearly all demands for goods of society.

Linh strongly defended the party's decision to "recognize the existence and development of the private economic component". He castigated the persisting prejudices against that economic form, the failure to accurately evaluate the contribution of the private component, and the instinctive attempts to limit the development of the constituent parts of a mixed economy. Importantly, he also identified the deleterious effects of a spontaneous, uncontrolled development of the new components. Linh encouraged guidance of the private and household economy towards investment in production and services, underwrote limits to the participation of those forms in trade and food catering businesses, endorsed continued state control and the right of the central government to conduct inventories of the goods and assets of these businesses, and generally supported the notion that these private components of the economy could be gradually nudged towards accepting socialist rules for economic activity.

Socialist Transformation

Linh argued for a judicious use of law and leverage in government attempts to control the economy, and against forceful and disruptive exertion of state prerogatives.[138] He sought to blunt the potentially costly use of intrusive enterprise registration policies, state-mandated limits on products authorized for sale by private businesses, and rules governing the ways in which goods produced above the level defined in the state plan could be used by producers. Instead, Linh favoured a more orderly means of guaranteeing compliance with price management policies, assessment of profit and collection of taxes, and protection of the role and prerogatives of the state in controlling the market in an increasingly decentralized system. In Linh's words,

> It is mainly through the process of using management, regulation, inventory and control by the socialist state that we orient the capitalist economy towards different low and high forms of state capitalism.

Linh was against the excessive use of state intervention that had been directed against the southern economy in the 1978–79 Socialist Transformation of Private Industry and Commerce,

> There is no need to use the sabre-rattling word, transformation, that scares people because its former impression still remains heavy. The former simplistic and rude transformation procedures have disabled the production force of private individual and capitalist economies that are always essential to our society.

However, the plenary session communiqué enshrined the term "socialist transformation" as an expression of the continuing commitment to the "socialist road", an indication that supporters for the more cautious implementation of economic reforms could still muster enough votes to impose caveats on the unrestrained use of capitalist economic mechanisms. According to the communiqué, the reformist agenda — including the adjustment of the economic structure through the use of investment capital and renovated mechanisms of investment, and the implementation of the policy on multi-component economic structures — brought into focus issues of "long-term strategic significance relating to the rules governing the road to socialism from small production". That path towards socialism consisted of both an effort to "democratize" the economy by guaranteeing the freedom to all citizens to make a living in accordance with the law, and a simultaneous attempt to effectively carry out socialist transformation in accordance with the policies of the Sixth Party Congress.

However, Linh was not prepared to argue for uncontrolled reorganization of the economy. Though he strongly maintained that administrative orders cannot replace market relations, Linh favoured the planned management of the commodity economy. In Linh's words, the regime's policy was to make "full use" of the commodity-money relationship and market relations "as objective existing relations to link through market activities producers with consumers and to spur competition to make production more dynamic and effective". However, "full use" of market relations to propel the socialist reform involved a dimension of planning and authoritative regulation of the market mechanism. Linh, for example, argued that the state must influence the money commodity balance. In his words,

> We must continue to promote market developments so as to allow for equal and legal participation by all economic components. Nevertheless, control and guidance should not be relaxed. It should also be pointed out that the market does not negate planning, for the major factors of market − purchasing power, stocks of commodities − should and can be planned to a certain extent.

While the communiqué reflected Linh's position that controlling inflation is the most pressing task, and reiterated the commitment to renovating the mechanism of economic management, it also reflected the Central Committee's diminished desire to authorize broad licence to use markets and other economic levers to modify the socialist structure. Thus, the communiqué emphasized the extent to which structural, tactical and policy change did not depart from the overall ideological ends of the Vietnamese revolution. Renovation, according to the communiqué, does not mean changing the goal of socialism. Instead, it means "ensuring the effective realization of that goal through the adoption of correct concepts of socialism and suitable forms, steps and measures". According to the communiqué,

> Marxism-Leninism always serves as the ideological foundation of our party and guides the entire revolutionary undertaking of our people. Renovation in thinking is designed to overcome erroneous concepts and enrich correct concepts about our time and socialism for creative application and development, rather than to break away from the principles of Marxism-Leninism. Renovating the organization and operational mode of the political system is meant to strengthen

the party's role of leadership and the state's managerial efficacy and to develop the people's right to mastery — that is, to enhance the strength and efficiency of the dictatorship of the proletariat and make the organizations of the political system operate in a more dynamic and effective manner.

To Linh, the economic situation required new thinking, new definitions and flexibility, which did not signal abandonment of overarching goals but rather demanded a practical recognition of economic necessity. In his closing speech Linh stated that,

> Comprehensive socio-economic renovation inevitably entails renovation in the organization and operational mode of the political system along the line of continuing to broaden socialist democracy. This is an area in which we do not have much experience, but we must act with determination, caution, and careful preparation so as to preclude otherwise unavoidable adverse consequences.

Linh, in short, placed more emphasis on solving problems and making socialism work better than on hatching enduring rules and axioms to describe the reforms and their role in the enterprise of the Vietnamese revolution.

The Role of the Party

According to the General Secretary, some quarters had sought to "weaken or nullify" the party's leadership role, and to create a "political counterweight" to the party through the enfranchisement of various interest groups and other components of the activated society.[139] Those interests took the position that the party stood as an impediment to reform, and that broadened political participation by social groups would generate political and economic change. Linh called the critics of the party's leadership role a "small number of ill intentioned people". He defended the party's central role in the reform process, and supported the enhancement of that role rather than efforts to diminish the party's power. Linh, however, urged the development of a partnership between the party and the state characterized by a sharing of power and adherence to a stringent division of labour.

To Linh, the party played a central role in broadening democracy through parallel efforts to improve the organization of government mechanisms, enhance the role of the National Assembly and elected organs at all levels, and develop the role of mass organizations. However, in his words, "we advocate broadening democracy and reaching a consensus through debate, but we do not tolerate pluralism. Democracy needs party leadership; and conversely, party leadership must be based on democratic methods".

The plenary communiqué was somewhat more categorical about the limits to the process of democratization, and the obligation to protect the centrality of the party,

> We must criticize the tendencies to negate or belittle party leadership, and at the same time we must attentively listen to and accept sincere views of shortcomings in party leadership and party building.
>
> Broadening democracy in all fields of social life and developing the people's right to mastery is both the goal and the driving force of building socialism. This is socialist democracy, not bourgeois democracy. Democracy must go together with centralism, discipline, the sense of responsibility as citizens, and respect for the law. Democracy requires leadership, and leadership must be aimed at developing democracy in the right definition and through correct democratic methods. Democracy is applied to the people, but strict punishment must be meted out to those who undermine the gains of the revolution, security, and social order.

The Meaning of the Plenum

Linh's manoeuverability was further constrained by the sixth plenary session, which more stringently defined the operating assumptions of the increasingly cautious Central Committee without foreclosing on the reformist goals. Linh was reminded that his formula for remaking the economy and the party-state relationships was limited by the reluctance of at least a plurality of party decision-makers to accept major departures from the political, ideological and organizational core of the revolution. The plenum demonstrated basic endorsement of the sweeping changes that had taken place, and acknowledged that the party had missed its cues,

The party's leadership task and the state's management work have displayed many shortcomings. For instance: there has been a lag in efforts to review the actual situation in order to clarify a number of viewpoints and steps to advance in the process of renovation. The institutionalization of various party resolutions remains slow and there have been cases where this work is not carried out correctly and consistently. The renovation of the party's and state's tasks regarding party building and cadre organization are slow. The task regarding ideological guidance lacks self-motivation and there has been a failure to anticipate erroneous tendencies that may arise in the process of renovation for timely correction.[140]

However, the plenum defined the limits of the Central Committee's willingness to engage in social engineering, massive political change, and free-wheeling economic experimentation.

Conspicuous by its absence was an authoritative statement about foreign policy changes and priorities, and Vietnam's explanation of its position on Cambodia. According to Western press speculation preceding the plenum, Nguyen Co Thach was scheduled to address the Central Committee on the party's foreign policy plank. Hun Sen had paid a short visit to Hanoi on or about 19 March, prior to the opening of the plenary session, and several of Hanoi's ambassadors had been summoned home at the same time, presumably for consultations on the Vietnamese troop withdrawal proposal that was articulated in a joint Indochinese statement on 5 April. Major new twists had been added to the contours of Vietnam's foreign policy on Cambodia, on relations with the West, on Indochina links, and on relations with the Association of Southeast Asian Nations (ASEAN). The party had not issued a major declaration of foreign policy goals and intentions at any of the plenary meetings since the December 1986 Party Congress. As a result of all these changes, the party had a good deal of ground to cover in formulating a summary of developments in foreign affairs since the national meeting and providing a formulaic expression of fundamental foreign policy aims as they had emerged under Linh's direction. An expanded Politburo session, including select Central Committee members, was reported by the Western media to have occurred prior to the convening of the plenary session, and though this meeting was not discussed in the Vietnamese media it is conceivable that the party's foreign policy was the subject of a high level review at such a special, closed session.[141] Nevertheless, the plenary communiqué is devoid of any indication that the party was prepared to offer a capsule statement of foreign policy aims. Apart from isolated axioms about internationalist obligations and caveats about the unbridled expansion of foreign trade relations, the plenum's summary document gave every indication that the Central Committee was unable to devise a consensus statement about foreign policy.

Issues in the Aftermath of the Plenum

By mid-April, the party had formulated six principles for renovation that were to guide the enterprise of reform:

1. Advancing to socialism is the inexorable way of our country and the judicious choice of President Ho Chi Minh and of our party. The building of a socialist Vietnam is the objective and ideal of our party and people. Renovation, far from altering the socialist objective, is aimed at effectively achieving this objective through correct concepts about socialism, in appropriate forms and with appropriate steps and measures.
2. Marxism-Leninism is always the ideological basis of our party guiding the entire revolutionary cause of our people. Renovation of thinking is aimed at overcoming incorrect concepts and enriching the correct perceptions of the era and socialism while creatively applying and developing the principles of Marxism-Leninism instead of abandoning them.
3. Efforts to reform organizational work and the activity of the political system are aimed at strengthening the leadership of the party, the efficiency of state management and promoting the people's right to mastery, in other words, strengthening and increasing the efficiency of proletarian dictatorship and making the political organizations or system function with more dynamism and efficiency.
4. The party's leadership is the decisive factor for our people's cause of building and defending our socialist motherland. We must criticize the tendencies to negate or lower the party's leadership

while listening to and welcoming all frank criticisms of the shortcomings in the party's leadership and party building work.
5. Democracy must be expanded to all domains of social life. To promote the people's right to mastery is at the same time a motive force and an incentive in building socialism. Democracy here is socialist democracy, not capitalist democracy. It must be carried out along with centralism, discipline, the sense of responsibility of citizens and law observance. It must be a guided democracy so that it may be developed in the right direction and by democratic means. Democracy is applied to the people, while strict punishment must be meted out to the saboteurs of the revolutionary gains, security and public order and safety.
6. Combining patriotism with proletarian internationalism and socialist internationalism, combining the strength of the nation with that of the era in the new conditions.[142]

The principles stood as the regime's uncontrovertible bottom lines on the role of the party as ultimate arbiter of strategy and acceptable levels of flexibility in the reformist programme. A 1 April *Nhan Dan* editorial forcefully expressed this point,

> All renovations must comply with and must not go beyond these fundamental principles.
>
> Renovation does not mean to change our goal of socialism, but to enable this goal to be achieved effectively through correct concepts about socialism and through appropriate forms, courses of action, and measures.
>
> Renovative thinking does not mean distancing oneself from Marxist-Leninist principles, but applying and bringing these principles into play in a creative fashion and to enrich correct concepts about our times and socialism.
>
> Renovating organizations and the working method of the political system does not mean weakening the system of the dictatorship of the proletariat, but strengthening the party's leadership role and the state's management efficiency and bringing the people's right to mastery into play.
>
> Renovating the party leadership does not mean to negate nor downplay, but to intensify the party's leadership role, regarding

this as a decisive condition for the success of our revolutionary undertaking.

Renovating one's attitude and broadening democracy does not mean to embark on capitalist democracy, but to develop socialist democracy, guided democracy, and people's democracy while strictly punishing saboteurs.[143]

The editorials that followed the plenary session acknowledged that the six principles were far short of a "firm theoretical basis" for renovation. The authoritative party position was that they represented the first practical steps towards "building the political programme of the party". The editorial in the April issue of the party's theoretical journal stated that the Sixth Plenum had been unable to satisfy the demand for a clear definition of the transitional period and the "socialist pattern" appropriate to Vietnam. The six principles, however, articulated the basis for the "next steps and tasks of our current process". Interestingly, the formulation of those principles, according to the April *Tap Chi Cong San* editorial, "removed the worries from not a few people about the progress of socialist construction in our country".

Notwithstanding the party's claims to have allayed these worries by clearing the air about authority and direction, the differences of opinion over the economic reform programme that were given expression during the course of the March plenary session were not muted by the six principles that the party sought to establish as articles of faith. Rather, serious disagreements over the fundamentals of the reform programme prompted a reassessment of tactical choices and strategic decisions. For instance, an early April conference sponsored by the Central Committee's Propaganda and Training Department concluded with the acknowledgement that "practical and epistemological issues" required a re-evaluation of the "fundamental spirit" of Resolution Ten, a basic document laying the groundwork for the renovation of the mechanism of economic management in agriculture. The conference also recognized the need to re-examine the various decisions adopted by the party's Secretariat and the Council of Ministers in the service of Resolution Ten's provisions on signing contracts with the state, taxation, and the entitlement to dispose of production at the discretion of the individual agricultural producer.[144]

The Media in 1989: Restraining the Ombudsman

In 1987 Linh sought to involve the media in a process of public inspection of the party structure and membership intended to root out corruption. He urged that journalists focus on hitherto sacrosanct realms, including the process of party and government cadre selection and personnel advancement. Linh took steps towards turning his own public commentary, the "NVL" columns, into a self-sustaining instrument for protecting organizational standards. In 1988 Linh persisted in according the press virtual ombudsman responsibilities in the reformist campaign. In a mid-year conference of journalists and party secretaries, Linh acknowledged early opposition to his outspoken and publicly critical approach to problem-solving, and emphasized the manner in which the "NVL" columns supported the reformist, anti-corruption trends. By mid-1988 the leverage that Linh was able to bring to bear in sustaining the momentum of reforms through extra-party structures, an unleashed media, and newly enfranchised political interests had been diminished by the reaction of more cautious influences mindful of the party's prerogatives and inclined to reassert the basic formula for political power that favoured party dominance.[145]

In 1989 Linh's ability to use the media as a countervailing power to support his reforms in contests with conservatives diminished further as the party defined legal obligations and roles for the press, and established more effective levers of control over publishing houses and the electronic media. In April the party embargoed the issuance of new publication permits for a five month period until 30 August in order to establish a more formal control over the proliferation of publishing houses and the distribution of printed matter, original works and translated books.[146] In June, the Council of Ministers announced a decision on the management of press and publishing activities. According to the decision, the Ministry of Information would serve as the key instrument through which the Council would exert the state's influence over the media. The Ministry was given instructions to draft the necessary laws to facilitate that responsibility, and to enforce existing press, publishing and printing laws. During June and July, the party urged the quick drafting and submission to the

National Assembly of a law on publishing and on the media, and the establishment of control and inspection teams to govern publishing, printing and the circulation of printed matter.[147] The party spoke against the publication of privately-owned newspapers, and issued strong reminders of the need to sustain the role of the party in guiding the media while integrating some of the "new features" of the media — openness, sensitivity to public opinion, a freer hand at presenting news and reporting complaints — into operating instructions for the press.[148] In mid-year publishing houses were disciplined for publishing books that deviated from the list of prescribed topics, for printing without proper government authorization and permits, and for altering approved texts before publishing manuscripts. Journalists were held accountable before formal courts for articles alleged to be fabrications and other violations of the criminal code and decrees and directives governing the profession of journalism.[149] The Executive Committee report to the October Congress of the Vietnam Journalists Association underscored the importance of "renewing" the party's leadership and the state's managerial authority over the press, and squarely opposed the commercialization of the media,

> The ideological task in general, and for the press in particular, cannot be geared toward operating like a business with mere economic profits. It was previously correct and necessary to subsidize the press. If the press was left to run its own business and earn a living it would lead to harmful consequences.[150]

Do Muoi's speech to the Fourth Writers Congress in late October cautioned against allowing literature to "smear the party and state leadership and erode the people's confidence in the party and state". Ceaseless, unorganized debates could only be debilitating, he argued, and would detract from the character and process of socialist literature. Freedom of writing, criticism, debate, and diversity were not intrinsically threatening to the socialist order, but must be anchored to a well-defined plan presided over by the party and the government in order to avoid chaos.[151]

According to authorized media reports, the greatest controversy swirled around the draft press law, which was subjected to intense, "heated" debate in the December National Assembly session. The draft was revised after open discussion, and ultimately required special votes on the four most contentious issues contained within the 31 articles, 21 of which were modified as a result of debate.[152] The four issues that were brought to separate votes prior to the adoption of the modified legislation were (1) private sector operation of newspapers, (2) the requirement that papers seek permission to publish before beginning operation, (3) the role of the state management commission in appointing and relieving editors, and (4) the rights of and obligations to confidentiality of press sources, and the exceptions to the rights of confidentiality available to the chief procurator of the people's organ of control and the chief judge of the provincial people's court.[153]

At least three lines of argument over the press law emerged during the 26 and 27 December National Assembly debate. The first was strictly procedural, and focused on the extent to which the rules guiding the preliminary debate of draft legislation constrained effective discussion by placing a primacy on quick passage and limiting the time available for revision of the bill. Several Ho Chi Minh City delegates were credited with tabling this argument at the Ba Dinh Conference Hall debate in defence of a "legislative pattern" that was predicated on ample lead time – in excess of one month – for preliminary discussion of bills, revision preceding further discussion, and final passage of the draft law at a second National Assembly session.[154] The second line of argument addressed the issue of authorizing private ownership of newspapers by stressing the need for ownership forms to conform to economic realities. In a circumstance where private ownership was an artificial, unnatural economic accommodation, private holdings of newspaper licences would have to reflect the basic economic reality, i.e. the pre-eminence of collective and state-run sectors.

The third line of argument that emerged in the discussion of the press law focused on the implications of a free press for socialism and party leadership. The objection to the proposal for private newspapers did not seem to be that competitive views would trouble the party, but that a private press was simply incompatible with the character of socialism because private newspapers would reflect the class interests of their financiers, not the needs of the working class. This line received support from former Third Force activist Ms Ngo Ba Thanh, a National Assembly delegate from the south. Objections to her case were presented by other Ho Chi Minh delegates who noted that private newspapers could not jeopardize the rule of the party since power was already situated in the hands of the people. Other delegates argued that a ban on private newspapers would compromise the constitutional recognition of freedom of the press. According to media accounts of the proceedings, many southern and central delegates reacted to those views by supporting the position that freedom of the press was amply protected by the draft law itself, and making the case that sufficient vehicles for political expression already existed in the form of newspapers, radio and the force of mass and social organizations.

Security, Social Deterioration and Cultural Pollutants: Mai Chi Tho's Anti-crime Campaign

In 1988, the farmers marched in protest of the land laws. The protests prompted quick government attention to their complaints. In 1989, students in northern college campuses organized demonstrations against the harsh circumstances of student life.[155] General Secretary Linh's activation of the media made it easier to get a hearing in the press for complaints against the state and party bureaucracies. These circumstances caused concern among the more cautious party leaders who had seen the traditional formulae for political leadership altered in a manner that compromised the party's unfettered control over all aspects of social and economic life.

In 1988 the Politburo reacted to some of Linh's decisions by re-imposing controls on the media, reasserting the party's prerogative in decisions over the pace and scope of the reforms, and by bringing into focus the party's concerns over security and stability through the Movement Against Crime and Social Pollutants, another means of extending the party's reach back into areas over which it had always had a primary influence. The Movement continued in 1989 under the auspices of Minister of Interior Mai Chi Tho. In 1989, Tho sought to take on the increasing nationwide crime rates and the "serious deterioration" of public security. He was central to the organization and management of the mass movement for national defence and security, husbanding "progressive models", organizing regional conferences to survey local accomplishments in bringing civil and criminal violators to justice, and orchestrating co-operation between ministries, mass organizations and party Central Committee executive committees. In July and August the media carried stories about the proliferation of provincial security units and assault youth units established to work closely with provincial public security forces and army units to suppress illegal activities in the provinces.[156] Urban subwards and rural villages established social order and safety councils. The central government called for a more systematic application of existing laws; more rapid prosecution of criminals; an integrated approach to crime that combined centre-periphery, party-state and mass organization resources; and increased expenditures on public security forces to modernize equipment and facilities, and to upgrade cadre salaries.[157] By the last quarter of the year the media was trumpeting concerted actions against armed and organized criminal gangs, and the swift prosecution of violators.

As part of the task of controlling "social pollutants", the regime sought to limit access to foreign and domestic videos and literature judged to be offensive. The Ministry of Culture was made responsible for controlling commercial video screenings in co-operation with the Public Security Force cultural teams, for screening all videos intended for public viewing via the Central Cinematographic Corporation, and for co-operating with central and local government administrators to halt the import of video players for private use with the help of a high, punitive tax. The Ministry of Information, in co-operation with the National Assembly, was responsible for monitoring the media, preventing the circulation of unauthorized material and unapproved newspaper supplements, and preventing the publication of culturally or socially inappropriate original works and translations of foreign books through a system of licensing planned publications. The Ministry of National Defence devolved responsibility for resolving the issue of illegal video screenings within the military to unit commanders and unit party secretaries directly subordinate to the Ministry, the general departments and the Military Regions.[158]

Power Sharing

During 1989, the party reaffirmed its leadership role over the state, but accommodated to the need for reforms that accorded administrative structures and governing bodies more leeway and independence in decision-making. According to this argument, "The party does not need to become involved in administrative work, which is the function and responsibility of the state organizations or economic and technical organizations."[159] An early December analysis of social democracy and party leadership carried in *Nhan Dan* echoed a familiar refrain, "The party has interfered too deeply in state management, has reduced the effectiveness of state management, and at the same time, caused its leadership quality to decline." The cure involved infusing the state with political and legal power, emphasizing public and direct dialogue between the constituent parts of the policy process, according importance to the public dissemination of information on issues, and mandating public supervision and scrutiny of the policy process.[160]

The Sixth National Assembly session, convened from 18–28 December, went further than the fifth session towards granting the Assembly considerably more legislative authority. The party did not publicly convene a prefatory plenary session to set the pace for the parliamentary proceedings, repeating the departure from long-standing norms that marked the fifth session. Keynote National Assembly delegates – especially Politburo member and Chairman of the Council of State Vo Chi Cong – drew attention to the party leadership's conscious recognition of the need for a *modus vivendi* between the party and the state that would enable the legislature to flex its muscles and make decisions on legal and budgetary issues. National Assembly delegates formed internal alliances over specific issues and legislation to strengthen their respective positions, and voted in identifiable geographic blocs. Delegates were measurably more concerned with the impact of proposed national legislation on their constituencies, and were generally more focused, attentive to issues, and serious about their responsibilities as representatives. They closely questioned aspects of the proposed state plan in a manner that demonstrated their increasing mastery of economic issues. In his speech to the Assembly meeting, Vo Chi Cong reiterated the regime's view of the division of labour between the party, responsible for defining platforms, strategies and basic objectives, and the state, charged with implementing the basic goals.[161] In the planning realm, for example, the Politburo, Cong observed, provides the "major orientations", the Council of Ministers works out the details of the national economic plan, and the National Assembly utilizes its decision-making purview over specific legal and budgetary issues to promulgate legislation that will enable the plan to proceed.[162]

The regime stressed the limits of the party's purview over administrative committee activities, reiterating the importance of a minimal role for the party in selecting and vetting election lists for people's committees and people's councils. Delegates to the second session of the Vietnam Fatherland Front Central Committee plenum, held in Ho Chi Minh City in mid-August, unanimously agreed that the "old system" whereby the local party committee reviewed candidates before submitting approved election lists to the Front was no longer tenable. The campaign for a new people's council organizational law, which was submitted to the National Assembly in mid-year and passed by the fifth Assembly on 30 June, and the preparations for the three-level people's councils elections in November emphasized the need for an independent representative body, and a more scrupulous constitutional interpretation of the distinction between the legislative and executive organizations in the localities.[163]

One of the bolder statements on the necessity of reshaping the system by restoring power to the local elected bodies was made by Le Khac Thanh in the pages of the Army's daily newspaper in mid-January. Though Thanh couched his argument in terms supportive of a "reassumption" of the party's "rightful position", his more pressing agenda was constructing an argument for the empowering of people's councils. Thanh made the case that the party's penchant for uninhibited micromanagement violated basic Leninist precepts, and that the restoration of law as the central power of the system would allow a redefinition of the party's leadership role more in synchrony with the original revolutionary intent for a party that guides fundamental policy and leaves the driving to elective and appointed state bodies. Thanh criticized the extent to which the national assembly had abrogated its role as the organ of supreme power over the state machinery to the Council of Ministers, which ran the mechanisms in accordance with the resolutions of the Politburo, Central Committee, and the party Secretariat. He endorsed participation in politics by a broader slice of Vietnamese society, the "institutionalization" of the authority of the National Assembly in the Constitution, the reliance on juridical and constitutional power to reshape the political system, and the elimination of the practice of empowering individuals to hold concurrent legislative and executive positions.[164]

The party also focused closely on its shifting relationship with mass organizations as local representatives of non-party interests. The Thai Binh Provincial Party Committee, for example, reportedly urged the provincial Fatherland Front organization to redefine its own relationship with the provincial administrative committee by drafting a regulation encapsulating that connection, and recognized the importance of allotting more provincial leadership positions to Fatherland Front cadre who were party members. The party Committee also reflected on the necessity of broadening the participation of Fatherland Front chapters to include private economic "delegates" and families with relatives overseas. The Thai Binh Party Committee chairman took the position that the Fatherland Front should shoulder greater responsibility for arbitrating local conflicts involving Front members. He also urged the Front to organize itself in a more effective, committee-centred fashion to facilitate taking responsibility for more specific areas of local and provincial administrative work. Fatherland Front and party activities in villages and districts discussed similar themes, and complained that the Front, the People's Council, the peasant association, Youth Union and women's association had become "flower pots", mere displays whose functions had been usurped by local party structures.[165] Party newspapers decried declining membership in youth unions and progressively lower yearly levels of union members eligible for party cards.[166] The party stressed the importance of paying greater attention to fine-tuning relations with religious groups, ethnic minorities, and ethnic Chinese-populated areas, and developing "vocational" mass organizations.[167] The party, editorials urged, should not do everything for the mass organizations, but neither should the mass organizations seek an environment free from party influence. Editorials and articles in party-controlled publications stressed the right of private citizens to run for public office, and the rights of non-party "social organizations" to table their own recommendations for candidacies. The regime authorized the Vietnam Fatherland Front to prepare caucuses of such social and mass organizations to discuss candidates independent of the party.[168] The aim was a "harmonious" system that balanced improving the efficiency of the state and broadening participation with ensuring the party's leadership role. The party understood that expanded economic rights had engendered an interest on the part of the greater number of players in expressing their political preferences. The party also understood that the emphasis on the wider dissemination of information had developed an atmosphere of "openmindedness" which placed a premium on public discussion and frank debate. However, though the party sought a demure and incremental renovation of the balance of political power in the Vietnamese system, the possibility of delicately controlling the "new developments" receded as opportunities for self-expression and the formation of like-minded groups of economic and social actors increased.

A case in point is the formation of southern communists, intellectuals and army cadre into the Club of Former Resistance Fighters, founded in 1988 by General Tran Van Tra, former Saigon party Committee Secretary Tran Bach Dang, and former Ho Chi Minh City People's Committee Chairman Nguyen Ho. In 1989 the Club, which had established branches in some southern provinces and in Ho Chi Minh City, clandestinely printed its own newspaper that expressed dissatisfaction with the party and its leadership, and supported the democratic election of a prime minister through secret ballot and the neutralization of the VNCP's role in such an election. The prestige of the founding members of the Club, who were all first generation revolutionaries, was of sufficient concern to the regime to prompt the confiscation of the Club's first printing of its newspaper, *The Tradition of Resistance*, and to launch the party on a concerted effort to co-opt and control the Club. The activism of distinguished retired general officers and senior party officials, and the political atmosphere encouraging frank, critical and constructive dialogue in the press and increased activism within legislative bodies ultimately prompted the leadership's preoccupation with re-establishing the primacy of the party, and the near obsessive criticism of pluralism.[169] By mid-year the party acknowledged that the reforms had produced uneven results, and that the goal of "democracy" had been complicated by a local-level backlash of party organizations unwilling to accommodate changes, surrender prerogatives, and enforce new laws.

The Steadying Hand of Orthodoxy: Foreign Policy Direction and the Seventh Plenum, August 1989

The party held its seventh plenary session from 15–24 August under the chairmanship of General Secretary Nguyen Van Linh. The meeting focused on the impact of world currents on socialist revolutions and the influence of internal reform processes on Vietnam's role in the socialist community. The plenary communiqué and Nguyen Van Linh's closing speech marked a turn to the steadying hand of orthodoxy by the party leadership.[170]

The plenary session took up the issue of the party's international plank in a public session for the first time since the 1986 National Congress. However, in the General Secretary's "important speech" to the session, the business of the meeting was described as relating to "ideological work in the face of the current internal and international situations". The party had not gotten much closer to a consensus on practical matters of regional and foreign policy. The Central Committee did not offer to sanctify party policy on relations with China, the approach to ongoing negotiations on Cambodia, or the current status of U.S.-Vietnamese relations. There had been few publicly announced special Politburo sessions to consider fast-breaking international events. Foreign policy was being run out of a few vest pockets via tightly controlled consultations at the highest levels of the political command structure.

Linh's closing speech to the seventh plenary session had the uncharacteristic ring of a stiff ideological message. The General Secretary urged adherence to party discipline, respect for the unity of the socialist community and continued attention to internationalist responsibilities. From December 1986 when he ascended to the post of General Secretary, Linh studiously avoided speaking in the idiom of ideology, demonstrating an adeptness at balancing a respect for the icons and the founding ideas of revolution with a recognition of the need for a new flexible manner of speech and thought for socialist thinkers, planners, and managers. His seventh plenary closing speech marks a departure from his less strident manner. Linh made the case for orthodoxy in language that sounded alien in his voice: Marxism-Leninism appeared as "the lodestar guiding us on our path", and while Linh urged avoiding servile imitation and rigid attitudes, he mapped out a rather determinist course of progress for the economic and social reforms implemented under his auspices that hinged on the inevitable progress of socialism and the inexorable process of imperialist decay.

Linh made five basic points in his seventh plenum speech. First, the basic forces of competition between capitalism and socialism continue to drive history. Though the capitalist world had generated a significant standard of living, this magnified the contradictions that exist between the Third World and the capitalist countries. Imperialism had escalated the nature of conflict to an extremely militant point that involved competing nations in massive and deadly nuclear arms races. The bottom line remained unaltered: socialism will prevail, but imperialism will not be dispatched by a simple, rapid action. On the contrary, it will linger, perhaps for centuries.

Second, in this context Vietnam's initial choice remained the correct and judicious one: to strive to build socialism by carrying out the bourgeois revolution before waging the socialist revolution.

Third, the instrument for achieving this socialist end is the Vietnamese Communist Party. "This is the party that represents the will and interests of the working class and labouring people and is armed with creative Marxism-Leninism..." Creative Marxism-Leninism had led the party to a programme of comprehensive reforms and an effort to clarify the characteristics of socialism in Vietnam.

Fourth, the reforms necessitated the introduction of democracy into every corner of the economy and polity. However, the introduction of democracy did not entail the introduction of political pluralism, the creation of multiple competing parties, and the denial of the centrality of the communist party.

Fifth, the preservation of socialist advances depended in large part upon sustaining the community of revolutionary countries and movements. Vietnam, Linh noted, owed a profound debt to fraternal parties and friends, and the Vietnamese revolution has in turn exerted an important influence on the development of "revolutionary currents" in the world.

From December 1986, Linh framed his pronouncements on regional relations and foreign affairs in tough language, and stated the Vietnamese position on foreign policy issues in firm and conservative terms. Though he presided over some distinctive changes in fundamental foreign policy strategies, Linh obviously had an interest in strongly defending the Vietnamese revolution. It is conceivable that Linh had reserved the realm of foreign policy as the plane on which he would take the more orthodox positions, as the price necessary to convince the conservative interests to refrain from scuttling his internal reform programme. It is also likely that he considered himself to be at a disadvantage in the foreign policy realm in the company of such policy czars as Nguyen Co Thach, and had taken the path of least resistance by stating Vietnam's foreign policy positions in conventional and conservative terms. In the past that allowed him to take some bold steps on the domestic scene while sticking to the mainstream visions of Vietnam's regional and international role.

Restating Ideological Bottom Lines

Two lines of thought crystallized during January and February, and gained a momentum in the context of the sixth plenary session of the Central Committee in late March.

The first centred on the question of the overall theoretical foundation of the reform programme, and the efficacy of the economic decisions that were at the heart of the reform programme in the early 1980s. The party leadership had acknowledged responsibility for the failure to fix the economy at the sixth National Congress in December 1986 and at the end-of-year plenary and National Assembly sessions in 1987. The leadership admitted to squandering opportunities, to being overly cautious and sluggish in their responses to problems, and to inadequately understanding basic economic danger signs. The critical retrospective that took shape in early 1989 sought a more systematic definition of key causes of failure. In Le Khac Thanh's words, the problem was not simply the failure of a certain organization, section or individual to make changes, "Something more of a general character is the root cause of contradiction."[171]

The second line of thought centred on the role of the party in the reform effort. Discussions of this issue developed as a reaction against escalating criticisms of the party's management of economic problems and the overall capacity of the VNCP to regain popular confidence and perform its leadership role.

These two lines of thought and other conflicts over theory and direction were addressed in several philosophical discussions of the first principles of socialism that appeared in the party's daily newspaper and its theoretical monthly journal. The writings, part of a continuing effort to more firmly anchor renovation to the enterprise of socialist revolution and to the mainstream of Marxist theory, made several essential points.

1. *Socialism is a vibrant, fluid system of ideas, not a complex of rigid definitions or a fixed ideal in whose image reality must be contoured to achieve revolutionary ends.*
   This argument enabled abandonment of limiting concepts of the socialist path, and allowed emphasis on "national characteristics" and the freedom of innovation. In a January article in *Tap Chi Cong San*, Nguyen Dang Quang, editor of *Tap Chi Giao Duc Ly Luan* (*The Journal of Theoretical Education*), wove his case from the Marxist and Leninist classics,[172]

> Our teachers clearly said that communism is not... an ideal that must be duplicated in reality, but it is a real movement for eliminating the present condition. Lenin specifically explained that: "With a view to replace 'imaginative' definitions bearing the scholastic and untrue nature... (what is socialism, what is communism), Marx analysed what people may call steps toward economic maturity of communism." "Marx did not imagine or think of any new society ... Marx studied the emergence of a new society from the old one. He studied various forms of transition from one society to another and regarded this a natural historical process."... In this spirit, we should not tie ourselves to such rigid and one-sided "definitions" to describe socialism. We should begin answering the question "what is socialism?" by analysing the real situation of the Vietnamese nation and people at a turning point of history and analysing evolutionary steps in conformity with the law to develop the people's democracy to the initial path of socialism.

Quang supported a flexible, adaptable application of socialist principles that would allow for the recognition of evolving circumstances and local peculiarities,

> We may have to debate extensively on socialist characteristics according to the current concept. But we have to consistently perfect our "definitions" of socialism to keep pace with the era's development. During the past half century we did very little in reviewing this scientific task because we contended that capitalism has been proceeding to its final stage, and that what should be continued or eliminated Marx, Engels, and Lenin had already defined for us. As a result, our awareness of socialism has become increasingly backward as far as the reality of socialist society and of the era is concerned. This is a root cause creating confusion and oscillation for us. To overcome this confusion and oscillation by reasserting totally the existing principles of socialism is not enough. Only by reforming the existing socialist model on the basis of developing "definitions" of socialism covering all the modern features, will we be able to consolidate confidence in the communist ideal. Also, the newest definitions of socialism must not be considered as the last theoretical model.

2. *The "transitional" step in the revolution — moving from precapitalist,*

colonial, semifeudal society with a poorly developed economy to socialism, bypassing the stage of capitalist development – entails development of "productive forces" through flexible economic rules permitting multi-component forms.

Productive forces are to be developed through precisely the complex of renovative economic policies put in place by the party at the Sixth National Congress that urged the empowering of unique combinations of economic forms and forces in order to increase productivity, invigorate economic exchange, and sustain a basic standard of living during the prolonged period of transition. That argument enabled the party to take as its starting point for reforms the notion that "modern capitalism" can still influence socialist concepts to continue developing to perfection. Quang forcefully made the case for supporting continued experimentation with non-socialist forms through historical analogy,

> The NEP [New Economic Programme] was an experiment...which rapidly paid off. It saved Russia and brought to the Soviet people a new social beginning that was then acceptable. At that time some communists, who firmly upheld the maxims of socialism, clamored that in carrying out the NEP Lenin was renouncing socialism and going against Marxism. They called for absolute revolution and even demanded an immediate world revolution. Lenin's successors, due to their failure to understand and capitalize on his ideas concerning the NEP and socialism in reality, terminated the NEP and instituted a kind of "bureaucratic state socialism", thus twisting socialism out of shape and infesting the new society with negative aspects which are now being resolved by the current restructuring process.

This history lesson is useful when we try to answer the question, "what is socialism?" Under current conditions, while we are renovating in greater conformity to the spirit of socialism, freeing ourselves from the kind of voluntaristic socialism that is imposed from the top and the outside, and building a socialism that is realistic, genuine, dynamic, creative, and typical of each country's special characteristics, some people criticize that we are renouncing socialism while they want to distance themselves from socialism. When we are trying to base ourselves on "the truths about the movement" to create the beginning of a socialist society that the people may accept, some people view this as a step backward and the destruction of the revolution's gains. No, we are moving forward, trying to take firmer and wiser steps on the road already chosen, and protecting the revolution's gains in all our alertness. However, as Lenin said, we are determined not to "turn ourselves into longstanding Bolsheviks...who have on many occasions played a deplorable role in our party's history. For instead of studying the characteristics of the new, vivid reality, they keep re-using in a stupid manner the formula they had learned by heart."

Nguyen Huy, Director of the Institute of Economics of the Social Science Commission, sought a definition of the transitional stage to socialism that would admit more energetic, innovative possibilities, including the hybridization of structures of economic ownership.[173] Huy stated that,

Explaining and correctly applying the dialectics of the switch from the national people's democratic revolution to the socialist revolution is the most important theoretical and practical task of the Vietnamese Revolution. To accomplish this we cannot overlook K. Marx's concept which follows: "No social system will collapse when all the production forces the environment for whose development is fully created by that social system have not yet become developed; and new, higher production relations will never emerge when the material conditions for their existence have not yet fully ripened within the old society."

In Huy's argument, the efforts to assiduously improve productivity through the distinctive capitalist mix of production forces remains an indispensable requirement for the continued economic life of society in the transition from precapitalism to socialism,

This means that we can only dismiss the capitalist socio-economic configuration — naturally in all the stages of its development — but not the efforts to develop the production forces, create the material and cultural conditions for a socialist society as well as for the switch to the socialist revolution in the transitional period. Far from being rejected, the capitalist production relations, being production relations which are more progressive than those of the precapitalist period and which are needed for the development of the production forces in the transitional period and especially during the stage of the people's democratic revolution, must be considered as a necessary part of the system of transitional production relations without which we cannot successfully skip the stage of capitalist development to advance from a precapitalist society to socialism.

In structural terms, this means that the process of establishing a socialist economy depends on the development of a "multicomponent people's democratic economy", which is organized through the application of rules of nationalization, and the construction of a sector under state auspices. In Huy's recipe,

> The capitalist economic component represented by the national bourgeoisie and the individual economic component comprising small peasants and handicraftsmen are allowed to freely develop in accordance, naturally, with the policies and the law of the people's democratic state. The state capitalist component, which includes the marketing co-operatives of small peasants, should especially be encouraged to develop. Only the patriarchal economic component should be eliminated. All this is aimed at developing the positive character of the private and individual economic components brought about by the success of the national democratic revolution, rapidly accelerating economic restoration, and proceeding with national industrialization along the line of establishing and developing the people's democratic commodity economy. From a general viewpoint, the people's democratic revolution has the duty to prepare the material and spiritual prerequisites as well as cadres – with regard to their democratic conduct and civilized trading practices – for the implementation of the basic tasks during the transition to the socialist revolution.

3. *The ideological element in the development of the reformist policy – the "new theoretical thinking and the new political orientation" – retains the sanctity of Marxist-Leninist thinking without becoming inhibited by that system of concepts, theories and action plans.* Innovative, argumentative discourse is a hallmark of, not a departure from, communism. The Vietnamese Revolution encourages "free

intramural discussion" of the theoretical issues in the context of the party's firm "political orientation" towards renovation, thus allowing ideological leeway while staying the course defined by the party. That argument encouraged inventive thinking and the taking of conceptual liberties with classical, theoretical assumptions of Marxism. Early in the year, Tran Trong Tan, Director of the party Central Committee's Propaganda and Training Department, attempted to explicate the circumstances that mandated new, clever ideological work and to establish the limits to the elasticity of the basic theoretical framework of socialism. Tan spoke of increased ideological disaffection and diminishing faith in the system and urged an active party response that would protect socialist ideology,

> There is an increase in the number of people within the party and the society who show signs of vacillation. Due to a lack of proper knowledge of Marxism-Leninism, of the true nature of the self-criticism movement in the various parties, and of the ways to conduct the socialist revolution in the past years, a small number of people have shown signs of vacillation hardly seen before. This vacillation has something to do with the socialist path and Marxism-Leninism. This is something very serious. It is easy to understand that people may remain indecisive in the face of a specific policy or at a certain point in time. Yet, if they lose their belief in socialism or doubt Marxism-Leninism, then this is something unusual. Nowadays some people feel ashamed when they have to say something about the superiority of socialism. Noteworthy is the fact that if they happen to hear somebody scoff at socialism, make fun of Marxism-Leninism, or extol capitalism to the point of worship, some people keep silent as a sign of approval. Others want to show disapproval of what they hear or a determination to protect Marxism-Leninism but simply do not know how to fight back. This is where the danger lies. There are other manifestations of vacillation arising from a lack of proper knowledge of the new policy towards development of our commodity economy and multicomponent economy. . . Vacillation to such an extent means deep-rooted doctrinal and ideological indecisiveness. It would be dangerous if the party fails to establish ideological orientations to cope with such a situation. Because the enemy of socialism is trying by all means to take

advantage of this situation to conduct sabotage against us, we must remain very vigilant.[174]

In his closing address to the Sixth Central Committee Plenum (20–29 March), Linh identified competing views that had emerged regarding the role of the party in the reformist enterprise, the nature of the party-state relationship, and the impact of "social democratization" on the party. Linh defended the party as central to the reform process, calling for enhancement of that role rather than efforts to instal checks and balances within the system of power. Linh, however, did endorse changes in the methods of party leadership, and urged the development of a partnership between the party and the state characterized by a sharing of power and adherence to a stringent division of labour. To Linh, the party played a central role in broadening democracy by improving the organization of government mechanisms, enhancing the role of the National Assembly and elected organs at all levels, and developing the role of mass organizations. However, the process of remaking the institutional bases of power and developing democracy should not pre-empt the party by supporting unbridled pluralism. In Linh's words, "we advocate broadening democracy and reaching a consensus through debate, but we do not tolerate pluralism".

Linh reiterated that position in his September National Day speech. He emphasized the need to avoid "extreme democracy" and attempts to "misuse" democracy to serve the ends of individuals. Linh stressed the differences between the economic reforms which had enfranchised different forms of the private sector, and the political reforms that in some arguments should have enfranchised multiple interests and allowed them to operate as political parties. In Linh's words,

> The real or nominal character of democracy depends not on whether there is one party or many parties. The essential thing is what segment of the population and what class in the society it serves.[175]

The party was unequivocal about the threshold level of tolerable reforms beyond which the system should not venture. Challenges to the position of the party and calls for a multi-party system were clearly unacceptable and elicited strong opposition from the leadership. The party castigated pluralism as inappropriate and dangerous, and viewed the challenge in the context of world-wide trends that diminished the power and manoeuverability of ruling communist parties, wrecked one-party regimes, and produced a potentially threatening popular activism. The Vietnamese response to those trends and their potential for impact on the domestic situation was two-fold. The party took a hardened stance on Vietnam's place in the world, and became more active in defending the status quo.

four
1990: Economic Crisis, Organizational Failure and the Conflict over Reformist Goals

Introduction

During 1990 the debate over political and economic renovation took on a sharper, more intense edge as economic problems mounted. Key social and political interests grew disillusioned with the inability of the reformist course to respond to the collapse of socialist regimes in Eastern Europe, the end of Soviet largess, the slow development of foreign investment, and the intractable structural deficiencies of the economy. The party continued to contend with the difficulties of adjusting to decentralized economic decision-making, increased authority for the market-place and the emergence of newly enfranchised private traders. The party bore the burden for the miscalculation that the withdrawal of combat forces from Cambodia would end the Cambodian predicament and result in the flow of Western capital and foreign aid into Vietnam that would finance economic recovery.

The party confronted an accelerating decline in cadre quality and membership levels as increasing numbers of card-holders petitioned for release from the party or met with the axe as the result of ongoing efforts to purge corrupt and ineffective cadre and party leaders. The political scene was further complicated by the emergence of a more complex relationship between the party, mass organizations and special interests with their own increasingly independent organizations which had begun to claim roles in the political system. Corruption and incompetence of district, provincial and central level party leadership led to strong criticisms of the party and significant internal disputes over basic doctrine and reformist strategies. Elements of the party leaned towards political reform and endorsed diminished party control over administration, governance and economic strategy. Organizations and associations concerned with social, literary and environmental issues were formed without the authorization of the party in a calculated though modest challenge to the monopoly of party control over all dimensions of social, economic and political life.

The party responded by placing a firm lid on debate over the need for political reform, strongly criticizing advocates of simultaneous political and economic reform, working quickly to co-opt or neutralize the effect of unauthorized organizations, unceremoniously dropping the leading proponent of political reform from the Politburo, initiating a wide-ranging crack-down on domestic dissent under the control of the Ministry of Interior, and stepping up the anticorruption campaign to eliminate glaringly ineffective party leaders and moribund cells.

The Crisis in Eastern Europe

The collapse of communist regimes in Eastern Europe, the emergence of effectively led and organized challenges to Eastern European communist parties, and the outpouring of popular discontent and anticommunist sentiment in the crumbling Soviet bloc caught the Vietnamese leadership off guard and as unprepared for these events as the rest of the world. Hanoi's considered response to the collapse of communism and the birth of reformist regimes in Eastern Europe was to reinforce the distinctiveness of the Vietnamese road to socialism, review the pace and scope of the reform and restructuring process, and recommit to basic Marxist orthodoxies without abandoning the commitment to economic change and improvement.

In 1990, authorized media commentary about the crisis in Eastern Europe crystallized several important themes:

- The antisocialist activism of imperialist forces profited from a

moment of political crisis and effectively undermined communist parties in various socialist countries.
- In the face of dwindling membership and declining popularity, communist parties lost nerve. The dismal performance of dominant parties led important interests to question the wisdom of one-party systems and the core values reflected in basic communist party platforms.
- Changes, especially the trend towards sharing power with new leaders, new parties and newly enfranchised interest groups, took place hurriedly and without preparations. These changes led to a near anarchic situation where a multiplicity of competing parties contended for power in an ideological and political vacuum.

In early 1990, editorials and feature-length articles made the case that the crisis in Eastern Europe had revealed the contradictions that had developed in the process of building socialism, in large part as a result of "serious mistakes" committed by communist parties. The most serious mistake was the failure to "design a correct, effective social leadership mechanism". Parties had become lethargic, corrupt, privileged and distant from their constituencies. The antidote to this situation was an active effort to inculcate self-discipline. In response, the party advocated recognizing (1) the "special characteristics" of national development that required inventive formulations of the path to socialism, and (2) the "inevitable trend" towards renovation and the need for "democratization" to preserve close relations with the people. The party also acknowledged the continued threat of imperialist interventions and the concomitant need to move cautiously into relationships with imperialist countries.[175]

Articles during the early months of 1990 focused on the political vacuum created by the collapse of Eastern European communist parties, and the emergence of disorganized, "unhealthy" political parties to fill the gap.[176] By mid-year the articles had become more clearly defensive and didactic, drawing lessons from the decline of communism in Eastern Europe to help repair the damage to a discredited Vietnamese party organization that sought to urgently fend off its own demise. A late-May article in *Quan Doi Nhan Dan* noted that,

> Many lessons must be drawn from [the] historic events [in Eastern Europe]. Nevertheless, the most urgent lesson to learn while seeking ways to resolve the internal conflicts arising from restructuring, reform and renovation must be the need to remain vigilant in the face of imperialism's dark schemes of peaceful evolution.[177]

The arguments in articles and editorials centred on a more shrill sense of Vietnam's vulnerability to conspiracies by familiar enemies, and a more forcefully stated opposition to insidious "political pluralisms". Articles spoke of "dark schemes" aimed at instilling a multi-party system, concocted by "imperialist forces and their reactionary exiled henchmen". Remnants of former Government of Vietnam (GVN) parties including the Dai Viet, Quoc Dan Dang, Xa Hoi Dan Chu, and Can Lao Nhan Vi in the centre and the south were said to be at the core of some of the threatening counter-revolutionary activities. Newspapers noted what was observed to be the re-emergence of Nguyen Van Thieu, Nguyen Cao Ky, Tran Thien Khiem and Nguyen Khanh as commanding figures in Overseas Vietnamese circles, clearly a misinterpretation of an embarrassing attempt by Ky and Thieu to address audiences of Viet Kieu in the United States.[178] The media also fixed on the clear and present danger posed by pluralism, the "battering ram" and "spearhead" used by antiregime conspirators to manipulate "legitimate desires" and political concern for freedom and democracy in order to discredit and disable the VNCP.[179]

The Movement Against Crime and Social Pollutants continued to focus on crime suppression activities and took on the added task of responding to the threat of antiregime activity. In 1990 the Movement relied increasingly on normal chains of local governmental authority for guidance and direction, instead of the combined party, security bureau and ad hoc assault youth groups and subward-village social order and safety councils that were called upon in 1989 to power the Movement.[180]

The fifth phase of the campaign, launched in April 1990 to implement Council of Ministers Directive 135, focused on anticrime activities and enforcement of economic laws.[181] It was accompanied by a crack down on unauthorized activities by grass-root and social organizations; the detention or close monitoring of the movements of

Catholic priests, student leaders, and other potential dissidents; and the restriction of travel by visiting foreign journalists, businessmen and aid workers. The crack-down was a response to the perceived potential for antiregime protests on the fifteenth anniversary of Hanoi's victory over the U.S.-backed southern republican government (15 April), the one-hundredth anniversary of the birthday of Ho Chi Minh (19 May), the demise of Eastern European communist regimes, and the severe cut in Soviet bloc assistance to Vietnam.[182]

Coinciding with this mid-year period, critical essays published in major papers acknowledged that there was support for political pluralism in Vietnam. These mid-year articles noted support for the emergence of countervailing centres of power and challenges to the VNCP's monopoly, and for the removal of democratic centralism from party regulations to free political minorities from organized discipline and the obligation to respect the view and rule of the majority.[183] The party-controlled press portrayed these views as being little more than the result of activist antiregime campaigns under the control of imperialist forces rather than reasoned and serious viewpoints held by legitimate interests within the party.

"Pluralism" and the Party

The party responded to the challenges posed to the Vietnamese political order by the disintegration of Eastern European communism by restating the basic terms of reference that governed the party's relationships with the other parts of the Vietnamese political universe: the party is the vanguard of the working class, the labouring people, and the nation. The people are the ultimate powers. The party is the guardian of the people. The state is entrusted by the party with the role of executive agent for the people's will, and is empowered to govern through the formal expression of that will, the law.

To the party, pluralism was a fragmenting force that would work towards overturning the social and political balance of power achieved by the party.[184] Early in the year, the party cautioned against viewing the deliberate efforts to nurture a multi-sectoral economic structure — family, private capitalist and petty bourgeois "economies" — as a means of allowing "economic pluralism" to lead the way to political pluralism.[185]

To fend off the consequences of pluralist trends, and uphold Marxist-Leninist orthodoxies, the party sought to co-opt and control the panoply of new forces and interests unleashed by the economic reforms that empowered private market activities and limited economic activity by households and individuals. In the terms of a late 1989 *Nhan Dan* editorial,

> The major factor deciding the nature of socialist democracy is whether the leadership of the party can develop the role of the state and mass organizations, and whether power truly lies in the hands of the people. Multiple parties can still be democratic in form only and one party still can be truly democratic. The problem is the need to create a political system and mechanism that considers the realistic structure of society, and the diversity of interests and inclinations of all classes, strata and social and ethnic groups.[186]

The Central Committee's draft platform, circulated for comment in early February, stressed the party's role as the organizing force for these new interests and the party's ability to respond inventively to the needs of new social and economic groups:

> The party supports and actively helps the people gather together in social organizations, and operates to meet the occupational demands and diverse interests of the people along the line of benefiting all families and the country as a whole in accordance with the law.[187]

The draft platform sought to make a virtue out of necessity by recognizing the natural tendency of new groups and constituencies to seek an organized state. The party attempted to graft these organizations to the system while minimizing the possibility that such forces could supplant the party. It carefully imposed limits on the process of openness, and unambiguously opposed processes that would compromise the centrality of the party,

> We should overcome the pessimistic and vacillating thoughts and erroneous views that deny our revolutionary gains, lower or deny

the party's leadership role, and advocate political pluralism and multi-partyism.[188]

The Eighth Plenum, March 1990
The Draft Platform

The Eighth Plenum, convened from 12–27 March, was prefaced by the public circulation of the Central Committee's draft platform in early February, an unprecedented step. The draft platform argued that the shortcomings of the reform programme resulted from the party's truancy in renovating itself. Further, the draft platform asserted that the party's problems also stemmed from the failure to understand the role and importance of mass proselytizing and the relationship between the party and the people. The draft platform urged the improvement of the party's representative role, and supported consolidation of the mass organizations and special interests with their own increasingly independent organizations which had begun to claim roles in the political system. These aims were discussed under the rubric of perfecting socialist democracy and ensuring the retention of power by the people.

The reform policy introduced a "new stage" in which "diverse interests" in the form of new social groupings, new economic entities and interests, and more complex political and social aggregations of people impinged on this formula of political relationships. Those "diverse interests" required the system to be capable of flexible response to changes. The draft platform stressed the party's role as the organizing force for these new interests and the party's ability to respond inventively to the needs of new social and economic groups. The new social groupings were to be strong and capable, not merely "decorative symbols" but active and independent organizations,

> The party and state respect the people's independence from the organizational standpoint, promote the initiative and creativity of the people's social organizations, and oppose the paternalistic and authoritarian attitudes of party cadres and the administration towards politico-social and social organizations of the people, and, at the same time, the bigoted or nonchalant attitude towards mustering the people's forces.[189]

The draft platform noted that the party "must never neglect the people's interests, but should not be demagogic nor allow the development of parochialism, departmentalism, and localism", a reminder of the party's position on political pluralism.

The draft platform contained some obligatory positions on economic improvement, including admonitions to overcome the problem of unemployment, develop the family-based economy, and adjust taxes and salaries to promote effective income distribution. It also called for improvements in health and insurance services, family planning, and national care for veterans and the handicapped. The draft platform urged legal recognition of the "legitimate right" to conduct business, own land and inherit or transfer land.

However, the real crux of the draft platform was the prescription for specific organizational change. The document endorsed,

- the "consolidation" of people's organs of control and the melding of the work of those organs with the state inspection system;
- the development of state "information networks" for population centres;
- the institutionalization of party-managed sessions to monitor and guide the civil proselytizing work of fundamental party units and youth unions;
- the institutionalization of regularly scheduled public criticism sessions focused on the actions and behaviour of individual party members and party chapters;
- the examination of party practices in the realm of long-term assignments for specialized cadre;
- the strengthening of National Assembly standing committees, the encouragement of active communication between National Assembly delegates and voting constituencies, and the improvement of the decision-making process of the National Assembly, Council of State and People's Councils;
- the reduction of intermediary administrative levels of state bureaucracy, and the restriction of the authority of state management agencies over grass-root installations and private and family businesses; and

- the party-supervised improvement of mass organizations, including efforts to reform the management, cadre selection practices, and funding situation of mass organizations aimed at increasing their operational independence.

The draft platform focused most closely on the last goal, and provided specific, detailed guidance on the steps necessary to upgrade the organization and performance of mass organizations.

Most of the goals endorsed by the draft platform were not new additions to the programme of reform. The distinction of the draft platform was that it set these organizational reforms in the context of an expanding political system, with new organizations and interests claiming roles alongside established mechanisms. The draft platform clearly anticipated the burgeoning of organized interest groups, "In the near future, there will be more social societies". The various mass organizations were given more explicit responsibilities for organizing subsidiary groups. The Ho Chi Minh Communist Youth Union was the "key centre" for encouraging youths to join appropriate organizations – student associations, youth association chapters, the General High School Student's Association. The draft platform reaffirmed the Peasants' Association role in establishing professional groups of producers and specialized farmers, and re-emphasized the Women's Union role in developing "operating mothers clubs and midwifery groups".

Public Debate

The draft document was the subject of public meetings, party study sessions, expanded provincial party committee conferences and intensive media coverage for the month leading up to the opening of the Eighth Plenum. Discussions of the draft document focused on the need to further refine the party's approach to its relationship with mass organizations, the concrete steps necessary to establish new social organizations, and the importance of empowering those new organizations to function with the promised autonomy and financial independence.

Publicized meetings of mass organizations stressed the importance of formulating the platform to include more precise commitments to employment and welfare programmes, and more stringent measures of official accountability. Such sessions also endorsed a reinvigorated anticorruption process that would rely more directly on the court process and involve mass organizations in investigations of allegations of impropriety. The party was heavily criticized for the failure to sustain important links to interest groups and social organizations, and for equivocating on the formation of the Vietnam War Veterans Association after the concept for this organization had received Politburo level support. The party was castigated for failing to implement programmes to correct even the most basic abuses and lapses of its bureaucracies, and for neglecting citizen rights. Public sessions called to review the draft document endorsed electoral reforms and the institutionalization of election campaigns to afford basic choices to voters.[190]

Central Committee member Tran Bach Dang's 5 March essay on the draft document echoed many of these criticisms. The draft platform, Dang argued, was a disappointment. The programme for improving party-mass organization interaction was little more than a rehash of long-standing precepts of party reform. It reflected antiquated concepts of social organization, and inaccurately depicted reflections of the progress of social and political renovation. The platform neglected the dialectical symbiosis between the party and mass organizations, in Dang's view, and contributed little to understanding the impact of current social forces on the party. In Dang's argument, the draft platform delved into unnecessary detail on the mode of operation of mass organizations instead of reserving such choices for the organizations themselves and confining the party's role to defining the "general orientation". Dang asserted that the draft platform presented a flawed picture of social forces, and confused religious and mass societies,

> Moreover, classification of mass societies is not made in a renovative manner while only a brief description is made on such social components playing an important political role, such as groups of citizens, workers, intellectuals and ethnic minority people, including the Chinese, Khmer, Cham, religious and bourgeois groups as well as the overseas Vietnamese. There is a regrettable mistake in the section on mass and religious organizations, that is the

Catholic Solidarity Committee is regarded as a mass society while the Vietnam Buddhist Association is recognized as a religion. It is not appropriate for the programme to go into detail on the organization of religious groups while failing to set forth a renovative policy on this matter.[191]

To Dang, the draft platform viewed the Vietnam Fatherland Front more as a passive umbrella organization than as the crucial connection between the party and the mass organizations. He emphasized the importance of the draft as a tool for establishing a programme that would recognize and respond to changes in social forces, and compel the party to modernize its relationship with these newly enfranchised interests.

The month-long public discussions of the draft platform revealed numerous competing views within the party on critical issues, such as the course of the reforms and the principles guiding party-mass organization relations. While "almost all people and cadres" were predisposed to support reforms that would reinvigorate the party and "consolidate" its influence, by implication a significant yet undefined number was not inclined to support a reform process that would return the party to a level of strength, internal coherence and unrivalled influence achieved during the revolutionary war. Some argued that laws should be written to define the relationship between the party and mass organizations in a manner that would delimit the party's purview and specify obligations of the interacting parties.[192] There was no consensus on the draft platform itself. Opposition to acceptance of the document focused on what some provincial and subordinate party committee participants saw as ineffective and incomplete descriptions of the roles of the individual mass organizations.[193] There was also some slight disagreement with the decision to circulate the document for comment prior to the plenary session.[194]

By late March the public airing of views on the draft platform had picked up a significant head of steam. Some of the controversial views, according to one media review, implied "a lack of good will towards the party".[195] Finally, there was less than unanimous agreement on the independent role to be accorded mass organizations, and on the extent to which the party had failed to integrate representatives of mass interests into the process. "Many" registered the view that the party had become "distanced from the people" and had lost popularity and trust. "Many" suggested that the party should reform its working relationship with, and be more sensitive about, cadre assignments to mass organizations.[196] However, media treatment of the public review of the draft platform reiterated unanimous opposition to pluralism and continued confidence in the party.

The Ousting of Tran Xuan Bach

The plenary communiqué tersely announced the removal of Tran Xuan Bach from his positions as Politburo member, Central Committee Secretary, and Central Committee member for having "seriously violated the party's organizational principles and discipline, leading to many bad consequences". Bach was said by a variety of sources to have vocally supported rapid liberalization in the political realm and to have flirted with pluralism in public speeches during late 1989.[197] However, his infidelities to the more cautious views of reforms were less likely to have earned him the censure pronounced at the Eighth Plenum than his violations of party rules against criticizing policies defined by consensus. Bach's views on the need for political change did not go far beyond the position that Linh had staked out. Linh supported the necessity of linking economic reforms with political renovation, and the widening of local party responsibility for the reformist agenda. In a 7 December 1989 speech to an "economics club" in Hanoi, Bach outlined the connection between the economic and political reforms,

> Commodity economy and social democratization are two new, progressive trends originating from the renovation line of the Sixth Party Congress. The commodity economy is breaking up the artificially partitioned market and the rigid, inefficient planning process. The commodity economy has introduced its own law of value into the national economic battleground, creating a material premise for the law of socialist economics to be tested and to have an effect on realistic socialism.
>
> Social democratization is breaking up the centralized, bureaucratic

mechanism of management and "state socialism" and is creating material and moral premises for scientific socialism to appear in its true humanitarian, democratic, equitable, progressive and modern form and character. The creative worker is the centre of society.

Commodity economy offers the worker benefits and responsibility as the real master in both production and consumption, abolishing authoritarianism and promotion of personal and factional interests in both production and consumption. Social democratization is returning to the party its role as a political nucleus, a moving force of social progress, and is eliminating the malady of the party turning into civil servants agencies. Renovation is infusing our society with a fresh vitality and restoring our people's confidence in the party.[198]

In a 13 December 1989 speech to a Club of the Union of Vietnam Scientific and Technological Associations, Bach asserted that economic and political renovation should be synchronized,

> One problem has emerged from these two issues: what are the viewpoints on economic and political renovation? Some countries think they do not need renovation while others carry out economic renovation quickly but have been sluggish about political renovation. Other countries have vigorously engaged in political renovation but have been slow about economic renovation. However, all these countries have faced a very tense situation. Some countries have been able to carry out both economic and political renovation, but it has not been a harmonious process and they have encountered difficulties. Renovation must be carried out harmoniously step by step in these two domains; it cannot be conducted more intensively in one domain than in the other. Nor can it be carried out entirely in one domain.[199]

In late January, Bach participated in an "exchange of views" on party building and leadership sponsored by the Standing Committee of the Hanoi Party Committee. The meeting, which convened city and district level cadre responsible for party work and education, aired views on the party's role and leadership, the connection between social democracy and proletarian dictatorship, and renovation of the economic mechanism and the political system.[200] In a 11 March "exclusive interview", Bach told a *Mainichi Shimbun* correspondent that Vietnam's reform programme "is getting on the right track in both the economic and political sectors". Thus Bach, at first a supporter of the more cautious approach to the programme of renovation, had begun to articulate the necessity of a parallel track of political reform to match the economic reforms. He did not venture into support for "pluralism", though he did emphasize the importance of social processes unleashed by the new economic policies, including the emboldening of social groups seeking roles in the economy and making demands of the political system. Bach saw the party as having an obligation to "crystallize" these trends. In his 13 December speech Bach said that,

> Of late the question of party competence has emerged as a key issue. We can no longer use power in lieu of competence. Every era has its own intelligentsia, and the party must have intelligence which matches the era. Although our society has improved as pressures from inflation and market pressures have decreased somewhat, there is still unrest among the people. They are demanding more democracy and more social justice, and want our cadres, party members and party as a whole to surge forward to the vanguard position. The party must crystallize national traditions and the intelligence of the epoch. This is the guarantee for the party's role of leadership. We should not blame reorganization, renovation and reform. Renovation is a mirror which allows us to look at ourselves. The problem now is to renovate uniformly and generally both the economic and political institutions and to raise the requirements for creative thinking of theory.[201]

In his *Mainichi Shimbun* interview, Bach argued that a market economy, expanded democracy, and more open participation in the world economy could be introduced under the auspices of the party's leadership. Bach told the Japanese correspondent that, unlike other countries, "the Vietnamese Communist Party faces no leadership crisis and still enjoys the deep trust of the people". He added that "we should not make fools of the people by introducing a multi-party system haphazardly." While Bach did not speak in as explicit terms as Linh had about the inappropriateness of a multiparty system for Vietnam, he did reaffirm the party's role and abjured an early introduction of such a multi-party system in Vietnam.

Bach's support for these ideas paralleled Linh's commitment to empowering social organizations, non-party groups and the media to take a more vocal role in issues, and to scrutinize party rule and policies. Bach's views also replicated Linh's conviction that a more coordinated approach to political and economic change was required to sustain the programme of reform. In some ways, then, censuring Bach was an indirect slap at Linh's rather bold initiatives. With Bach as the target, such criticism did not risk discrediting Linh, bringing disgrace to the highest office of the party, and suggesting that the party was badly split over the reforms.

Plenary Communiqué

The plenary communiqué, issued on 28 March,[202] catalogued the successes of the three years worth of renovation, noted the rough spots and the partial achievements as well as obstacles to continued progress,

> With regard to the domestic situation, the plenum unanimously asserted that in the past three years or more of implementing the Sixth National Party Congress resolution, our party and state have set forth many renovation guidelines to adjust the economic structure; develop the multi-sectoral goods economy; eliminate the system of subsidization; vigorously shift to socialist business accounting; expand foreign economic relations; simultaneously renovate economic management on a large scale in the domains of planning, distribution, circulation and finance; adjust the strategy of national defence; intensively assure security and order; better implement democracy in the party and society; and initially renovate party leadership, the activities of popularly-elected agencies, state management, and the activities of mass organizations.

The Central Committee's bottom line was that the "socio-economic" crisis had not abated, in spite of the efforts taken on all fronts to improve the economic system. The pressures born of the system's inability to reverse the economic downslide had led to conflicting views regarding the next steps. Such differences were made exceedingly clear in the month of debate over the draft platform that preceded the plenum. The plenary communiqué antiseptically acknowledged the existence of conflict over policy, restated the party's concern over increasingly divergent policy views and criticism, and emphasized the need to "correct" the situation,

> Good results have been achieved initially. This proves that our renovation guidelines and steps are correct. However, we still face many difficulties and obstacles. Our country has not extricated itself from the socio-economic crisis. Moreover, in the process of renovation, differences will continue to emerge. This requires that we be highly alert in order to detect and promptly overcome them.

The Central Committee's recipe for success took as its starting point the need for political stability and the preservation of the party's leading role. The communiqué enumerated a set of very conventional tasks as the centre-pieces of the plan for party improvement: increased political and ideological indoctrination, renovation and strengthening of leadership, enhancement of the party's vanguard role, maintenance of unity, the cultivation of strong party-people relations and the broadening of socialist democracy. The Central Committee's key point was that the system must cohere and survive before change could be safely and effectively engineered,

> To implement these tasks, we must consistently and firmly maintain stability in the political, economic and social domains, especially political stability. Only when we achieve political stability will we be able to stabilize and develop the socio-economic domain, gradually overcome difficulties, and improve the people's daily life, thereby creating conditions for triumphantly implementing the cause of renovation. These are tasks each citizen and party member must clearly realize and implement, especially in the current seething, complicated situation.

The party muted the criticism trenchantly made during the month of debate over the draft plenary programme, disingenuously proclaiming that the outpouring represented broad confidence in the party. The party downplayed public discussions of the need to expand participation and enfranchise the active interests and organizations that had, in one form or another, entered the political arena. The communiqué merely acknowledged that the opinions had been noted, a resolution on the strengthening of the party-people connection had been issued, and that the resolution would be made public in the near future.

Party Resolution

On 24 April, one month following the public issuance of the plenary communiqué, Hanoi Domestic Service broadcast the text of the resolution.[203] The resolution offered prescriptions for ameliorating the heavy-handedness of party bureaucracies, avoiding leadership lapses and repairing unco-ordinated relationships between party and mass organizations.

The resolution called for the renovation of the party's mass mobilization work, and the strengthening of the link between the party and the people through,

- developing the "all people solidarity bloc" of workers, peasants and socialist leaders;
- paying increasing attention to the individual interests of citizens;
- establishing various new mass organizations on a self-governing, self-financing basis to accommodate the new interests emerging in a more and more complex socio-economic setting; and
- linking the mass organizations to the "co-ordinated political system" led by the party and based on a division of labour between the state, party and mass organizations.

Reflecting decisions established in the communiqué, the resolution endorsed an invigorated role for the Vietnam Fatherland Front, a pre-eminent role for the party as the galvanizing agent for all social and professional organizations, and more intensive efforts to "motivate" various interests to participate in Fatherland Front activities. The document also emphasized the importance of inventive new approaches to organizing social and cultural groups and professional interests.

The resolution called for increased sensitivity by party organizations to the independence of mass organizations, a more sophisticated approach to staffing mass organizations including rotational assignments that would require cadre to spend long periods of time at the grass-root level, and the authority for mass organizations to produce and engage in commerce within the limits of the law in order to generate income to cover operating expenses. The document also stressed the relevance of party reform, and reiterated the importance of upgrading grass-root party leadership, purifying the party's ranks of corrupt and ineffective leaders, and instituting state inspection systems to supervise the implementation of laws and policies governing the cleansing of party and state organizations.

Whereas the communiqué gave voice to serious concerns about the threats faced by world socialism, the resolution offered a more conventional expression of concern over the "wicked plots and manoeuvers of imperialism and reactionary forces inside and outside the country". Those forces were, according to the resolution,

> ...aimed at opposing and sabotaging our people's socialist construction, dividing our party's internal ranks, separating the people from the party, breaking our national solidarity bloc, and dividing our people from the Soviet, Lao and Cambodian peoples and other socialist countries.

The communiqué expressed concern over "imperialist and reactionary forces" that were "thoroughly exploiting the difficulties of socialist countries in order to intensify their intervention and sabotage and to carry out peaceful developments with the aim of wiping out socialist countries". The resolution did not dwell on the disarray of the socialist world, and the need for vigilance against imperialist forces seeking to exploit vulnerabilities in socialist countries experiencing important changes in the same way as the communiqué did. Rather, the resolution described the national responsibility for defence and security tasks, connecting these concerns with the agenda for cleansing and strengthening the party bureaucracy and leadership with an end to promoting "political security".

The Central Committee required an additional month to formulate the resolution following the closing of the plenum. The resolution stated the convictions of the Central Committee in more moderated terms. It focused on the interactive process that bound the growing number of mass organizations and the state bureaucracy to the party via a range of new behaviour that included consultations, elections, freer choices in nomination and selection of key cadres, and checks and balances through rigorous inspection work. The resolution did not, however, veer recklessly towards support for broadened democracy, and accepted some limits on the process of openness by emphasizing the importance of "political and ideological tasks". The resolution offered support for an educational system that would "create the conditions for the intelligentsia to develop their talents", and support for a system of co-ordination that would measure the responsiveness of public officials and administrative cadre. It also supported a system of political obligation intended to preserve the trinity of the party, the state and the mass organizations. The resolution also manifested the same unambiguous opposition as the communiqué to processes that would compromise the integrity and centrality of the party.

Linh's imprimatur was decidedly less evident in the eighth plenary session than in preceding Central Committee meetings. He gave the opening and closing speeches at the plenum, none of which were given any significant attention in the media. The eighth plenary session marked a further decline in his fortunes. However, the dramatic early airing of the draft platform and the attentiveness to expanding participation and its consequences for the party worked to his advantage by focusing the party's attention on the need to utilize non-party groups in the renovation programme, at the same time as he articulated the majority's will to treat "pluralism" as an unacceptable compromise.

The Ninth Plenary Session, August 1990

The Ninth Central Committee plenary session, held from 16–28 August, took up the two basic draft strategic planning documents commissioned by the party and the five year plan that together would guide the economy through the year 2000. General Secretary Linh chaired the Subcommittee for Drafting the Platform for Socialist Construction in the Transition Period, which had generated ten drafts since convening in early 1987. The tenth draft was put before the Ninth Plenum which offered suggestions for revision, none of which were amplified in either the plenary communiqué or the resolution. The plenum mandated Politburo involvement in the redrafting work of the Platform Drafting Subcommittee, and left the Politburo the task of circulating the penultimate document for public evaluation prior to the convening of the Seventh National Party Congress.

Politburo member Do Muoi, Chairman of the Council of Ministers, chaired the Socio-economic Strategy Drafting Subcommittee responsible for the Draft Strategy for Socio-economic Development until the year 2000. That Subcommittee, formed in 1989 or 1990, organized regional seminars on development in early 1990 where party officials, technicians and managers at the central and provincial level discussed the economic development strategies. According to the ninth plenary resolution, the Central Committee "entrusted" the Politburo and the Strategy Drafting Subcommittee with "perfecting" the document, and defining the process for soliciting public commentary on the socio-economic strategy in advance of the National Party Congress.

The communiqué noted that the Central Committee session was characterized by "lively discussions and debates" about these two basic draft documents, and that the plenum elicited "many important suggestions of high quality" intended to assist in the re-drafting of the documents. The communiqué called for further revisions of the two planning documents prior to submission to the Seventh Party Congress. The resolution implied that the Central Committee was responsible for perfecting the two drafts, "on the basis of suggestions received during the plenum".

According to the communiqué, the plenary session also discussed the "main orientation" of the 1991–95 Five Year Plan and "some urgent socio-economic problems". These agenda items were not mentioned in the unusually brief plenary resolution. The communiqué reiterated the party's commitment to renovating the economic management mechanism, taking "profit-and-loss accounting along socialist lines" as the point of departure for all economic activities, enhancing the conditions of the "regulated market economy", and increasing responsiveness to the "new demands of foreign economic relations". The communiqué enumerated the accomplishments of the first half of 1990, including the achievement of grain self-sufficiency; the reorganization of key, centrally run industrial sectors; the increase of the profit margin in several state enterprises; the upgrading of communications and transportation; and an encouraging trend in the export index for January to July 1990. The communiqué acknowledged that despite these achievements, socio-economic weaknesses persisted as the result of uncontrolled inflation, the problems associated with allowing a regulated market to begin the governing of a centrally planned economy, and managerial inexperience in the new multi-sector system. Corrupted bureaucracies; persistently stale and unresponsive banking and credit policies; a reluctance to take strong measures against bribery, violation of laws governing planning, pricing and the market contributed to the economic muddle. The communiqué indicated that the Central Committee had called for "urgent and effective" measures to correct these deficiencies during the 1991–95 Five Year Plan, in accordance with the guidance of the Sixth National Congress regarding economic renovation.

The resolution issued at the conclusion of the plenary was terse and did not provide helpful guidance on the next steps in the reform programme. General Secretary Linh made the opening and closing speeches that were acknowledged in only the most perfunctory manner in the communiqué. He derived more status from his chairmanship of one of the two planning document drafting subcommittees, and in that context was given equal billing alongside of Do Muoi, representing a net gain for the more conservative Central Committee interests.[204]

Organizational Weaknesses and Approaches to Renovation

In articles and editorials throughout the year, the party catalogued organizational weaknesses that led to confused relations between echelons and a proliferation of conflicting policies at the grass-root level. Party committees subordinate to ministries, commissions, agencies, unions, and party cells were basically moribund and ignored. Interaction between committees and directors of low-level organs had virtually ceased, leaving party organizations marginalized. A study of 30 provinces and municipalities concluded that approximately

30 per cent of basic level key cadres were effective in their work. A third of the basic party cells were deficient, poorly led, overstaffed or tended to usurp the managerial responsibilities of production and business entities.[205]

Standards for recruiting had declined during the late 1980s, when 80,000 members were brought into the party. One 1990 survey of 29 provincial and municipal party organizations concluded that in several unspecified party organizations over 70 per cent of the newly recruited members were subjected to disciplinary action. More than 64,000 members had been subjected to some form of disciplinary action during 1988–1990, and 20,000 had been expelled. During the third quarter of 1990, municipal and provincial party organizations publicized reports on the progress of the campaign to consolidate basic party organizations, including accounts of the number of disciplinary actions – reprimands, dismissals from official position, and expulsions from the party – taken against party members. Hai Hung Province expelled 2,800 of its 55,600 members, and Hau Giang expelled 107 of a total membership of 23,500 for the most serious violations of party roles, suggesting wide variations between provinces in the implementation of the Party Purification drive.[206] Overall recruitment levels had fallen from the 1985 high of 105,000 new members, though the intake level exceeded the 1984 recruitment of 64,000 members.

Newspaper articles reporting critical studies and surveys noted that the party membership had grown older and that the number of retired cadres in the ranks had grown steadily. In 1986, 23.5 per cent of the membership were younger than 30 years of age. In 1988 that figure was 21.3 per cent. Retirees, who accounted for 18.2 per cent of the total national party membership, dominated village, subward and township party organizations. In Ho Chi Minh City, 57 per cent of subward and village members were pensioners. In some organizations 70 per cent of the membership were retired cadre.[207] In 1990, workers constituted from 9 to 11 per cent of the national membership, representing a serious decrease from 1985 when 15 per cent of the newly enrolled members were workers. The number of party members admitted after 30 April 1975 climbed to 44.19 per cent. The majority of party members who were petitioning for release from the party had been admitted to membership after 1975.[208]

Clearly, an unhealthy percentage of basic party organizations and chapters, the party's cells, were considered to be in a "prolonged state of weakness". As one early 1990 article put it,

> Many basic cells have failed to firmly grasp their own functions and tasks, thus leading to two commonly-seen tendencies: party cells have either taken for themselves the work of other people — in this case, they have interfered too deeply in the management and direction of work of the administration, economic organs, or mass organizations — or they have just let things go uncontrolled, thus negating their own leadership role. Party cells leadership over mass organizations is still carried out for forms sake, and is heavily characterized by red tape.[209]

Clashing views of the role of grass-root organizations complicated efforts to sort out the problems of basic organizations. According to one view, grass-root organizations were "total and decisive" structures with clear responsibilities for every primary level activity. An opposite perspective stressed that as the "nucleus" of political leadership, the grass-root organizations had absolutely no responsibility to make decisions concerning the tasks of local government or management agencies in which party entities were located.[210] "Fragmentation" characterized the sectoral level party grass-root organizations, leading to functional confusion at the committee and chapter level. A tendency for the missions of specialized district level agencies to dominate the subordinate party committees at the agency level prevented party organizations from developing a coherent relationship to party echelons beyond the interagency party committee. The emergence and proliferation of municipal level specialized party entities tailored to the needs of unique organizations complicated the hierarchies, relationships and flow charts. In Hanoi, party affairs committees were invented to serve as the connection between the municipal party committee and party grass-root organizations in colleges, though the majority of party organizations at grass-root levels outside of colleges were directly subordinate to ward and district party committees. Membership in basic party organizations was generally unevenly distributed, creating lopsided primary level party units in some organizations. Some party entities were composed of diverse, unrelated and organizationally incompatible "primary level formations" which complicated efforts to centralize the minor party chapters. As one August article in *Nhan Dan* stated of the situation in Hau Giang Province,

> Some party organizations consist of many different primary level formations. The Domestic-Foreign Trade Service party organization has production enterprise, joint venture, trade corporation, and career administration agency party chapters. Because some chapters are located far from their parent sectors, the party organization assigns management to the local area but the province and district have no grasp of the professional work of these primary level units. Some block party committees such as the province's party administration party committees, in charge of 86 primary level party units comprising 3,300 members, are extremely confused in their work because, by only providing ideological management with no grasp of the professional task, they encounter a great many difficulties in disciplinary action, party member development, and cadre projection.[211]

Basic party organizations in production and business sectors were often organized in a manner that was not consistent with the "new mechanism" empowering production enterprise autonomy in economic decision-making. Mid-year articles stressed the party's role at the grass-root level as the "leadership nucleus", not as an "authoritarian organization deciding every matter like a management agency". Those articles restated the importance of the 1988 party and state decisions on autonomy and the party-state division of labour.[212]

To a considerable extent, the confused pattern of organizational relations complicated the ability of the party to communicate regulations to localities, especially concerning new and ungoverned activities authorized by some of the economic reforms. By early 1990, for example, there was still no centrally articulated regulation governing the degree to which grass-root level party members were permitted to engage in private economic activities, and on how to establish party entities in joint ventures involving foreign partners, leading to a very confused application of policies at each location. By the third quarter of the year, the party was being urged to consider transforming enterprise federation party committees into "specialized sector basic unit secretary councils" to overcome the gap between existing basic party organizations and the new economic mechanism. The establishment of new "rural party chapters" and distinctive "populated area chapters" was meant to respond to the need for unique organizations created by the application of the new contract mechanism in rural areas.[213]

As a means of improving basic party organization management and leadership, the Ho Chi Minh City Party Committee leadership backed the premise behind an intermediate party organization between basic level organizations and precinct and district party organizations. The basic organizations established within sectors and municipal committee subordinates would report to this intermediate organization. The municipal party committee had experimented with a system of party organizations above the basic level, on the authority of the Central Committee Secretariat beginning in 1982. However, because the intermediate level was not recognized as a legitimate party entity, some sectors and municipal party committee subordinates had only haphazardly staffed those levels. In part, the municipal committee leadership regarded the continued weakness of the party bases as a result of the failure of production and business sectors, professional units, and rural villages to provide leadership and staff for this level of organization.[214]

Vietnam's Chicken and Egg Argument: Political and Economic Reform in 1990

The debate over the relationship between political and economic reform turned on the question of timing – which must come first, economic or political reforms – and primacy between the two reforms, which was of immediately greater importance. The baseline for discussion was established early in the year: economic reforms must come first for the time being, without neglecting the need to make political repairs to the structure, and without negating the basic symbiosis that existed between economic and political reforms.

Linh's position was that economic renovation should be realized "without causing political instability and creating opportunities for bad elements to sneak in and cause trouble". He believed that political renovation should be carried out "gradually and steadily", in a manner "consistent with [the] country's concrete conditions".

Some very slight shadings emerged around this basic orthodoxy. One fairly literal interpretation preserved the "economics in command" approach while recognizing the need to keep the polity honest, free of red tape, and functioning effectively. Another interpretation preserved the recognition of the parallel importance of economic and political reform while tacitly admitting the possibility that political reform might be a more pressing matter than economic reform.

Nguyen Duc Binh, the Director of the Nguyen Ai Quoc Institute, spoke the basic orthodoxy in an early February article published in *Nhan Dan*,

> Actual practice has also shown that effective economic renovation will create a favourable environment for political reform. A new economic mechanism not only stimulates political renovation but also accurately points out the requirements and courses needed for political renovation . . . This does not mean that economic renovation must be completed before political renovation is undertaken. First of all, there is no way that the matter could occur in such a distinctive manner. Economic renovation is impossible without simultaneous political renovation. The problem here is at what degree and what steps to choose in political reform to both ensure the need for creating a political premise for economic reform within each step without creating political chaos that obstructs economic reform . . . Nevertheless, the thing I want to emphasize in the relationship between economic and political renovation is that in our party, during the initial period, economic renovation has been taken as the primary element. Besides the reason that this is a most urgent demand of life and the results attained, although only initial, of economic reform, must regain the confidence of the people in the party and the renovation task, there is also another important reason: that political renovation requires a period of necessary preparation, and cannot have an attitude of simplicity and neglect. . . .[215]

Phan Anh, Vice Chairman of the Vietnam Fatherland Front

Central Committee, took a different view in an early January conferenceon democracy. Anh noted that political and economic reforms must be understood to be complementary,

> Some comrades ... said: Our renovation should concentrate not only on the economy but on the political domain as well. We should be alert and sensitive politically. We must consider politics and the economy on the same level because these are two aspects of the "comprehensive democratization" issue clearly specified by our party at the Sixth Congress. I concur with this view, and ask the party to emphasize the political issue in its coming political activities, such as preparing the resolutions of the party Central Committee's Eighth Plenum and the Seventh Party Congress.[216]

Linh's position allowed considerable flexibility and local initiative in the decision on how to proceed with parallel political and economic renovation,

> As in the past, we stand for parallel renovation in both economic and political fields with emphasis on economic renovation. Renovation in the political sphere ought to be carried out actively but steadily so as to bring about realistic results, causing no political instability and doing no harm to renovation in general. Renovation is a new cause; it could only be carried out through experimental and probing steps. The important thing is on one hand to study and master the basic principles of Marxism-Leninism, creatively applying them to Vietnam's conditions. On the other, we should penetrate more deeply into realities, analyse them, evaluate the experiences of the localities, branches and the grass-roots. In this cause, the party must mobilize the wisdom of the entire party and people, especially that of the social and natural sciences and of the technological circles.[217]

Anh's words stood as a steadying influence in an argument that threatened to rapidly become arcane and detached.

The Tenth Plenum, November 1990
The Communiqué and the Plenary Resolution

The tenth party plenum was held from 17–26 November. General

Secretary Linh delivered the opening and closing speeches. The communiqué, broadcast on the closing day of the meeting, stated that the central committee discussed and passed three documents:

1. A resolution on the orientations for directing the 1991 socio-economic development plan;
2. A resolution on a draft of the report on party building and on the revision of party regulations; and
3. A revised draft of party regulations to be submitted to the Seventh National Party Congress.

According to the communiqué, Politburo member Nguyen Duc Tam, Chair of the Subcommittee for Drafting a Report on Party Building and on the Revision of Party Regulations, briefed the Central Committee session on the process of preparing the two documents on party reform. The Central Committee scrutinized the documents, "contributed many important suggestions" on the drafts, and empowered the Politburo to organize the process by which comments on the draft documents would be elicited from party members before the documents were submitted to the Seventh Party Congress.

The plenary resolution, publicized on 27 November, focused exclusively on the Central Committee's decisions on the party building report and the amendments to the party regulations. The party did not issue a resolution on the plenary session's adoption of the two draft economic strategy documents, the "Strategy of Socio-economic Stabilization and Development Up To The Year 2000", and the "Platform for Building the Nation in the Period of the Transition to Socialism". The "adoption" of these documents was mentioned in a 2 December Vietnamese News Agency transmission.[218]

Neither the resolution nor the communiqué mentioned the party platform, a key document that would be presented to the Seventh Congress following party-wide discussion. On 1 December the regime made public an outline of the six chapters that would comprise the platform, prefaced by a simple call for public views on the major issues represented by the chapters.[219] The platform included two chapters on socio-economic stabilization and development until the year 2000 (discussed in Chapter Three entitled "Socio-economic Development"), and on building socialism in a transitional period (discussed in Chapter Two, entitled "The Transition to Socialism In Our Country"). The ninth plenary resolution contained a brief statement that the party had debated two draft documents comprising the Platform for Building the Nation in the Period of the Transition to Socialism and on the strategy for socio-economic development.

However, the platform was first unveiled and subjected to scrutiny by the party at a national cadre conference in Hanoi during 10–13 November 1990, over which the secretariat presided. Dao Duy Tung presented a draft platform for Building the Nation in the Period of the Transition to Socialism that had six chapters. The first chapter, on the lessons of the Vietnamese revolution, focused on the achievements, general lines and objectives of the party. The second chapter was an explication of the transition from capitalism to socialism in a "complex international" environment. Chapter Three on "Socio-economic Development" explored the new economic concepts and the reforms including the commodity-based economy, the link between planning and the market, the multi-sectoral economy, landownership, private capitalism's role in the transition to socialism, and social classes in the transitional period. Chapter Four was about "national defence, security and foreign relations policy". Chapter Five, entitled "The Political System", examined party-state relations. The sixth and final chapter was on the role of the party in socialist construction. General Secretary Linh endorsed the document and the plans for nationwide discussion of the contents of the draft platform. Those plans, announced at the cadre conference by party Central Committee office chief Hong Ha, provided for an initial stage of review by all echelons of party committees, which was to begin in early November. The review process was to proceed through the cycle of provincial and municipal party congresses, which were scheduled to conclude in mid-April.[220]

An examination of the communiqué, the resolution, and radio broadcasts following the conclusion of the plenum suggests basic agreement within the Central Committee on the need to sustain the economic reforms. The communiqué endorsed a 1991 socio-economic development plan that continued the emphasis on producing grains and food, consumer goods, and goods for export; curbing inflation and controlling prices; improving basic social welfare policies and expanding markets. The communiqué gave strong support to efforts to attract foreign investment and gain access to foreign technology; and to eliminate state subsidies and encourage the continued shift to "socialist business accounting". The communiqué stressed the importance of transferring ownership or disbanding state-run economic entities that failed to produce or turn a profit; intensifying managerial reforms; and encouraging family based economic entities.

Importantly, the communiqué accorded a decidedly secondary place of importance to the party reforms, paying desultory attention to the draft documents that encoded new party rules which were tabled for discussion at the plenary session. Though the resolution focused exclusive attention on the instruments of party reform, guidance on the development strategies broadcast after the closing of the plenum reflected commitment to an approach that sought to "realize" development "along the socialist road", to build an open economic system with a "multi-sector structure and many forms of ownership", and to diversify external economic relations. However, neither the plenary communiqué, the resolution or the authorized broadcasts that followed the conclusion of the plenum spoke of the "vanguard role" of the party as a "decisive factor" in the same terms and firm tone as the mid-November national cadre conference which unveiled the party platform. Linh emphasized the central importance of a "politically, ideologically and organizationally strong party with blood and flesh ties to the people" to the economic reform process in his speech to the cadre conference. In his words,

> With a view to satisfactorily formulating our party's programme as well as the socio-economic strategy, we must raise the question of building a truly wholesome, firm and strong party. Only when the party is firm and strong, and the quality and ability of its members [are] good, can we implement the programme and this socio-economic strategy. This is a major issue. All party cadres and members should mull over many questions, make democratic contributions, and consult the masses to supplement the programme and the socio-economic strategy as well as the party-building issue.[221]

That sentiment was muted in the communiqué, and absent from the resolution, which merely offered a bland notice that the Tenth Plenum had discussed the three drafts on party building and party regulations. The plenary session passed the resolution on the orientations for directing the 1991 socio-economic development plan with a close vote that did not merit the customary observation concerning the concord of views within the Central Committee.

Do Muoi and the 1991 Plan

Do Muoi's report on the socio-economic situation in 1990 and the 1991 development plan did not attract noteworthy support, though the rather downcast appraisal of the implementation of the 1990 plan was "discussed and unanimously assessed".

Muoi's report stressed the economic impact of the substantial drop in Soviet and Eastern European assistance levels and focused on the consequences of simultaneous increases in import prices and the undiminished costs of debt servicing requirements, alongside of "natural calamities" which cut into agricultural productivity. Muoi stressed the importance of maintaining political stability, repairing monetary and banking systems, reducing inflation and controlling wasteful spending and excessive capital construction plans. The three major economic programmes — production of grain and food, consumer goods, export items — remained central to the 1991 development plan. Muoi emphasized the need to,

- expand relations with foreign countries to develop markets for Vietnamese products, attract increased foreign investment, and obtain access to foreign technology;
- sustain efforts to eliminate state subsidies to production, business and capital construction;
- rationalize state policy towards state-run economic installations to encourage disbanding or transferring ownership of unproductive, unprofitable entities on the basis of strict economic measures of success;
- encourage family-based economic entities; and

- emphasize the well-being of the population by reducing unemployment, creating more jobs and undertaking regional development plans.[222]

Muoi's report represented a restatement of the regime's basic economic survival policies.

The Draft Platform, Socialist Transition and the Role of the Party

The Draft Platform for Building the Nation in the Period of the Transition to Socialism reaffirmed the VNCP's commitment to nurturing a democratic process, and firmly supported reforms which would define and limit the party's purview, restrict the party from "substituting" itself for other bodies in the system, and hold party members and officials to a strict measure of accountability.

The Draft Platform began with a confession by the party leadership of error and heavy-handedness in supporting rapid transformation, acceleration of heavy industry development, and flawed price and wage policies implemented in the late 1970s.

Following that introduction the document offered an explication of the role of the multi-sector economy, diversified forms of ownership, and "consolidated and developed" state-run and collective economic sectors in a commodity economy. The Draft Platform enumerated social policies that were to be wedded to the plans for the new transitional period, including full employment, reasonable state support for housing, and environmental production. It also described national security and foreign policy priorities, including efforts to sustain friendship and co-operation with the Soviet Union, Laos and Cambodia; restore relations with China; broadening links with Asian, African and Latin American developing countries; and enhance friendship and co-operation with all countries on the basis of non-interference in internal affairs and respect for sovereignty.

The final two chapters focused on the political system (Chapter Five) and the party's place in socialist construction (Chapter Six). Chapter Five accorded a role to the various structures in the political system — the state, mass organizations, the Vietnamese Fatherland

Front, and "social institutions" — alongside of the party and prescribed basic individual rights for every citizen including the right to freely do business, travel, chose one's place of residence, vote, stand for election, and speak freely. The chapter concluded with a strong reminder of the importance of proper party-state relations,

> The pivot of the renewal and consolidation of the political system consists of clear demarcation and correct definition of the respective functions of and the relationship between the party and the state, between the party and mass organizations, and between the party and social institutions.

The role of the party would be constrained by other parts of the system that had their own legitimate mandates and equities. The party is the "leading body" in the system, and at the same time is a "constituent part" of that system.

Chapter Six stressed the freedom of members to express their views within party organizations and to "express reservations" concerning strategies and policies without fear of censorship, punishment or "discrimination". The Draft Platform reiterated the importance of party discipline and unity, and support for the majority rule as expressed in party resolutions. It also endorsed measures to reorganize the relationship between the central committee, the state, the Vietnam Fatherland Front, and "mass societies", and to control the "abuse of power" by party organizations. Those measures would include means of periodically holding the party publicly accountable for policies and membership choices, a systematic and regulated process of selecting delegates for the party congress; and a more responsible means of reviewing cadre selection and training.[223]

The Plenary Session and Continuing Policy Issues

Beginning in December 1988, the party had sought to avoid preempting the National Assembly. The party aimed to escape from the circumstance in which the Assembly was seen to be merely the rubber stamp for the pronouncements of the customary end-of-year plenary session, which had generally preceded the legislative session until December 1988. The tenth plenary session preceded the convening of the National Assembly by ten days, reverting to the pre-1988 practice. Though the party sought to reaffirm the importance of the legislative body in the communiqué, it was clear that the party had in fact attempted to seize a guiding role in a moment of economic weakness and confusion triggered by Soviet austerity measures that portended the elimination of virtually all aid and assistance. The Tenth Plenum was the third central committee session for the year, the second time the party had met for a third plenary session since the Sixth Congress — beyond the customary two annual sessions — to address issues pertaining to the economic reforms since 1987. The party tabled strong lines on budget balancing, inflation control, banking reform, taxation, and management practices. However, there was no easy agreement within the Central Committee on the nature of the party's role in the economic reform process, reflected in the absence of decisive references to the party's role in economic reform in any of the documents generated by the plenary session.

The plenum left some questions on the relative strength of the plenary performance by Nguyen Van Linh and Do Muoi. Linh's speeches prefaced and concluded the session, though they were not accorded anything more than perfunctory, passing reference in the communiqué. Do Muoi's speech on the socio-economic plan was highlighted in the communiqué, and was in fact the main working document of the plenary session which focused on economic issues in so far as its publicly acknowledged agenda was concerned. Muoi, however, failed to argue convincingly to the Central Committee about the party's economic role, and did not achieve a respectable level of support for the plan that was adopted. A range of issues presented the sticking points. The apportionment of responsibilities for implementing the plan between the party and the state, which in the past had merited detailed attention in such meetings, received hardly any mention in the public documents of the Tenth Plenum. The clipped section of the communiqué that focused on the consequences of the virtual cessation of meaningful Soviet largess (the "impact of the world situation") suggested that there may have been serious differences in the assessment of the consequences of the Soviet austerity decision and the manner in which the VNCP should react to it. The primacy accorded "political stability" suggested that the debate over pluralism had not abated, though the multiplying economic problems had compelled the party to refocus its attention on basic planning and management issues.

The Leadership in 1990: Losing Face, Losing Ground

During 1990 the Vietnamese leadership was unable to make the breakthroughs in economics and foreign policy necessary to achieve critical dividends. The regime could not reach agreement on the steps necessary to take the economic reforms to the next plateau, including the question of fully abandoning state-owned companies, opening "strategic goods" under government control to the market, and instituting radical tax and revenue collection policies. Consequently, the regime confined itself to exhorting agreement to the basic reformist achievements, and engaged in arcane debates over unproductive points of philosophy — such as the relationship between economic and political reform and the importance of "stability" versus radical and rapid change.

The leadership could not agree to the basic terms that would put an international solution to work in Cambodia. Instead, the party concerned itself with the extent to which the proposed United Nations plan would accord China undue advantage and continuing influence in Cambodian affairs and would require Hanoi to cut and run from an erstwhile ally, and the impact this would have on Vietnam's reputation and future maneuverability in the region.

It had become a lot more difficult for the inner circle of the Politburo to reach consensus decisions on these and other issues. The glue that held the collective decision-making process together — the common revolutionary experiences, the personal bonds and shared ideological commitments — was not an effective cohesive force for an ageing leadership group that had been required to abandon key articles of faith to reform and survive, and that had realized the need to quickly rejuvenate and hand over critical portfolios to younger leaders with very different revolutionary credentials and a distinctive world view.

The leadership also had to contend with a more activist and energetic set of interests, such as the nationwide network of veterans organizations, organized for the first time as distinctive groups with independent, though modest agendas and political aims, and fully prepared to criticize the leaders. The leadership also had to cope with a more confident and serious group of National Assembly delegates who did not shrink from calling ministers to the carpet for close and critical questioning, forcefully suggesting alternative policy courses to ministerial representatives and government bodies, and demanding accountability from the party and the state.

A serious group of dissidents emerged, emboldened by General Secretary Linh's opening of the press and encouragement of criticism, and obviously not deterred by the conservative backlash. Colonel Bui Tin, deputy editor-in-chief of the party newspaper, *Nhan Dan*, travelled to Paris in November 1990 and delivered a "citizen's petition" to the Vietnamese Ambassador in which he argued that a new and genuine commitment to "build a democratic system really based on the people" should be adopted. In early 1991 Nguyen Khac Vien, a respected historian, wrote a letter to the chairman of the Vietnam Fatherland Front in which he detailed the loss of confidence in the Politburo and the party and accused the party of intruding into affairs of state and basic governance, and criticized the party for refusing to grant greater freedom of thought, press and assembly. Literary figures, such as the novelist Duong Thu Huong, criticized the party and made clear their serious lack of confidence in the leadership.[224]

Finally, newer, less senior Politburo and Central Committee members gradually moved up in the ranks, profiting from vacuums created by "natural selection". Ministerial reorganizations and slowly shifting political alignments contributed to the fluctuation of political fortunes for the likes of Le Duc Anh, Nguyen Co Thach, Mai Chi Tho and Nguyen Thanh Binh.

Some leaders adjusted to this more effectively than others. In the absence of the kingmakers, especially following the death of Le Duc

Tho, the shape of alliances and the rules of political interaction began to change and power began to shift away from certain interests and individuals. For example, Le Duc Anh, who had taken on added significance in December 1984 by authoritatively defending Hanoi's Cambodia policy, had criticized the Foreign Ministry's policy of winding down the war in Cambodia, unsuccessfully resisted the plans to withdraw operational combat units in late 1989, and in the end relented from a position of weakness as a result of the regime's financial inability to sustain the war effort. In 1990 Anh took a "pro-Chinese" position, urging rapprochement in more vigorous terms than the architect of that policy, Nguyen Co Thach, but on the basis of narrow interests in securing Chinese military assistance which the Vietnamese military felt − with no basis in fact − would become available to Hanoi if the leadership accommodated itself to Beijing's position on Cambodia. As another but opposite example, Nguyen Co Thach had been especially sensitive to Tho's continuing interests in and attentiveness to the U.S. prisoners of war/missing in action (POW/MIA) issue from at least the late 1980s, and had upon occasion shaped the Foreign Ministry's positions to reflect Tho's strong, hardline views on this issue. In late 1990, presumably following Tho's hospitalization and until Tho's death in October, Thach had a much freer hand to set policy and determine the tone of Vietnamese governmental responses to U.S. positions on the POW/MIA issue. Indeed, he sought to strike a more reasonable, co-operative note in his approach to the issue, and was a good deal more flexible in his October 1990 meeting with Presidential Emissary General John Vessey, Jr., than he was in positions taken prior to his late 1990 visit to Washington, D.C.[225]

Finally, less senior Politburo and Central Committee members moved gradually up in ranks during the year, profiting from vacuums created by natural selection, ministerial reorganizations, and slowly shifting political alignments. Periodic fluctuations in the Politburo line-up imperfectly reflected changes in status and rank for Le Duc Anh, Nguyen Duc Tam, Nguyen Thanh Binh, Dao Duy Tung and Mai Chi Tho during the course of the year. Nguyen Thanh Binh and Mai Chi Tho were net winners according to this index of relative political status. They rose a modest notch or so in various protocol listings of

Politburo members, while Le Duc Anh, Nguyen Co Thach, Vo Van Kiet and Dong Sy Nguyen on the whole seemed to lose some ground or remained frozen in place while others achieved some slight and often fleeting upward mobility.[226]

Conclusion

In 1990 the party fought a rearguard action against irrelevance, dealt with a slightly emboldened population empowered to make individual economic decisions, and an increasingly complex group of social organizations prepared to articulate modest individual agendas.

Important elements of the party bridled against continued efforts to define the party's role as being limited to decisions of fundamental policy and direction, while administration was returned to the control of the state. The conservatives compelled the reimposition of controls over the media and reasserted the party's prerogatives in decisions over the pace and scope of reforms. Conservative elements attempted to reinforce the party's wide-ranging role through the campaign against crime and corruption. That campaign served as a measure of the extent to which old ways and practices could be used to slow down what party conservatives saw as the reformers' rush in an inappropriate, incorrect direction.

Central Committee plenary sessions continued the debate over the party's role in economic reforms at a moment of economic weakness and confusion triggered by Soviet austerity measures. The Central Committee meetings also tabled strong lines on budget balancing, inflation control, banking reform, taxation and management practices. Linh's shifting fortunes were evident in his standing at the three plenary sessions in 1990.

Throughout the year, especially in conjunction with several nationwide conferences, the late President Ho Chi Minh's name was evoked to add a dimension of legitimacy to the party's efforts to combat "bureaucratism, corruption and waste", and to lend a patina of respectability to the regime's programme of reforms and foreign policy.[227] Commentaries pointed to Ho's support for establishing a stable system before seeking to implement his "struggle for national independence and construction".[228] Commemorative articles highlighted Ho's commitment to "constant renewal and creation", and drew parallels between Ho's "vast dream" and efforts to renew the Communist Party's leadership, "enhance" the VNCP's "vanguard role" and "reinforce the ties between the party and the masses".[229]

In February and March the regime stressed the importance of effectively implementing the newly promulgated press law, and policing the profession of journalism. In early April a symposium sponsored by the Vietnam Journalists Association and its Hanoi office reviewed the profession's responsibilities under the new law. Essays published in the party's daily newspaper and speeches by key leaders during the middle of the year strongly criticized (1) the tendency for newspapers to abandon political and ideological responsibilities, (2) the proliferation of publications not firmly anchored to the party, and (3) publications intent on writing for the market rather than for the public good.[230] In his June address to a meeting at the Hanoi Press Center on the occasion of Vietnam Press Day, Nguyen Van Linh praised what he characterized as effective coverage of economic, cultural, social and defence issues; a healthy involvement in renovation efforts and the anti-negativism campaign; marked improvements in "forms and styles", and efforts to make newspapers more attractive and appealing to consumers. Linh also praised the efforts to provide an outlet for views of individuals, mass organizations, organized labour and party organization members in the pages of the press.[231] Linh stressed the importance of the party's leadership role over the press and mass media, acknowledged the need to improve local and central party relations with the press, and restated the need to control unlicensed or improperly licensed publications.[232]

In June and July the party took legal action against unlicensed publications. Party secretariat directives on cultural, artistic and press publication work were disseminated to "clarify" party leadership and define the "state management role" over these activities, especially the authority to ban and limit publications and to remedy the "anarchic situation" in publication work.[233] In the third quarter of the year the regime continued to take legal action against publications that failed to hew to the publishing regulations, strictly enforcing the rules down to the province level.[234]

In October General Secretary Linh emphasized these themes in speeches on the occasion of the fortieth anniversary of the army's daily newspaper, and during visits to media offices.[235] The Council of Ministers issued its resolution on "intensified control over press and publication work" in early November, calling for a reorganization of central and local news media, specifying requirements for granting operating licences for publications, authorizing the printing of foreign books in Vietnam, and providing for the training of specialized media cadre.[236]

Linh had obviously been required by the conservatives to accept a modified version of his early, relatively unrestricted guidance on media activities in Vietnam. He remained firmly committed to an activist, inquisitive press, and did not abandon his own efforts to utilize the media as a means of making important points on his programmes. For example, in late September Linh published several articles under his "NVL" byline, exhorting people to support the "three economic programmes" by using foreign currency to import goods necessary to sustain production in the service of these reforms – fertilizer, insecticide, fuel, raw materials – and to refrain from importing or smuggling luxuries and banned goods into Vietnam.[237]

The Anti-Crime Movement

The 1989–90 Movement Against Crime and Social Pollutants was another means of extending the party's reach back into areas where it had always had a primary influence. Interior Minister and Politburo Member Mai Chi Tho presided over a return to a multi-sectoral campaign in which exhortation played as large a rule as organization, and an opportunity for the Ministry of Interior to reclaim centre stage in partnership with the party. The campaign was a restatement of the fundamental importance of basic internal security issues.

During the first quarter of the year local public security services formulated plans for a "fourth drive" to crack down on crime and restore order, in keeping with Council of Ministers Directive Number 135 of late 1989. The fourth phase of the campaign commenced in early March and focused on the "suppression of professional criminals", as well as continuing efforts to eliminate corruption, and reduce "serious crimes" and violations of public order.[238] Interior Minister Mai Chi Tho, addressing a meeting of the "leading cadres" of Saigon Giai Phong and other newspapers on 6 March, stressed the importance of monitoring police forces throughout the country. Those forces were to bear the brunt of the operational responsibilities for the co-ordinated anti-crime drive in 1990. Tho also restated the crucial role of party leadership in this movement. He noted the role of the state, the importance of public participation, and the contribution of the media, which had played an important part by undertaking "exposes" of organized criminal activities, and unearthing information through "investigations" that ultimately supported the work of local governments and the Ministry of Interior.[239] A month later the fifth phase was initiated with a major sweep of known organized criminal rings in the north.[240]

In May, the regime cracked down on southern dissidents, arrested several foreigners including an American businessman in Vietnam, took measures against what were presumed to be nets of anti-government activists and organized espionage.[241] The Interior Ministry's Counterintelligence General Department managed a co-ordinated effort against unlicensed foreign businessmen, people in Vietnam without proper papers, and "reactionary organizations" in conjunction with the public security and the armed forces.[242] The Interior Ministry presided over a major reviewing conference in early June and issued a joint circular in association with major judicial entities and the Ministry of Justice on accepting the surrender of criminals and determining their eligibility for lenient treatment.[243] In early June provinces began establishing People's Security Teams, youth assault units and other forms of amalgamated security organizations under provincial administrative committee control, in order to undertake a more manageable and organized campaign against criminal activity.[244] In late June the Council of Ministers issued a decision on a co-ordinated law enforcement crack-down on corruption, embezzlement, and bribery. In mid-July the regime amended the criminal procedures law.[245] In August the Council of Ministers established two special anti-smuggling committees under the direct supervision of the Office of the Chairman, drawing staff from the Ministries of Trade, Interior, Finance, Culture and Information, and the Customs General Department as well as the military.[246] Linh gave his support to this effort with a mid-September "NVL" article against commerce in counterfeit goods, and a second article in late September urging severe punishment for smugglers.[247]

In the last quarter of the year the campaign focused on arresting and bringing to trial suspected anti-regime organizations, bringing cases against party members for serious acts of corruption and violations of party discipline, and expelling from the party unredeemable party members and officials accused of major lapses and criminal activities.[248] The campaign represented a major reassertion of the prerogatives of the security-conscious, conservative Central Committee interests, and reduced Linh's maneuverability.

The Plenary Sessions

Linh's imprimatur was decidedly less evident in the eighth plenary session than in preceding Central Committee meetings. He gave the opening and closing speeches at the plenum, none of which were accorded any significant media coverage. During the public discussion of the Draft Platform, Linh was obliquely criticized for his September National Day speech. The eighth plenary marked a further decline in his fortunes, but the dramatic early airing of the Draft Platform and the attentiveness to expanding political participation reasserted Linh's approach to party reform. He was able to fix the party's attention on the need to utilize non-party groups in the renovation programme, at the same time as he bent to the majority's will to treat "pluralism" as an unacceptable compromise.

The Ninth Central Committee plenary session, held from 16–28 August, discussed the two basic draft strategic planning documents commissioned by the party and the five year plan that together would guide the economy through the year 2000. Clearly, the Central Committee was so riven with basic disagreements over approaches to economic renovation that it was unable to define a resolution that could serve as an authoritative basis for further orders, decrees and decisions on the reform tasks. General Secretary Linh made the opening and closing speeches that were acknowledged in only the most perfunctory manner in the communiqué. He derived more status from his chairmanship of one of the two planning document drafting subcommittees, and in that context was given an equal billing alongside of Do Muoi, representing a net gain for the more conservative Central Committee interests.

General Secretary Linh delivered the opening and closing speeches to the tenth party plenum, held from 17–26 November. The plenary resolution, publicized on 27 November, focused exclusively on the Central Committee's decisions on the party building report and the amendments to the party regulations. The plenum left some questions regarding the relative strength of the plenary performance by Nguyen Van Linh and Do Muoi. As noted above, Linh's speeches prefaced and concluded the session, though they were not accorded anything more than perfunctory, passing reference in the communiqué. Do Muoi's speech on the socio-economic plan was highlighted in the communiqué, and was in fact the main working document of the plenary session which focused on economic issues insofar as its publicly acknowledged agenda was concerned.

Linh's fortunes were not boosted by these proceedings. By midyear, rumours of his plans for retirement were circulating in Hanoi in full force, alongside of other rumours suggesting that Linh would not retire because a suitable candidate to replace him could not be agreed upon. Linh would, according to these stories, become a figurehead General Secretary with limited support, waning credibility and diminished ability to perform the job in anything but the most perfunctory way.

five
1991: Fashioning Consensus
Towards the National Party Congress

Introduction
During the early months of 1991, party organizations discussed the Central Committee's draft documents: the platform, economic strategy, the political and the party-building report, as well as the party statute amendments. This process had begun in the first quarter of 1990 with the establishment of five subcommittees assigned by the Central Committee to collect and summarize views on the documents expressed by grass-root level party organizations. Key cadre conferences made plans to hold party organization conferences, distributed the appropriate versions of the drafts for dissemination, and issued instructions to the lower echelons on how to conduct discussions on the platform and companion statements about development strategies.[249] District party organizations established steering committees to manage the process of convening key cadre conferences.

The earliest meetings criticized the failure of the drafts to crisply define development strategy, and to address institutional and leadership problems. The meetings underscored the importance of serious discussion of state authority and party power, and the need to balance and reorganize institutions. The early, lower echelon conferences also drew attention to the omission from the draft documents of any real consideration of military modernization and reorganization, national defence priorities and security issues, troop reductions, the status of militias and national defence budget issues.[250] Finally, early party meetings critically assessed the endorsements in the draft documents of a key role for the state sector in the multi-sectoral economy.

The direct criticisms of strategic concepts, approaches to socialist development, assessments of basic practices of governance, leadership, and party organization set the pace for discussions at the first round party congresses, and defined the issues that were thrust before the Central Committee at the National Congress in June.

Preparatory Party Congresses: From Grass-root Sessions to the Provincial Organization Meetings

Grass-root party organizations, including pilot units, held first round congresses during February and March. According to initial media reports, the first round congresses at the lowest levels were not particularly well organized. The participation by younger delegates was disappointing. Efforts to elicit criticisms of, and suggestions concerning, the draft political report yielded meagre results. The majority of delegates elected to attend upper-level party congresses were cadres; few party members from production lines or "non-governmental economic sectors" were elected.[251]

The party began making plans for convening party organization congresses in early January. Key cadre conferences discussed the goals for the local preparatory party congresses, including the election of delegations to the meetings of the higher echelons. The preparations for local party organization congresses proceeded alongside campaigns to "purify" membership, improve recruitment procedures to attract a better quality of cadres and members, oppose corruption and review and improve production plans.[252]

During April and May, provincial and municipal congresses of delegates pressed conservative themes. According to media accounts of some of the party meetings, the summary reports and communiqués rejected pluralism and "multi-partyism", and urged continued development of the leading role of the state-run economy. The communiqués also endorsed methods to preserve the system of agricultural co-operatives by transforming some entities into service co-operatives, streamlining organization and leadership, and gearing the co-operatives to the size of communities. The most radical departure from standard policy and practices endorsed by those congresses entailed support for granting rights of inheritance and transfer of wealth, and the right to use land and rice fields for 20 to 30 years.

By late February, some provinces could only report partial completion of the first round local congresses. Several provinces, including Ha Nam Ninh, held leading provincial cadre meetings to review the process of convening local party meetings. Those sessions focused on how the key documents were to be examined and criticized during the local party meetings.[253] Early March projections suggested that the grass-root party congresses would proceed through early April. The local party meetings in the south took place more slowly and casually.[254]

The schedule for the National Congress began to slip in late February, moving from the original May date to June and later July as the result of the disorganized state of the local congresses and the intensity of disagreement over the draft documents, reflected in the enormous number of "suggestions" made by local delegates at party conferences.[255]

By mid-March, party chapters and grass-root organizations had finished the first round congresses, completed the selection of delegates to upper level congresses, and generated hefty commentaries on the five draft documents.[256] Minh Hai and Kien Giang were among the first provinces to announce the results of efforts to purge the party apparatus of errant members and cadre.[257] Also, in March various higher level party organizations conducted grass-root party congresses in organizations directly subordinate to their control, and municipalities such as Ho Chi Minh City directed "experimental" first round congresses in grass-root organizations.[258] The results of district party committee congresses were initially reported in the media in late March. Provincial party organizations began to convene in the last two weeks of March to review completed first round congresses.[259] Ministerial level party organizations convened their first round congresses in late March and early April. Military region party congresses were convened in early April.[260]

Provincial party organization meetings were under way by the third week in April. Media accounts indicated that many of the issues raised in the draft documents provoked "lively debate" and pointed discussions. For example, the treatment accorded the landownership question in the draft document elicited a great deal of attention at the provincial meetings. Most provincial congresses conceded the key point, made in the various draft documents, that land "must be placed under all-people ownership". The majority of delegates to the Ben Tre Province meeting suggested that the state enact policies on the right to long-term use of land, land inheritance, and the right to transfer landownership. Some delegates, however, opposed permitting private ownership of land on the grounds that such authority would lead to the rise of an exploiting class.[261] Approximately one-fifth of the delegates to the Ha Nam Ninh Province Congress supported long-term allocations of land to peasants, but rejected inheritance rights to land or the right to transfer ownership, preferring that the state have the authority to reallocate land in response to population increases, the return of demobilized soldiers to native rural homes, or the return of unemployed handicraft workers to the countryside. The majority of delegates supported long-term landownership grants and government-authorized land transfers to peasants, with co-operative executive committee approval. The Ha Nam Ninh delegates were divided over granting ownership of residential land, as opposed to granting authority for specific land use exclusive of ownership rights.[262] Thai Binh delegates agreed that land use authorizations for cultivated land should be broad though controlled, and that those occupying residential land should be entrusted with certificates so the land could be sold at its real value and the transaction subjected to taxation.[263] Hoang Lien Son delegates came to the more conservative view that the right of land use should be closely co-ordinated with production cycles, and that the state should reduce taxes on reclaimed land.[264]

Provincial delegates to the Thai Binh Congress debated the status of the labour force as a commodity in a multi-sectoral economy, and the right of party members to conduct private business under strictly controlled limitations and in close accordance with existing government laws.[265] Dong Thap Province delegates were divided over the issue of according party members the right to engage in private trade. Many delegates supported the proposition, but some called for further clarification of the terms of this provision.[266] Delegates to the Ha Nam Ninh Province meeting "animatedly debated" the role of the state in economic management, agreeing on the state's responsibility for eliminating subsidy-dependent management practices and for passing sensible economic laws which encouraged development.[267] A minority of the Hoang Lien Son delegates stressed the "guiding role" of the state-run economy over key economic components, disagreeing with the majority which supported the efforts given encouragement in the draft documents to develop state-run collectives and private economic activities.[268]

The proceedings of other provincial congresses, such as the Quang Binh meeting, focused attention on the need for a more profound treatment of cultural, press and literary issues and matters concerning mass organizations in the draft documents. Minh Hai Province delegates raised the issue of the modernization of the armed forces, and the budgetary concerns of city, ward and village level administration, and urged that the Seventh Congress pay close attention to these and other matters not sufficiently treated in the draft documents.[269] Provinces in the mountainous region, such as Lam Dong and Hoang Lien Son, urged further attention to highland development and to their regions' ethnic minority group issues. Ha Tuyen delegates proposed party support for formulating mountainous area investment plans.[270] Some provinces, including Hoang Lien Son, Quang Binh and Ha Tuyen, raised social welfare policy issues — public health services, education, family planning, literacy campaigns — which had not received detailed consideration in the draft documents. Delegates to those meetings suggested specific approaches to cultural development problems, public health issues, and educational improvements.[271]

Provincial congresses also debated the nature of the "transitional period" to socialism, the question of pluralism versus a multi-party system, and basic Marxist orthodoxies including the utility of democratic centralism in changing times, the leading role of the party, and Ho Chi Minh's contributions to the ideological core of Marxism-Leninism.[272] On these issues, according to media coverage of the provincial congresses, the delegates generally endorsed the conservative positions articulated in the draft documents, including opposition to multipartyism and strong support for the central role of the party.

Provincial and municipal party organization congresses, and party organization meetings within the central military command structures, the military regions, and central party blocs debated the manner in which the draft documents handled the key issue of the party leadership's responsibility for strategic errors.[273] The Congress of the Air Defence Corps, for example, urged that the Central Committee and the Politburo take responsibility for having committed mistakes in "strategic leadership". The Congress of the Ho Chi Minh City party organization Science and Technology Committee "heatedly debated" the issue of party "shortcomings and mistakes". The committee was divided over the question of whether the party had erred in failing to define a "model" and to clarify the "objectives of socialist construction" in the early, post-Liberation period, or had merely erred in the implementation of the general line.[274] Some delegates to the Hanoi Party Organization concluded that the party had, upon occasion, erred in formulating lines and policies, not merely in the implementation of those policies.[275]

Party organizations were often unable to fashion consensus positions on key issues. Media accounts summarized point-counterpoint exchanges without indicating the manner in which a problem was resolved, suggesting that major differences over fundamental issues persisted as late as the provincial and central bloc meetings.

The Draft Political Report: Public Review and the Eleventh and Twelfth Plenary Sessions

A draft version of the Political Report was publicized in early April, after months of discussion, debate and criticism of the shape and substance of the report at local and provincial party conferences.[276] A committee formed by the Politburo began to compile the platform and the economic strategy in 1987. In March 1990 the Central Committee established five subcommittees of its own to accomplish the task of collecting and summarizing views of the draft documents expressed at the local, provincial and central bloc party meetings. Apparently, both committees generated several drafts of each document, including the Political Report, before the document was declared ready for presentation to the Central Committee.[277] General Secretary Linh presented the draft report to the Central Committee at the opening session of the Eleventh Plenum, convened from 7–11 January. The plenary communiqué, broadcast on 13 June, described the draft as "an important document that summarizes the renovation realities in our country, examines the implementation of the Sixth Party Congress' renovation line, points out achievements and the extent to which they have been attained, and discusses outstanding issues, shortcomings, newly emerging problems and their causes, and lessons learned from experience".[278]

During the plenary meeting, Linh emphasized the need to critically assess the reforms that took place during 1987–90 in order to appraise the plans for future reform activities. Linh stressed the importance of comparing pre-Sixth Congress policies to the post-Congress record to properly assess the evolution of the reforms and the political and economic situation on the eve of the Seventh Party Congress. The Central Committee subjected the draft to close criticism, and charged the Politburo and the drafting subcommittee with the responsibility of writing and disseminating the final document. Linh concluded the plenary session with an admonition to work hard to complete preparations for the local congresses.

The twelfth plenary session, held in Hanoi from 18–29 May, "unanimously" approved the Draft Platform for Building the Nation in the Period of the Transition to Socialism, the Draft Strategy of Socio-economic Stabilization and Development, the Political Report, the Report on Party Building and the draft amended party statutes. The terse plenary communiqué, broadcast on 29 May, noted that Linh delivered "important" opening and closing speeches at the meeting.[279] The communiqué acknowledged the "heated debate" that characterized discussions of the documents at all levels of party preparatory conferences, and reviewed the many views and criticisms that led to the redrafting of the documents. Finally, the plenum set the dates for the national Party Congress, which was to be convened from 24–27 June.

Though the resolutions passed by the Twelfth Plenum were not released, and the only communiqué publicized was a brief, antiseptic document that provided the barest description of the proceedings, later references to the meeting suggest that the Central Committee tussled over significant issues raised in the Political Report and reached some strong, conservative decisions. For example, in his Seventh Party Congress summary of the Political Report, Linh took a strong position on land use leases. He argued that land and rice fields "belong to the entire people and are allocated to co-operative members' households for long-term use". Linh pointed out that in contrast the party Central Committee's Twelfth Plenum held that it is "impossible to privatize land and rice fields because it will lead to serious division of classes, impede planning for construction of infrastructures and other material bases, and put further strain on the problems of the already complex problems of land disputes".[280]

The two last plenary sessions before the Seventh Party Congress were given minimal media coverage. The meetings avoided public airing of sensitive debates, in keeping with the party's directive to control discussion over the more touchy issues, and sought to project maximum popular support for the draft documents.[281]

The Draft Political Report: Content and Issues

The Draft Political Report consisted of two parts, each composed of eight points. The first part, focusing on the renewal of "social life", began with a review of the renovation process and progressed through a commentary on the process of reform in the economic, social, national defence and security, and foreign affairs realms. The last two sections of part one focused on reforms concerning state and party organization, followed by a conclusion evaluating the course of the reforms. Part two began with an outline of "major orientations and tasks for the 1991–95 period", and progressed through an inventory of objectives for economic development, social welfare policy, national defence and security, foreign policy, and reform of the state, party and mass organizations.

The Draft Political Report that resulted from the process of criticism and discussion at the preparatory party conferences was an anodyne document that sought political balance rather than creative solutions to lingering problems. The document skirted issues, weakly reviewed situations, and combined the best of local party organization suggestions with the worst clichés about repairing the economy, improving cadre discipline, raising standards of living, modernizing party organization, and improving the performance of government bodies. It was a flabby, patchwork report that veered across the spectrum of viewpoints to reach awkward and temporary compromises between conservative and liberal positions on central issues. The section on reforming the state and mass organizations, for example, stressed the need to develop and improve the legal system, reorganize the National Assembly and the Council of Ministers, improve provincial, district and village administrative systems and strengthen law enforcement mechanisms.[282] The draft report lacked the punch of some of the local and central party conference suggestions on election reform, revising the practices of candidate selection, and the pointed criticisms of ministerial-level work and organization that were tabled at the local and central bloc conferences. The draft report issued commitments to sustain the anticorruption struggle, to "rearrange and streamline" administrative organizations to achieve a "compact and effective" apparatus, and to promulgate a labour law that would define standards for state employees, without addressing the sharply critical observations accumulated during the months of local and provincial criticism of the draft documents. However, while the local, provincial and central executive committee bloc conferences were rather exact in their recommendations concerning ways to reduce and streamline central, ministerial and provincial administrative structures, the draft report avoided that kind of specificity.[283]

The section recommending renovations of the Vietnam Fatherland

Front and other mass organizations called for strengthening the close relationship between the party and mass organizations, and a "diversification" of the form and activities of mass organizations "in accordance with the principle of voluntarism and self governance under the party's leadership and in compliance with state law". The local and provincial conferences debated the question of the independence of the mass organizations, the necessity for a single, centralized means of monitoring mass organizations, and the importance of organizing hitherto untapped social groups and economic interests into mass organizations. Serious discussions of the role of the Fatherland Front and the basic precepts guiding mass organization and party relationships took place at the conferences. Much of that was not reflected in the draft report, which cursorily sketched the issues in an uncontentious manner. Clearly, no agreement had been reached on the manner in which the mass organizations – especially the new ones – would relate to the party.[284]

The portion of the Draft Political Report dedicated to party reorganization reiterated basic and long-standing reform goals in a conventional manner, tilting in the direction of restoring an emphasis on ideological purity, Marxist-Leninist orthodoxy and organizational authority. The draft report noted the importance of enhancing "the quality of ideological tasks", and of "upholding vigilance against all enemy plots and manoeuvres of division and subversion against the revolution of our people". The draft also stressed the need to "enhance the ability to apply Marxism-Leninism to the specific situation in our country, help formulate party guidelines and policies. . .and basically renovate political and theoretical education". On the core issue of organizational reforms, the report stated,

> We must revamp the party organization and machinery, create revolutionary changes in the organization and machinery at all levels, make party committees from central down to grass-root levels truly competent in terms of intelligence and leadership suitable to the requirements of each level, promptly replace or appoint additional party committee members whenever necessary without having to wait until the end of their tenure, continually perfect the various specialized sections of party committees along the line of

streamlining organization and staff to keep only competent cadres, revamp the organization and operation of basic party organizations to conform with changes in the socio-economic organizations and the procedures of party leadership for the new situation, and by all means overcome the problem of rotten basic party organizations.[285]

The draft report raised conventional themes, and highlighted the importance of preserving Democratic Centralism, enhancing the authority of central committees, improving methods of monitoring party membership performance, training new party cadre, and recruiting new party members. The draft report avoided some of the more sensitive issues concerning the party's role and specific prescriptions for change that preoccupied party members and officials during some of the local debates over the draft documents. The report emphasized the conservative preoccupation with internal security issues, studiously avoided straying into the need to modernize Marxist-Leninist canon, and skirted key arguments over issues such as "political stability", the relationship between political and economic reform, the invigorated role for mass organizations, and the role and authority of grass-root party organizations.

The Party Congress

Top Leadership Changes

The Seventh National Party Congress, the Congress of Wisdom, Renovation, Democracy, Discipline and Unity, convened on 24 June. Vo Chi Cong gave the opening speech. General Secretary Linh presented the Political Report. Do Muoi, selected to succeed Linh, closed the Congress on 27 June. The Congress elected a 146-member Central Committee, which elected a 13-member Politburo, a nine-member Secretariat, and a nine-member Control Committee. No alternate Politburo and Central Committee members were elected. In the past, the General Secretary was selected by the Central Committee but at the Seventh Congress this officer was chosen by the Politburo. The Politburo was elected by the new Central Committee at the first working plenary meeting of the Seventh Central Committee. In the past, the outgoing Politburo had elected its successor.[286] The Central Committee named Linh, Pham Van Dong, and Vo Chi Cong to positions as advisers to the Central Committee, and left it to the advisory group and the Politburo to draft a statute outlining the responsibilities of the group and providing for the selection of additional advisers, subject to Central Committee approval.[287] The new Central Committee shrank by 27 seats. The new Secretariat was four seats smaller than the one elected by the December 1986 Congress. The Control Commission grew by two seats.

Eight new names were added to the Politburo (Table 5.1) Ranks 6 through 13 of the Politburo were filled by newcomers whose average age was 60. At the 1986 Congress nine Central Committee members joined four Politburo members to form the Secretariat. The Seventh Congress chose five Central Committee members and three Politburo members to form the Secretariat (Table 5.2).

The National Congress elections did not result in a mass retirement of the elder party leadership. Though seven senior leaders,

TABLE 5.1
New Politburo Members

Rank	Name	Position at the time of Party Congress
6.	Vu Oanh	Secretary, Party Central Committee, in charge of mass mobilization
7.	Le Phuoc Tho	Secretary, Party Central Committee, in charge of agriculture
8.	Phan Van Khai	Chairman, State Planning Committee
9.	Bui Thien Ngo	Deputy Minister of Interior
10.	Nong Duc Manh	Head, Party Central Committee Commission for Nationalities
11.	Pham The Duyet	Secretary, Hanoi Party Committee
12.	Nguyen Duc Binh	Director, Nguyen Ai Quoc Institute
13.	Vo Tran Chi	Secretary, Ho Chi Minh City Party Committee

TABLE 5.2
Secretariat Members

Sixth Congress	Seventh Congress
Nguyen Van Linh	Do Muoi
Nguyen Duc Tam	Le Duc Anh
Tran Xuan Bach	Dao Duy Tung
Dao Duy Tung	Le Phuoc Tho
Tran Kien	Nguyen Ha Phan
Le Phuoc Tho	Hong Ha
Nguyen Quyet	Nguyen Dinh Tu
Dam Quang Trung	Trong My Hoa
Vu Oanh	Do Quang Thang
Nguyen Khanh	—
Tran Quyet	—
Tran Quoc Huong	—
Pham The Duyet	—

TABLE 5.3
Rank of Politburo Membership

Sixth Party Congress	Seventh Party Congress
1. Nguyen Van Linh	Do Muoi
2. Pham Hung	Le Duc Anh
3. Vo Chi Cong	Vo Van Kiet
4. Do Muoi	Dao Duy Tung
5. Vo Van Kiet	Doan Khue
6. Le Duc Anh	Vu Oanh
7. Nguyen Duc Tam	Le Phuoc Tho
8. Nguyen Co Thach	Phan Van Khai
9. Dong Sy Nguyen	Bui Thien Ngo
10. Tran Xuan Bach	Nong Duc Manh
11. Nguyen Thanh Binh	Phan The Duyet
12. Doan Khue	Nguyen Duc Binh
13. Mai Chi Tho	Vo Tran Chi
14. Dao Duy Tung (alternate)	—

including General Secretary Linh, "retired" from the Politburo, Do Muoi, Vo Van Kiet, and Le Duc Anh held on to their positions (Table 5.3). Vo Chi Cong, Chairman of the Council of State, and Dong Sy Nguyen departed from the Politburo, along with two relatively young members elevated at the Sixth Congress in December 1986: Nguyen Duc Tam, the chair of the Organization Department who did a rather lacklustre job, and Nguyen Thanh Binh. Minister of Interior Mai Chi Tho also vacated his Politburo seat and was replaced by a deputy, Bui Thien Ngo, who was named Minister of Interior at the National Assembly meeting in August 1991. Foreign Minister Nguyen Co Thach lost his Politburo seat.

The new line-up of the Politburo, Secretariat and Central Committee represented a net gain for the military and cautious reformers. Do Muoi, the new General Secretary, was widely regarded as a reformer and an action-oriented man with considerable experience in untangling Byzantine state bureaucracies. There was some confidence among Vietnamese officials that Muoi would continue the reforms. Though at first a lukewarm subscriber to the reformist line in the mid-1980s, Muoi quickly became an important voice for sustained economic change and policy flexibility. Minister of Defence Le Duc Anh became the second ranking Politburo member, and Doan Khue moved to the number five slot. Khue replaced Anh as Defence Minister at the August National Assembly session. Together, the positioning of Anh and Khue represented an important advance in influence for the People's Army of Vietnam (PAVN), which had been burdened with the need to slim down fast in the face of severe budget constraints, and had become embroiled in a debate over new national security requirements, Cambodia, and the role of the peacetime army.

The new Politburo and Central Committee left the Foreign Ministry without Politburo level representation. Four Foreign Ministry officials — Tran Quang Co, Nguyen Duy Nien, Vu Oanh and Nguyen Manh Cam — were elected to the Central Committee. The compelling influence that Thach wielded on foreign policy matters as a result of his Politburo post and his concurrent deputy chairmanship on the Council of Ministers was not to be duplicated by the appointment of Nguyen Manh Cam as the new Foreign Minister at the National

Assembly session in August. Altogether, this was a net gain for the two ministries that had been engaged in frontal combat with Foreign Minister Thach over the issues of national security, the rapprochement with China, diversifying foreign relations, and the U.S.-Vietnamese relationship. The new Politburo was a clear victory for the views espoused by Le Duc Anh in favour of a rapid normalization of relations with Beijing, and a clear loss for Thach's "balanced" approach to expanding and diversifying foreign relations, as well as a negative comment on Thach's approach to Cambodia and the United States.

Composition of the Central Committee

Forty-six (31.5 per cent) of the 146 individuals elected to the Central Committee at the Seventh Party Congress in July were new members. Sixty-four incumbents accounted for 68.4 per cent of the Seventh Central Committee. That number included 36 alternate members elected at the Sixth National Party Congress who were elevated to full membership at the Seventh Congress.

Classifying the Central Committee membership according to their primary responsibility and highest ranking job — central government, central party, provincial or military — reveals some interesting patterns (Table 5.4). The Central Committee consisted of an even balance of party and government officials, 60 (41.1 per cent) and 62 (41.8 per cent) respectively. Eleven military officials constituted 7 per cent of the total membership. The number of party officials in the Seventh Central Committee represented a slight increase over the percentage of senior party officials in the Sixth Central Committee. Military officials constituted a steady 7 per cent of the Sixth and the Seventh Central Committees.

Fifty-two of the 146 members (35.6 per cent) were provincial-level officials. Forty-nine per cent of the Sixth Central Committee were secondary level officials. Thirteen of the 52 provincial level officials in the Seventh Central Committee held concurrent positions as deputy chairmen of the provincial party committee and chairmen of the provincial people's committee.

The ratio of new to incumbent party officials roughly balanced

TABLE 5.4
Job Ranking and Responsibilities of Seventh Party Congress Leadership

	Party	Government	Provincial Party	Dual (Party-Government)	Military
Incumbent	10	34*	16**	0	4
Alternate at Sixth Congress	5	13	11	6	1
New Member	6	15	12	7	6
Total	21	62	39	13	11

* General Le Duc Anh, who was replaced as Minister of National Defence by Doan Khue at the August National Assembly meeting; Colonel-General Dao Dinh Luyen, Vice Minister of National Defence; and Lieutenant General Nguyen Trong Xuyen, Vice Minister of National Defence and Director of the Rear Services Department; and Doan Khue, are classified according to their ministerial assignments as "government officials" at the time of the Seventh National Party Congress.

** Trang A Pao, Chairman of the People's Council of Hoang Lien Son Province, held a dual district party and provincial government position during the tenure of the Sixth Party Congress. In the authoritative list of the Sixth Congress Central Committee members, he was listed as holding the chairmanship of the Hoang Lien Son People's Committee, and the secretary post in the Bao Thang District Party Committee. He is not listed as Bao Thang Party Secretary in the Seventh Congress list, only as the governor of Hoang Lien Son Province, and is counted in the ranks of the government incumbents for the purposes of this exercise.

the ratio of new to incumbent government officials. The Congress elected 42 incumbents whose primary responsibility was within the central party apparatus, and 47 incumbents who were central government officials, representing 28.8 per cent and 32.2 per cent of the total membership respectively. The Congress elected 18 new members whose primary responsibility was within the central party apparatus, and 15 new members who were central government officials, representing 12.3 per cent and 10.3 per cent respectively.

Three of the five deputy heads of Central Committee executive committees were newly elected members (Table 5.5). No new members held executive committee chairmanships. Three Central Committee incumbents were placed in charge of key areas and issues: agriculture, ideology, and mass organizations. Together with the other Central Committee members who held leadership positions on the executive committees, they underscored the extent to which the incumbents dominated the Central Committee: nine incumbents and four newly elected Central Committee members held membership or leadership positions on central executive committees or within the Central Committee structure itself.

TABLE 5.5
Rank of Central Party Officials in Seventh Party Congress Leadership

	Incumbent	Sixth Congress Alternate	New
Central Committee			
Committee Heads	2	1	0
Deputy Heads	2	0	3
Committee Members	3	0	0
Central Committee Members in Charge of Specific Areas	3*	0	0
Miscellaneous Central Committee Positions	2	3	2

* Three Central Committee members were listed as being in charge of specific areas: Le Phuoc Tho, in charge of agriculture; Dao Duy Tung, in charge of ideology; and Vu Oanh, in charge of mass organizations.

TABLE 5.6
Rank of Government Officials in Seventh Party Congress Leadership

	Incumbent	Sixth Congress Alternate	New
Council of Ministers Chairman and Vice-Chairman	3	0	0
Ministers	7	3	4
Vice-Ministers	9	3	3
Committee Chairmen	4	1	1
Other	10	6	8

TABLE 5.7a
Regional Representation of Provincial Party Officials in the Seventh Party Congress Leadership

	Incumbent	Sixth Congress Alternate	New	Total
North	5	6	5	16
South	5	3	5	13
Centre	6	2	2	10
Total	16	11	12	

TABLE 5.7b
Regional Representation of Provincial Party/Government Dual Officials in the Seventh Party Congress Leadership

	Incumbent	Sixth Congress Alternate	New	Total
North	0	3	6	9
South	0	2	1	3
Centre	0	1	0	1
Total	0	6	7	

Incumbents similarly dominated the ranks of the government officials elected to the Central Committee. Twenty-two ministers or vice ministers were incumbents (Table 5.6). Seven newly-elected Central Committee members were ministers or vice ministers.

Northern and southern provinces were evenly represented within the group of Central Committee members who held provincial party positions (Table 5.7a). Approximately 11 per cent of the membership who held provincial party positions were from the north; 9 per cent were from the south, and 7 per cent were from the centre. Northern provinces clearly dominated the Central Committee when the number of provincial officials holding concurrent provincial party and government positions are added to this number (Table 5.7b). In that case, approximately 17 per cent of the membership who held either party offices or dual appointments were from the north, 11 per cent were from the south, and 7 per cent were from the centre.

Four military region commanders were newly elected to the Central Committee (Table 5.8). Only one military region commander was an incumbent. Incumbent staff officers dominated the Seventh Central Committee membership.

Four Ministry of Foreign Affairs (MFA) officials — one Ambassador and three vice ministers — were elected to the Seventh Central Committee (Table 5.9). Vice Minister Tran Quang Co was elevated to full membership from alternate status. Four Ministry of National Defence (MND) officials were elected to the Central Committee. All were incumbents. The two Ministry of Interior (MOI) vice ministers elected by the Seventh Congress were incumbents. Thus, though the MFA had the same number of seats on the Central Committee as the more conservative MND, the MND officials were experienced second-term members. Additionally, the four MND incumbents coupled with the two incumbent MOI members gave those generally more conservative ministries a slight voting edge over the MFA.

TABLE 5.8
Rank of Military Representation at Seventh Party Congress Leadership

	Incumbent	Sixth Congress Alternate	New	Total
Military Region Commanders	1	0	4	5
General Staff	3	1	2	6
Total	4	1	6	

TABLE 5.9
Security Bloc Ministerial Representation in
Seventh Party Congress Leadership

	Incumbent	Sixth Congress Alternate	New	Total
Foreign Affairs Ministry	0	1	2	3*
Interior Ministry	2	0	1	3
National Defence Ministry	4	0	0	4

* Nguyen Manh Cam, one of the four Foreign Ministry officials elected to the Central Committee, held ambassadorial rank at the time of the Seventh Congress.

The MOI, MND and the MFA — the "security bloc" — placed about the same number of ministerial and vice ministerial officials on the Seventh Central Committee as did the "economic" ministries (Table 5.10). The MOI, MFA and the MND elected more vice ministers than ministers to the Central Committee than did the economic ministries. The economic ministries elected more ministers than vice

TABLE 5.10
Ministerial Representation in Seventh Party Congress Leadership

	Incumbent	Sixth Congress Alternate	New	Total
Security Bloc				
Vice-Ministers	5	1	3	9
Ministers	1	0	0	1
Economic Ministries				
Vice-Ministers	3	0	0	3
Ministers	5	1	2	8
Social Welfare Bloc				
Vice-Ministers	1	1	0	2
Ministers	1	1	2	4

ministers, and a slightly larger number of incumbents. Both the security bloc and the economic ministries promoted one member to full membership status.

Unfinished Business

The resolution adopted at the 27 June closing session of the Congress "approved" the platform for national construction in the period of transition to socialism. The resolution also "entrusted" the Central Committee with "compiling the document" on views expressed at the Congress before the official announcement of the platform would be made. Clearly, continuing differences of views required further changes to the "approved" documents before they could be adopted by a Central Committee resolution. Further, the resolution approved the "basic contents" of the strategy for socio-economic stabilization, and approved the Political Report. However, the resolution again "entrusted" the Central Committee with the responsibility of "supplementing and perfecting" the strategy and the Political Report, based on views expressed during the Seventh Congress, before those two documents would be given official blessing. Only the party building report and the amended party statutes were given unqualified approval, according to the resolution. Finally, there was no indication that the party had adopted a set of main guidelines and objectives for the five years of the Seventh Central Committee's term, as had been done as a matter of course at the conclusion of previous National Congresses.

In editorials prefacing the Congress, briefings prior to the opening meeting, and in speeches on the first day of the session, it was made quite clear that the central task of the Seventh Congress was to pass a political platform defining the course for "national construction in the transition period advancing to socialism", and approve the development strategy for the period up to the year 2000. In his opening speech, Vo Chi Cong said,

> The paramount significance of the Seventh Party Congress lies in the fact that for the first time the Congress will approve a platform, point out the viewpoints and basic orientation for the period of

transition to socialism in our country, and pass the strategy of socio-economic stabilization and development until the year 2000. These issues are related to the task of perfecting the party's political leadership over society, and will further strengthen the scientific basis of the party's major discussions.[288]

However, Vo Chi Cong went on to suggest that much of the work on key policy positions and general orientations, discussed in the draft documents, would have to continue beyond the Congress. Cong said that the documents themselves still required criticism and further rewriting,

> The delegates to the Party Congresses at all levels and the party Central Committee plenums have already studied, discussed, and adopted the draft documents. However, in my opinion, to arrive at the truth, one has to go through a lot of thinking and reasoning. It cannot be said that we have completed our discussions; it is important to remember that we did not focus on the various issues raised in the draft documents but only on fundamental issues that need further clarifications or that contain major different viewpoints.[289]

Others echoed this view. In his speech to the 24 June afternoon session of the Congress, General Doan Khue acknowledged that the party organization congresses of the military had "seriously discussed and achieved a high identity of views" on the contents of the draft documents, but that he had some lengthy, additional opinions on the subject of national defence which he hoped to express. Clearly, the head of the army party organization delegation felt that the military's views concerning the streamlining of the People's Army of Vietnam, Vietnam's "internationalist duty" to Laos and Cambodia, and the necessity for laws ensuring the stability of a budget and supplies for the PAVN were not sufficiently represented in the draft documents. Khue also felt the need to amplify issues pertaining to the reserve force, militia and self-defence forces, command and logistical-technical supply systems, military education, and efforts to enhance Vietnamese defence industry.[290] Dao Duy Tung, who summarized the views and debates over key issues in the draft documents heard by the Central Committee, noted that there were still differing views on some issues, and that these unresolved issues suggested that the Central Committee should "seek ways to amend and perfect the Congress documents before making them public".[291] An essay, broadcast on the closing day of the Congress, stated that,

> Each of us profoundly understands that congressional resolutions can only point out the major orientations and determine the major goals to be reached by us in a certain period. The application of these resolutions calls for the ability to calculate and weigh them, and creativity and boldness to think and act, making the spirit and words of the resolutions suitable to the circumstances of each sector and each locality.

The essay further noted that the resolutions would have to be turned into "specific guidelines and policies" through appropriate legislation. Further, the resolutions "passed" by the Congress, the essay argued, were not immutable, inflexible laws or dogma but rather positions that party members would have to "supplement, perfect and further enrich based on practical realities and experience".[292]

Delegate Speeches

In their speeches to the Congress, most delegates commented in quite conventional terms about lapses in party leadership and rank and file failures to sustain basic membership standards of education, technical capability, and organizational management. The delegates' commentary on the party platform stressed the leading role of the state in the country's economy, and the importance of reclaiming the key government role in industry and reaffirming Vietnam's commitment to communist orthodoxy.[293]

In one form or another, delegates commenting on economic policy echoed Linh's position,

> The state economy must be consolidated and developed in the key sectors and domains. We must control the vital businesses and trades, and assume those operations in which other economic sectors have no suitable conditions in which to invest.[294]

Pham The Duyet, head of the Hanoi delegation, endorsed implementing a market oriented economy under state management.[295]

Nguyen Minh Thong, representing the Ministry of Agriculture and Food Industry, spoke of the necessity of placing natural resources such as land and water surfaces under uniform state management.[296] Bui Xuan Son, head of the Ha Nam Ninh Province Party Organization delegation, stressed the central role of the state in managing agricultural projects and production plans.[297] Vo Tran Chi spoke strongly in favour of the system of "state capitalism", and supported the concept of "developing a multi-sectoral economy according to the market mechanism and under state management".[298]

Several delegates endorsed proposals to reform education and address unemployment. Ha Quang Du, delegate of the bloc of central mass mobilization organs, listed improvement of youth education as a key priority. Hau Giang Province delegate To Buu Giam called for a review of education reform policy. He also recommended that Marxism-Leninism become a mandatory subject. Du committed the Ho Chi Minh Communist Youth Union to participate in efforts to solve the unemployment problem. He also endorsed the establishment of a state organ to oversee implementation of the party's policies on youth organizations, education, employment and activities. Nguyen Van Tu, Chairman of the Vietnam Confederation of Workers, supported an activist approach to education reform, with an emphasis on vocational training programmes, business management training, career development work, and retraining workers for increasingly specialized vocations.[299] Tu and others, including Hau Giang delegate To Buu Giang, addressed the issue of income inequalities. Tu urged wage reform, and stressed the importance of housing, social security and "insurance of realistic wages" as central tasks.

Many delegates supported the concept of "national ownership" of land while endorsing long-term utilization rights for peasants, and urging the passage of more thorough land use laws and government regulations. In his speech to the Seventh Congress, Dao Duy Tung noted that the land use issue was the subject of "particular attention" at both lower level preparatory party meetings and the National Congress. He stated that 97.97 per cent of the delegates endorsed the position that "land belongs to the country and that it is given to peasants for their long-term use", and supported government regulation of the transfer of the right of use and the right of heritage and mortgage.[300] These views were echoed by Nguyen Minh Thong, speaking on behalf of the Ministry of Agriculture and Food Industry; Nguyen Ba, representing the Nghe Tinh province delegation; and Bui Xuan Son, head of the Ha Nam Ninh Provincial Party organization.[301]

Nguyen Co Thach, a delegate from Ha Son Binh, emphasized that Hanoi's diplomatic aim was to "broaden friendly relations and co-operation", and to stick to the "open door foreign policy". Vietnam, Thach said, "wants to be friendly with all countries in the world and strives for peace, independence and development".[302] This view echoed the position taken by Linh in his opening speech, summarizing the key points of the political report. Linh repeated the commitment to a "wide open foreign policy", and declared Vietnam's desire to be friends with all countries with a mutual interest in "peace, independence and development". He reiterated Hanoi's desire to "strengthen solidarity and co-operation" with the Soviet Union to satisfy "mutual" interests, and to continue to develop the "special relationship of solidarity and friendship" with Laos and Cambodia, committing Vietnam to renovating those relations with an eye towards improving "procedures of co-operation" and enhancing efficiency in the relationships. Linh clearly articulated Vietnam's interest in an early, comprehensive political solution to the Cambodian conflict, but was more elusive in his commitment to the Permanent Five framework for a non-military settlement of the Cambodian conflict, suggesting only that the issues should be resolved on the basis of the "respect for sovereignty of Cambodia and the United Nations Charter". Linh said that the remaining problems with China should be resolved through negotiations.

Bui Thien Ngo, the deputy Minister of Interior who replaced Mai Chi Tho on the Politburo, and assumed the Interior Ministry portfolio at the August National Assembly meeting, spoke on behalf of the party organization in the security forces, and emphasized the importance of an integrated approach to security issues. In his words,

> Realities in recent years show that national security including political, economic, cultural and social security must be incorporated in all economic, cultural, social and diplomatic activities at all levels.[303]

Ngo's speech indicated the extent to which foreign policy would no longer be the exclusive, unchallenged domain of the Ministry of Foreign Affairs. Security and foreign affairs would require the attention and co-ordination of various ministries. The integrated approach would necessitate "close and effective combination of the strategy of national security with the strategies of national defence, economy, culture, society and foreign relations. Stability and development in all fields of social life are the foundation of national security".

Socialist Esoterica and Standard Operating Procedures: Key Issues and Votes

Dao Duy Tung's 27 June speech to the Congress summarized the debates over 17 issues on which the delegates had focused. Those debates contributed to the formulation of the Central Committee resolution on the various documents and the amended party statutes. Tung clearly indicated that differing views on some of these issues still existed by the end of the Congress, even following critical discussion and revision of positions by the delegates.

The issues ranged from philosophical esoterica ("basic contradictions of our society in the transitional period" and the "class nature" of the party) to bureaucratic details (the name given to the Platform for Building the Nation in the Period of the Transition to Socialism); and from practical issues concerning economic reform mechanisms and objectives, to very functional matters regarding party statutes, delegate conferences, the election of central commissions, and the selection process for the party's advisory council.[304] Most surprising was the extent to which the delegates disagreed over basic organizational matters. In spite of the fact that at the Seventh Congress the General Secretary was chosen by the Politburo, the overwhelming majority of delegates (95.4 per cent) rejected the position that the General Secretary should be selected by the Politburo, and supported the election of the Central Committee by the party chief. Approximately 84 per cent of the delegates agreed that the Central Committee's role in forming the Secretariat should be confined to electing individuals to unassigned slots, and that the Politburo should have the responsibility of designating the remaining members of the Secretariat.

The statutes passed by the Central Committee reaffirmed that the General Secretary should be elected by the Central Committee, and rejected a proposal formulated during the drafting stage that the Politburo, following its election by the Central Committee, be empowered to appoint the General Secretary.[305] The approved statutes incorporated the proposal that the party Central Committee elect only the Secretariat members who are in excess of those Politburo and Central Committee members assigned to the Secretariat. According to Tung, the majority of the Central Committee (78.1 per cent) voted in favour of having the party Central Committee appoint the Party Committee Military Commission.

Slightly more than 75 per cent of the delegates voted in favour of excluding the issue of the selection of an Advisory Council from the statutes, and supported Central Committee selection of Advisory Council members rather than the formation of the Council based on voting by the delegates to the Congress. Only 62 per cent of the delegates agreed that executive committees of party organizations should hold delegate conferences between national congresses. Approximately 63.5 per cent agreed that enterprise sections, school departments and village hamlets with between 30 and 50 party members could set up party chapters, and 56.1 per cent agreed that grass-root party committees should hold monthly meetings. Thus, there was only slim agreement on the means by which the party would address the inadequacies of the local level organizations that had accumulated during, and been magnified by, the process of reform.

Linh's Valedictory Address

Nguyen Van Linh delivered an abridged version of the political report to the opening session of the National Party Congress on 24 June.[306] In his final statement as General Secretary, Linh stated his basic loyalty to Marxist-Leninist orthodoxies and Ho Chi Minh's "thoughts". At the same time, Linh acknowledged the necessity of accommodating new views and being flexible in responding to special, unique problems. Linh was very concerned with the world-wide failures of socialism and the collapse of communist parties in Eastern Europe and the Soviet Union, and with "ideological vacillation and rejection of past achievements". However, he was unequivocally clear in his last words, "persistence in following the socialist path is the sole and correct choice".

Linh emphasized several points in his speech. First, he repeated the conventional wisdom on the "common trend of the suggestions" made by the first round party congresses at various levels concerning the draft documents, noting that the majority of the criticisms indicated basic agreement with the viewpoints of the documents, while the slimmest minority of views took positions "alien to our party and people". Importantly, Linh suggested that many of the critical viewpoints would have a relevance beyond the revision of the draft documents, and some of those suggestions not included in the revision would have a bearing on the means by which the final resolutions were implemented. With this view he articulated a preference for doing business in a manner that involved wide canvassing of all levels of party and state bureaucracies, active criticism of central initiatives and policy choices, and systematic discussion of alternatives, yielding a kinder, gentler democratic centralism.

Second, he spoke in strong terms on the subject of the appropriateness of the socialist path for Vietnam. Linh stressed the unanimity of the views aired during the course of the basic party congresses concerning the fundamental choices and commitment to socialism made by Ho Chi Minh.

Third, Linh addressed the essential characteristics of socialist society, and the "fundamental orientations" aimed at building socialism, and summarized them as five basic credos,

> First, the labouring people are masters. Second, we must have an effectively developed economy based on a system of public ownership of all key production means, and a modern education system characterizing our national colour. Third, men will be liberated from suppression and injustice. They will work according to their capability, earn according to their labour, and are provided with conditions to comprehensively develop themselves. Fourth, people

of various nationalities in our country will be treated equally. They must strengthen their unity and provide help to one another to advance further together. And fifth, we must maintain friendship and promote co-operation with peoples of all nations.

Linh stressed the importance of flexibility in applying these fundamental concepts, arguing that the "correct path" must be matched with a "spirit of renovation" to help prevent repeating past mistakes. He very clearly emphasized the areas where flexibility was important to the Seventh Congress platform,

> ...in the past when we guided the implementation of the revolution of production relations, we advocated a quick elimination of the multi-component economy, called for the establishment of a public ownership system absolutely occupying superiority over the national economy, rejected the essence of goods production, and slowly eliminated bureaucratic centralism and state subsidies. In this platform, however, the guiding thought of the revolution of production relations carries a spirit of renovation while ensuring the path towards socialism with the following tasks: Efforts will be made to advance in line with the development of the production force; strive to build step by step production relations, from the lower to the higher levels with diversified forms of ownership; develop a multi-component commodity-based economy in accordance with the socialist direction, in which the state-run and collective economy will be gradually strengthened; carry out various forms of distribution... based chiefly on the results of productive labour and economic results.

Fourth, Linh discussed the issue of "proletarian dictatorship", and the importance of expanding the alliance of interests and sectors that comprised the state. Linh noted that,

> The new issue lies in the fact that the platform this time refers not only to the worker-peasant alliance, but also to the worker-peasant-intellectual alliance. The majority of our comrades, except for some, have subscribed to this viewpoint, considering it a very correct and essential supplementary point.

Linh emphasized the importance of "intellectualization", or defining an appropriate role for intellectuals commensurate with their increased importance in an increasingly complex industrial and economically developed society. He spoke of how according intellectuals their proper role should not downgrade the centrality of workers and peasants, how complex class attachments had developed as the result of political alliances formed during the anticolonial war, and how intellectuals had "descended" from other classes, indicating close, complex and interactive relationships that cut across class lines and complicated simple definitions of classes and interests. He registered his view of how modern politics must accommodate an increasingly complex array of such interests, alliances and competitions, using the expansion of the "alliance bloc" as an example of the importance of a flexible view of relations and social interests in a commodity-based, multi-component economy.

Fifth, Linh commented on the central aims of the reformist economic policy, advocating the implementation of the multi-sectoral economy with a socialist orientation, and the concomitant consolidation ("rearrangement") of the state economic sector, which must continue to control "vital businesses and trades". Linh supported renovating the collective economy. He spoke in favour of treating co-operative members' households as autonomous economic units, while cautioning that a strengthened co-operative management committee had a real role to play in the management of production and services that could not be undertaken by co-operative households in a manner more efficient than the collective economy. Linh supported a liberalized landholding policy, and a flexible approach to expanding business activities of the collective economic sector, allowing the development of co-operatives or joint ventures "under many different forms". Linh also advocated the expansion of the private capitalist economy, and joint state-private ventures. He favoured the strong development of the family and house-hold economy, but cautioned that this should not be considered an independent economic component. He restated a very open-minded approach to the market and free, unsupervised choice by business organizations, while noting the continued importance of a responsible state economic sector.

Linh disparaged the view which suggested that "outside sources of development" had to be relied upon to achieve development goals.

He encouraged a balanced approach to foreign economic relations based on "equality and mutual benefit", and the "maximum exploitation of all sources of development and advantages inside the country". In Linh's formulation, "the will for self-reliance does not contradict the effort to attract foreign sources of development". Linh also reaffirmed that agricultural development depended on industrial development; supported the gradual introduction of appropriate technology, and emphasized the importance of vigorous development of technical and scientific training.

Sixth, Linh addressed plans for simultaneous, step by step renovation of the political system. He cautioned against demagogic solutions calling for a redistribution of power between the party, state and the people in a manner that would downgrade the party's leadership role. He strongly supported continued efforts to "resolve" relations between the party and the state, to "enhance party leadership" and "consolidate state efficiency". Linh also noted the importance of institutionalizing the party's link with growing mass organizations.

Linh warned against "demagogic manoeuvres which take advantage of the democratic banner to stir up disturbances". Democracy "cannot exist without centralism, discipline, order and a sense of one's civic duties". He also reiterated his position on political pluralism in unequivocal terms,

> Some people maintain that only with the mechanism of political pluralism and the existence of opposition parties and factions can we have democracy. As a matter of fact, the presence or absence of democracy does not depend on the one-party or multi-party system; under the former Saigon puppet regime, there were dozens of political parties and factions, but no one thought there was much democracy then. The choice of a one-party or a multi-party system reflects and results from the balance of forces in the political and class struggles. Consequently, it is a product of the specific historical conditions of each specific country in a given period. In our country's situation, there is no objective necessity to establish an opposition mechanism of political pluralism and multi-partyism. To accept the multi-party system of opposition is to create conditions for the reactionary forces of revenge within the country and

from abroad to rear their heads immediately and legally to operate against the homeland, the people and the regime. Our people definitely reject this.

Seventh, Linh took up the issue of party renovation. He staked out a very strict constructionist view of the party as the working class vanguard, and the role of Marxism-Leninism as the party's "ideological base and compass for action", speaking in strong mainstream terms in defence of the ideology. He acknowledged the importance of the "united front" to the party, and spoke of the importance of all strata of people to the organization. Linh stressed the crucial importance of party renovation and reorganization as a means of "making the party stable and strong politically, ideologically and organizationally". Linh defended the tradition of Democratic Centralism, and endorsed the codification of "full democratic practices" as a basic right in the amended party statutes,

> First of all, efforts must be made to ensure the rights of party members, especially the right to hold frank discussions, at their organizations, on issues related to the party's lines and policies; the right to criticize and inquire about the activities of party organizations and of party members at all levels. The draft amended party statutes also expands party members' right to gain access to information and to defend their opinions. These revised regulations provide a condition for overcoming the situation in which party committees infringe upon the right of party members while the latter adopt a passive attitude. While encouraging full democratic practice, the draft amended party statutes strongly stress the need to observe discipline and maintain unanimity within the party. Experience drawn from history shows that when a party ignores the principle of democratic centralism, it will become the sort of club which will benefit opportunism, factionalism, and all types of anarchy that finally will lead to the disintegration of the party organization, that is the abolition of the party.

Linh emphasized unity, the need to improve education and skill levels within the party, and the continued commitment to vigilance against corruption.

Finally, Linh reviewed the game plan and initial accomplishments of the renovation since the Sixth Party Congress, and spoke on the issue of the future of the reform programme. Interestingly, he noted the "near unanimity" of the party membership views of the draft documents on the initial achievements of the reforms, and the "basically appropriate" steps taken towards implementing the reformist plans. However, the General Secretary recognized that there was room for improvement in the plans for reform. Linh concluded that the initial progress in the economic realm, coupled with "social democratization" and the "achievements in national defence and security" had contributed to restoring confidence in "the prospects of socialism" and the party leadership. The crisis had been "lessened in magnitude" by the reforms, which had done much to define and elucidate the "path to socialism". He stressed these original contributions to the political and social process, and was generally more optimistic than the Political Report about the reforms.

Linh also added a cautionary note advising against overestimating the achievements of the reform programme, and bluntly reminded the Central Committee that Vietnam had not yet extricated itself from the socio-economic crisis,

> We should not belittle factors that can cause political instability. The inflation rate still remains high. The causes of inflation have not yet been removed. Many areas of production are still at a standstill. The rate of unemployment or underemployment is still on the rise. The people still experience many difficulties in their daily lives. The quality of many cultural and social activities continues to deteriorate. The impact of corruption, injustice, and social negativism remains heavy. People still cannot enjoy a sense of public security and order. Law and social order are not yet strictly enforced.

Linh stated his strong, personal support for the switch to a multisectoral commodity economy. However, he cautioned that "it would be a mistake to believe that the market economy is a wonder drug". He listed the social consequences of switching to a market-oriented economy — the customary litany of social vices, economic opportunism, and political corruption — and concluded that a partnership between the party, state, the mainstream Fatherland Front organizations, and "other mass organizations" representing new economic and social interests and organizations, could fix the things that had come apart during the course of the reforms. He concluded by reviewing the "key tasks" enunciated in the Political Report. Linh departed somewhat from the format of the draft political report publicized in April, and articulated a more specific, practical list of "key tasks", which in his explanation was based on the Political Report. He stressed the importance of increasing productivity, improving economic management, addressing "pressing social problems", ensuring social order and stability, renovating cadres, and preserving and expanding foreign relations that contribute to international socialist development.

Linh's summary of the Political Report emphasized the importance of encouraging and protecting the free expression of views; of organizing and integrating new social and economic interests into the mainstream of culture, society and the polity; and of inventing practical solutions to special social problems that had emerged from the activation of new economic structures, rules and practices. His summary reflected consensus views on public security imperatives and the priority of national defence issues. He echoed the more conservative concerns regarding political opposition, the potential for organized, externally-supported trouble, and the need for a foreign policy organized around familiar friendships ("special relationships") with Laos and Cambodia, Cuba, India, and the Soviet Union, a normalized relationship with China, and broadened friendly relations with the region, Europe, Japan and the United States. He subscribed to the mainstream position on the need for a cautious, incremental approach to the market, and the continued role of the state economic sector.

Conclusion

The Congress left a considerable amount of unfinished business in its wake, including the critical matter of redrafting ("compiling") the party's platform, and completing ("supplementing and perfecting") the document on socio-economic strategy and the Political Report, whose contents had merely received "basic" approval during the review process. The Congress also put in place a leadership that was an uneasy amalgamation of veteran party leaders and bureaucrats, young technocrats with post-Liberation education, reform-minded Central Committee members, and conservatives concerned with preserving the party's role and prerogatives.

The new line-up of the Politburo, Secretariat and Central Committee represented a net gain for the military and cautious reformers. Though significant retirements did occur, the newly seated Politburo did not quite represent a successful transition to a new generation of leaders. The leadership change created a moment of suspended animation for the political system during which the aged élite could begin to step aside, and the new generation could start the process of forming working groups and alliances based on common interests, institutional affiliations and issues.

The Congress took up key issues concerning the pace and scope of economic reform and development plans, the rights of private businesses and other new economic forms to make independent decisions, the state's authority over the economic realm, and social problems that emerged in the new economic environment. The party leadership spoke in support of a cautious, incremental approach to the market, and the continued role of the state economic sector. The Congress accorded public security and national defence issues priority attention, and conservative delegates registered their strong concern regarding the potential for organized, externally-supported antiregime activities. Delegates and key party officials underscored the need for a foreign policy organized around familiar friendships.

The speeches of key leaders and provincial delegates, and Linh's own valedictory address, manifested a simple faith in the system, confidence in the efforts to resurrect and reform the party and the economy, and a belief that the party and the state could share power. At the same time, the leadership made clear to the Congress its preoccupation with the situation in the Soviet Union and the collapse of communist parties in Eastern Europe. Linh's words to the Congress in his final statement as General Secretary, for example, evinced a basic loyalty to Marxist-Leninist orthodoxies, while at the same time acknowledging the importance of flexible, inventive responses to new problems. Linh's criticism of "ideological vacillation" and the "rejection of past achievements" gave expression to his worries about the impact of the dramatic changes in the socialist world but, like other delegates to the National Congress, Linh reiterated his unremitting commitment to the socialist path.

The Seventh Congress was not a dramatic moment in party history, or a benchmark introducing startling institutional and leadership changes. Rather, it was the occasion for a reiteration of the importance of reforming slowly and carefully, without kicking the struts out from under a system that, in the view of the Congress, still had the potential to survive, and still commanded the support of a significant core of cadre and leaders.

six
Conclusion
Nguyen Van Linh and the "New Way of Thinking"

A Matter of Style

Nguyen Van Linh, a long-time southern activist and organizer, and twice Chairman of the Ho Chi Minh City Party Committee, was elected General Secretary of the Vietnamese Communist Party at the Sixth National Party Congress in December 1986. He quickly established himself as a forceful and forward-leaning leader, committed to a coordinated programme of economic change and party transformation. As General Secretary, Linh demonstrated flexibility and adaptability, and a penchant for the unorthodox twist to policy-making. Where his predecessor Le Duan had been unprepared to compromise, Linh was willing to break ranks and engage in tactical gambles. Linh developed a record for being quite frank about the limits of the political system and the inability of the party machinery, leadership, and the governing apparatus to organize rapid and effective change.

Linh's hallmark was his contemplative approach to problems. He encouraged examination of the "theoretical issues" at the core of specific problems, and took as his starting point the need to rethink fundamental assumptions about strategies, policies and practices. He was less fixed in his approach to problems than his predecessors and apparently not ill at ease with a style that abandoned prevailing paradigms and sought alternatives to nagging economic, organizational and personnel issues, including recruitment and training of party and government newcomers.

Linh was adamant about the need to end secrecy and to subject the entire policy-making structure and leadership to an open, public process of inspection. He urged full media coverage of attempts to root out corruption, and endorsed a prying style of journalism in sensitive and hitherto sacrosanct realms, including the process of cadre selection and personnel advancement within the party and the government. Linh defended his style by arguing that essentially unrestrained publicity was one means of accelerating the reforms. An open media would prompt an outpouring of complaints and confessions, and bring to public and official attention cases of organizational and cadre deficiencies and policy weaknesses that otherwise would have remained hidden. He steadfastly rejected the argument, made with increasing frequency in 1988, that his penchant for public criticism of the party ran the risk of discrediting the institution.

Linh thought of himself as a problem-solver and a catalyst uniquely capable of teasing out the hidden possibilities and potential from a deadened system. On his parish visits to provinces, districts and enterprises, he sought to rectify problems by mending organizational disconnections, proposing alternative means of implementing policies to local officials, and suggesting immediate means of addressing economic issues.

Plenary Session Report Card

Nguyen Van Linh used plenary sessions to carefully outline disputes over reform strategies and tactics that divided the Central Committee, and to table his own means of resolving problems. At first Linh was basically successful at turning plenary sessions into showcases for his reformist plans and policies. However, for a variety of reasons, including the generally dismal performance of the economy and the flagging ability of the reforms to make even the most minor difference, beginning in 1988 Linh was less able to respond forcefully to challenges to his views, and less able to establish alliances necessary to press beyond conservative coalitions seeking to control the reformist strategy.

Beginning with the second year of his leadership, Linh had less of an opportunity to set the formal agenda for the regime. In part, this was the result of the altered plenary session schedule. Four sessions in 1987 provided the General Secretary with a regular forum for his policy views. That forum was not afforded by the fewer, more irregularly scheduled Central Committee meetings in succeeding years.

It was also the result of the more strictly technical policy needs of the late 1980s and the early 1990s which focused on implementing special tax and managerial regulations, import-export rules, and regulations establishing limits on sectoral activities. The nuts and bolts tasks of implementing the reforms afforded a lot less opportunity for dramatic problem solving than defining the reforms themselves, and required a great deal more focus on routines and regulations. Linh's reliance on initiative, unique and experimental methods, and inventive approaches to problem solving was somewhat less appropriate to the task of making systems work than it was to inventing systems themselves.

The schedule of plenary sessions that emerged in 1987 — three evenly spaced sessions for the year — was broken in 1988, and the party reverted to the basic pattern established by the Fifth Congress. Linh had gained certain advantages from the 1987 plenary pace. He seemed to be able to set the agenda and more vigorously dominate the first two post-Congress sessions of the Central Committee, using the second and third plenary sessions as instruments for defending and advancing his renovations. At the Fourth Plenum in December 1987, however, Linh took several direct hits as a consequence of the worsening economic situation, and the inability of the reforms to dramatically improve things. His more restrained role at the fifth plenary session (14–20 June 1988) reflected some slippage in his political position, stemming from the increased questioning of the wisdom of the economic reform programme. Linh's address to the Fifth Plenum lacked the activism of his address to the second and third sessions. Linh's third plenary speech, which carefully outlined the disputes over economic reform strategy and tactics and articulated his own assessments of competing views, suggested that Linh was attempting to broker compromises between contending policy positions, and to function as an arbiter of policy disputes. In contrast, his fifth plenary speech lacked the incisive commentary about conflicting viewpoints within the party concerning party building that had been part of his previous statements. The speech was more of a recitation of issues, minus the synthesis of views and Linh's own recommendations on how to proceed.

By mid-1988, Linh's appeal for a wider use of extra-party entities and enhanced responsibility for local level parties in setting their individual reformist agendas had become singularly unpopular with a Central Committee intent on strengthening established chains of command. In his speech to the Fifth Plenum, Linh acknowledged that his perspectives were not widely shared, and seemed to vaguely indicate that his position on the matter of party building had not been incorporated into the draft version of the resolution. His performance indicated that he could not press beyond the consensus of his colleagues.

Linh's manoeuverability was further constrained by the sixth plenary session (20–29 March 1989), which more stringently defined the operating assumptions of the increasingly cautious Central Committee, without foreclosing on the reformist goals. Linh was reminded that his formula for remaking the economy and the party-state structure of power was limited by the reluctance of at least a plurality of party decision-makers to accept major departures from the political, ideological and organizational core of the revolution. Linh's speech to the Seventh Plenum (15–24 August 1989), which focused on the impact of world currents on socialist revolutions and Vietnam's role in the socialist community, had an uncharacteristic ideological stiffness about it. Linh urged adherence to party discipline, respect for the unity of the socialist community, and continued attention to internationalist responsibilities. Linh made the orthodox case in language that sounded somewhat alien in his voice, and while he urged avoiding rigid attitudes, he mapped out a rather determinist course for the economic and social reforms that hinged on inevitable progress of socialism and the inexorable process of imperialist decay.

Linh's imprimatur was decidedly less evident at the eighth plenary session (12–27 March 1990), which discussed the draft platform for the National Party Congress. He gave the opening and closing speeches at the plenum, neither of which were given a great deal of attention in the media coverage of the meeting. The eighth plenum marked a continued retreat to orthodoxy, underscored by his criticisms of "pluralism" as an unacceptable compromise with non-party interests. At the Ninth Plenum (16–28 August 1990), which took up the two basic draft strategic planning documents commissioned by the party and the five year plan that would guide the economy through the year 2000, Linh's opening and closing speeches were acknowledged in the communiqué in only the most perfunctory way. He derived more status from his chairmanship of one of the two planning committees, and in that context was given equal billing with Do Muoi, representing a net gain for the more conservative Central Committee interests. By the tenth plenary session (17–26 November 1990), Linh's speeches were overshadowed by Do Muoi's address on the socio-economic plan which was highlighted in the communiqué issued at the plenary meeting, and was in fact the main working document of the session.

The Party under Linh

Linh's approach to party reform was unique in several respects. He relied less on mobilizational instruments – campaigns, exhortation, symbols – and more on bureaucratically co-ordinated programmes with distinct organizational ends. Linh utilized combinations of resources to attack specific party-related problems, often calling on instruments hitherto considered external to the process of party reform to undertake the changes he set as his goals. He placed a special emphasis on restoring balance to the political Trinity of the "party, the state and the people" and stressed the necessity of disaggregating the party and governmental functions – separating the church from the state.

During the course of his tenure in office, Linh fashioned a comprehensive package of party reforms that was more ambitious and potentially more far-reaching than the reformist goals of his predecessors. That package included efforts to empower local organizations to take on more responsibilities, parallel with the increasing economic autonomy afforded enterprises. Linh also introduced a more flexible style of management, and increased sensitivity to modern organizational skills and management techniques, and a concomitant active support for the training of a skilled class of party managers. He sought to confine the party to a more limited role as the conscience of the revolution responsible for fashioning social and political direction and maintaining the integrity of the revolutionary inheritance, while allowing responsibilities for daily governance to pass to a body of qualified technicians and elected and appointed officials. Linh's aim was to guide the party towards a quality control in operational matters and membership policy, emphasizing responsiveness to direct, critical complaints against party personnel and organizations.

Under Linh, the party sought to implement these goals through a variety of organizations, committees and local and provincial meetings. Expanded sessions of provincial party committees were convened to facilitate the writing of Action Programmes, intended to communicate the importance of the "Three Economic Programmes" — food production, consumer goods production, and production for export. Provincial and subordinate party organizations were empowered to orchestrate local purification campaigns based on a system of branch, district and provincial level party committee meetings. Internal party and economic inspection teams were deployed during the first quarter of 1987. Those grass-root level teams were responsible for closely monitoring and supervising the personal lives and individual morality of party members. Linh urged compliance with plans for renovating the party through visits by higher echelon party officials to subordinate chapters during which those senior officials assisted with local party chapter performance reviews. He supported efforts by the party's Secretariat to implement portions of the revised party statutes put forth at the Sixth National Congress that shortened the length of the probationary period for candidates and allowed only minimal leeway for members adjudicated to be guilty of violations of the party's code of conduct.

In addition, under Nguyen Van Linh the effort was made to make the party more publicly accountable for policies and personnel choices, both through the activation of internal control mechanisms and empowering a long dormant media to aggressively watch party behaviour. The party sought to reinvigorate control department mechanisms at all levels with the aim of using them as ombudsmen-like structures to process the mass of complaints and accusations triggered by Linh's policy of public scrutiny of the sacred. Mass organizations were enlisted as adjuncts to the process of monitoring party discipline. The party took steps to factor itself out of the equation on issues of governance. It appeared to have supported the revision of the candidate selection process in advance of the National Assembly elections, advocating a minimal role for the party in determining candidate lists.

Linh's actions initiated the process of sharing power between members of the polity, and strongly argued that party building should properly include non-party entities. He stressed the division of state and party labour, in a manner intended to prohibit the party from tampering with governance. The adjustment of the plenary and National Assembly schedule to allow the Parliament to convene prior to the usual end-of-year Central Committee plenary session was intended to portray the Assembly as being vigorous and independent.

While Linh continued to seek means to broaden political participation by non-party entities and to maximize the independence of action of mass organizations, he also took pains to stress the extent to which the party would remain central to the process and would continue to exert a strategic influence.

Nevertheless, though forced to live by new rules, the party remained a stiff and distant organization. Leadership change was still centrally determined according to the discretion of a small inner circle of party elders. Corruption and malaise remained blots on the party's record. Media scrutiny, internal control and vigorous prosecution of offenders made only partial headway towards eradicating party scofflaws. Membership rolls were cut by 20 per cent to eliminate the most egregious violators of party laws, and the least desirable cadre. In the end the party suffered a serious shortage of recruitable young, technically able, educated and – most of all – willing candidates.

The party, however, became a very different creature than it was under Le Duan. To a large extent, that was due to Linh's own activism and reformist agenda, and his distinctive operational code that placed a primacy on experimentation, openness, and problem solving.

The Party and the Future

Under Nguyen Van Linh, the party began to learn the art of sharing power, admittedly in a very initial, tentative and reluctant way. The party began to share centre stage with the enlivened National Assembly, with new and increasingly well organized social and economic interest groups, and with established, strong and influential parts of the political system. These groups and interests competed for diminishing resources in an increasingly cluttered, fragmented system where the old alliances and rules of collegial political conduct had less and less meaning. Bureaucratic leverage, interagency strategies, and issue-oriented alliances began to count more than the old loyalties, shared revolutionary experiences, and personal relations. For example, in October 1990, during a meeting in Washington, D.C., then Foreign Minister Nguyen Co Thach made the point that he could convince the military of the need to participate in efforts to achieve the fullest possible accounting for missing American servicemen. Thach noted that he had shared a jail cell with Le Duc Anh, and was confident that he could make the necessary arguments and elicit the required support. However, it was Anh who challenged Thach's views on normalization of relations with the United States most forcefully, took exception to Thach's policy of withdrawing combat operational troops from Cambodia and questioned Thach's approach to China. Anh struggled hard for the limited share of resources for his problem-stricken army and gave no quarter to Thach in interagency struggles over budget and policy direction.

The party demonstrated some finesse in its relationship with these new social groups and interests, and took relatively reasonable and flexible positions regarding the roles and rights of these groups. For example, though Hanoi responded to the emergence of a voice for dissatisfied veterans in 1989 and 1990 by closing their unregistered newspaper and co-opting their putative organization, ultimately the party allowed the veterans group to stay together, under party rule. Other, more drastic alternatives were theoretically available to the party. The VNCP, however, chose to co-opt rather than destroy the organizations. The party dealt cautiously with these associations and with other temporary, issue-oriented groups of farmers and students protesting specific conditions.

However, by the end of Linh's tenure as General Secretary, the party was not prepared to, or capable of, coping with a non-communist movement or anti-party activism. The rules which said that the party should still be the pre-eminent political voice were still on the books. Those rules had been bent slightly, but not supplanted. The system was by no means prepared to accommodate organized political competitors, or challenges to the party's role as the key decision-maker. However, diminishing political resources and leverage, the dwindling faith of the membership, the virtual end of external support from like-minded systems, and the emergence of a less compliant legislature confounded the party's ability to keep its grip on the system.

At the outset of his tenure, Linh sought to nurture the ability to compromise, change political habits, and alter institutional rules. His goal was to turn the party into a flexible organization and abandon the practices that had made the party an ossified, unyielding, corrupt and uncompromising machine. Linh achieved some initial and limited success in making the party responsive to the altered political playing field, and capable of undertaking some organizational changes. Linh, however, could not push beyond the conservative majority and his own faith and political beliefs to provoke real change in the Vietnamese political world.

Notes

1. Hanoi Domestic Service in Vietnamese, 0500 GMT, 18 October 1988, *Foreign Broadcast Information Service-East Asia* (hereafter *FBIS-EAS*), 88-203, 20 October 1988, p. 65.
2. William Duiker, *The Communist Road to Power in Vietnam* (Colorado: Westview Press, 1981), pp. 141, 176-80, 187-90, 193-95, 221-24.
3. According to the 1968 Statutes, the plenum decides the size of the Politburo, the Secretariat and the Central Control Committee (Uy Ban Kiem Tra Trung Uong). In the 1977 and 1987 Statutes, the size of the Politburo and Secretariat is determined by a Central Committee plenum. The Control Committee is dropped from the formula. See Dang Lao Dong Viet Nam, *Dieu Le* (Hanoi: Ban Chap Hanh Trung Uong, 1968), p. 43; *Nhan Dan*, 3 February 1977, pp. 2-5; and Dang Cong San Viet Nam, *Dieu Le* (Hanoi: Nha Xuat Ban Su That, 1987). The 1977 and 1987 Statutes required the plenary session to present "essential issues" for the lower echelons to discuss. Those echelons were in turn required to communicate their views on these issues to the Central Committee.
4. Hanoi Vietnamese News Agency in English, 0500 GMT, 12 February 1987, *Foreign Broadcast Information Service* (hereafter *FBIS*), 17 February 1987, k. 11.
5. Hanoi Vietnamese News Agency in English, 0500 GMT, 3 March 1987, *FBIS*, 4 March 1987, k. 3; *Quan Doi Nhan Dan*, 1 April 1987, pp. 1, 4, and 3 May 1987, pp. 1, 4.

6. *Quan Doi Nhan Dan*, 3 May 1987, pp. 1, 4.
7. On the "Three Economic Programmes" (Ba Chuong Trinh Kinh Te Lon), see Hanoi International Service in English, 1100 GMT, 4 February 1987, *FBIS*, 5 February 1987, k. 10.
8. Hanoi Vietnamese News Agency in English, 2300 GMT, 3 February 1987, *FBIS*, 5 February 1987, k. 3; Hanoi Vietnamese News Agency in English, 1430 GMT, 4 February 1987, *FBIS*, 4 February 1987, k. 4.
9. Hanoi Vietnamese News Agency in English, 1100 GMT, 22 January 1987, *FBIS*, 23 January 1987, k. 9–11.
10. Hanoi Vietnamese News Agency in English, 1430 GMT, 2 March 1987, *FBIS*, 4 March 1987, k. 5.
11. Ibid. Hanoi Vietnamese News Agency in English, 0500 GMT, 3 March 1987, *FBIS*, 4 March 1987, k. 3.
12. *Saigon Giai Phong*, 8 January 1987, p. 1; and *Saigon Giai Phong*, 15 February 1987, p. 1.
13. Hanoi Vietnamese News Agency in English, 2300 GMT, 3 February 1987, *FBIS*, 5 February 1987, k. 3.
14. "Quy Dinh Ve Thoi Ky Du Bi Cua Dang Vien Va Thi Hanh Ky Luat Trong Dang", *Nhan Dan*, 20 February 1987, p. 3.
15. "Chat Luong Hang Tieu Dung", *Nhan Dan*, 8 May 1987, pp. 1, 4; Hanoi Vietnamese News Agency in English, 1100 GMT, 27 March 1987, *FBIS*, 29 March 1987, k. 7–10.
16. *Nhan Dan*, 22 June 1985, p. 1.
17. Hanoi Vietnamese News Agency in English, 1100 GMT, 27 May 1987, *FBIS*, 29 May 1987, k. 7–10.
18. Hanoi Vietnamese News Agency in English, 1100 GMT, 9 January 1987, *FBIS*, 13 January 1987, k. 3.
19. Hanoi Vietnamese News Agency in English, 1100 GMT, 22 January 1987, *FBIS*, 22 January 1987, k. 9.
20. Hanoi Vietnamese News Agency in English, 1100 GMT, 3 February 1987, *FBIS*, 5 February 1987, k. 9.
21. Chi emphasized the confined role of the party secretary who, in tandem with labour and youth union affiliates, was empowered to conduct "regular inspections" to determine the extent of the enterprise management's compliance with party and state policies and resolutions. See *Saigon Giai Phong*, 24 February 1987, p. 2.
22. *Saigon Giai Phong*, 26 February 1987, p. 2.

23. *Saigon Giai Phong*, 7 March 1987, p. 2.
24. *Saigon Giai Phong*, 1 April 1987, p. 1.
25. *Nhan Dan*, 21 June 1987, editorial, pp. 1, 4.
26. Hanoi Vietnamese News Agency in English, 0500 GMT, 3 March 1987, *FBIS*, 4 March 1987, k. 3.
27. Hanoi Domestic Service in Vietnamese, 25 July 1987, *FBIS-EAS* 27 July 1987, N. 4.
28. Hanoi Domestic Service in Vietnamese, 2300 GMT, 28 July 1987, *FBIS-EAS*, 31 July 1987, N. 1.
29. *Saigon Giai Phong*, 27 May 1987, p. 1.
30. *Nebszabagsaq*, 17 August 1987, p. 3, *FBIS-EAS*, 19 August 1987.
31. For the text of the Communiqué of the Second Plenary Session of the VNCP Central Committee, see Hanoi Domestic Service in Vietnamese, 1100 GMT, 16 April 1987, *FBIS*, 17 April 1987, k. 7–13. For the text of Linh's opening speech, see Hanoi Domestic Service in Vietnamese, 1100 GMT, 16 April 1987, *FBIS*, 17 April 1987, k. 1–7. For the text of Linh's speech at the closing ceremony, see Hanoi Domestic Service in Vietnamese, 1100 GMT, 17 April 1987, *FBIS*, 20 April 1987, k. 4–9. Also see the VNCP document, Dang Cong San Viet Nam, *Nghi Quyet: Hoi Nghi Lan Thu Hai Ban Chap Hanh Trung Uong Dang (Khoa VI – Giai Quyet Nhung Van De Cap Bach Ve Phan Phoi, Lu Thong)*, Hanoi, 9 April 1987.
32. Hanoi Domestic Service in Vietnamese, 0500 GMT, 29 June 1987, *FBIS-EAS*, 8 July 1987, N. 3–6.
33. Hanoi Domestic Service in Vietnamese, 2300 GMT, 2 July 1987, *FBIS-EAS*, 8 July 1987, N. 4.
34. *Washington Times*, 4 August 1987, p. 4; *Washington Post*, 14 July 1987; *Far Eastern Economic Review*, 23 July 1987, pp. 28–29.
35. Ngoc Son, "Viec Hoc Tac Kinh Doanh Thuong Nghiep Bi Loi Dung", *Nhan Dan*, 26 March 1987, p. 3.
36. Hanoi Vietnamese News Agency in English, 1504 GMT, 14 April 1987, *FBIS-EAS*, 15 April 1987, k. 4–7; "Dang Ky Kinh Doang Thuong Nghiep Va Dich Vu", *Nhan Dan*, 17 July 1987, p. 1.
37. Hanoi Domestic Service in Vietnamese, 0500 GMT, 17 July 1987, *FBIS-EAS*, 21 July 1987, N. 4; Hanoi Domestic Service in Vietnamese, 2300 GMT, 13 July 1987, *FBIS-EAS*, 16 July 1987, N. 8.
38. Hanoi Domestic Service in Vietnamese, 1430 GMT, 30 June 1987, *FBIS-EAS*, 1 July 1987, N. 1.

39. Hanoi Domestic Service in Vietnamese, 1100 GMT, 6 June 1987, *FBIS-EAS*, 16 July 1987, N. 3–4.
40. *Nhan Dan*, 17 July 1987, p. 3; Hanoi Domestic Service in Vietnamese, 1200 GMT, 22 June 1987, *FBIS-EAS*, 29 July 1987, N. 5–22.
41. Hong Kong AFP in English, 1354 GMT, 28 May 1987, *FBIS-EAS*, 87-170, 2 September 1987, p. 36.
42. Hanoi Domestic Service in Vietnamese, 2300 GMT, 31 August 1987, *FBIS-EAS*, 87-170, 2 September 1987, pp. 36, 40.
43. Hanoi Domestic Service in Vietnamese, 2300 GMT, 31 August 1987, *FBIS-EAS*, 87-170, 2 September 1987, p. 39.
44. Ibid.
45. Ibid.
46. Hanoi International Service in English, 1000 GMT, 31 December 1987, *FBIS-EAS*, 88-002, 5 January 1988, pp. 52–53.
47. Hanoi Domestic Service in Vietnamese, 1100 GMT, 28 August 1987, *FBIS-EAS*, 87-169, 1 February 1987, p. 41.
48. Hanoi Domestic Service in Vietnamese, 1100 GMT, 25 September 1987, *FBIS-EAS*, 87-187, 28 September 1987, pp. 33–34.
49. Ibid.
50. Hanoi Domestic Service in Vietnamese, 1100 GMT, 21 September 1987, *FBIS-EAS*, 87-186, 25 September 1987, pp. 36–37.
51. Hanoi Domestic Service in Vietnamese, 1100 GMT, 14 November 1987, *FBIS-EAS*, 87-223, 19 November 1987, p. 46. Thanh Hoa and Thuan Hai provinces had developed plans all the way down to the sectoral level by mid-November.
52. *Nhan Dan*, 4 November 1987, pp. 1, 4.
53. *Nhan Dan*, 5 November 1987, pp. 1, 4; *Nhan Dan*, 23 October 1987, pp. 1, 4.
54. *Nhan Dan*, 26 September 1987, pp. 1, 4.
55. See L.M. Stern, "The Vietnamese Communist Party in 1986: Party Reform Initiatives, the Scramble Toward Economic Revitalization, and the Road to the Sixth Party Congress", in *Southeast Asian Affairs 1987* (Singapore: Institute of Southeast Asian Studies, 1987), pp. 360–63.
56. Nayan Chanda, *Brother Enemy: The War After The War – A History of Indochina Since the Fall of Saigon* (New York: Harcourt, Brace and Jovanovich, 1986), p. 373. Bach's career was short-lived. He was removed from his positions as Politburo member and Central

Committee secretary at the Eighth Party Central Committee plenary session in March 1990.
57. "Nguyen Thanh Binh", U.S. Government Biography 1 NVN-6-1972.
58. Murray Hiebert, "Caught in a Downdraft: Vietnam Admits its Economic Problems are Worsening", *Far Eastern Economic Review*, 14 January 1988, pp. 48–49.
59. Hanoi Domestic Service in Vietnamese, 1100 GMT, 19 December 1987, in *FBIS-EAS*, 87-245, 22 December 1987, pp. 42–45; Hanoi Domestic Service in Vietnamese, 1100 GMT, 22 December 1987, in *FBIS-EAS*, 87-248, 28 December 1987, pp. 47–49.
60. Hanoi International Service in English, 1000 GMT, 22 December 1987, *FBIS-EAS*, 87-246, 23 December 1987, pp. 32–33.
61. Hanoi Domestic Service in Vietnamese, 1100 GMT, 19 December 1987, *FBIS-EAS*, 87-245, 22 December 1987, p. 42–45.
62. Hanoi Domestic Service in Vietnamese, 1100 GMT, 20 December 1987, *FBIS-EAS*, 87-244, 21 December 1987, p. 46–47.
63. Hanoi Domestic Service in Vietnamese, 0500 GMT, 21 December 1987, *FBIS-EAS*, 87-244, 21 December 1987, p. 46.
64. *Nhan Dan*, 14 December 1987, pp. 1, 4.
65. Hiebert, "Caught in a Downdraft", op. cit., p. 46. In largely pessimistic tones, Kiet noted:

1. the two per cent drop in 1987 agricultural production, matched by a two per cent increase in the population growth rate;
2. the steadily low value of exports to socialist countries in 1987, and the unsatisfactory implementation of programmes of production co-operation with the Soviet Union; and
3. diminishing foreign currency earnings and unexpectedly low levels of remittances from Overseas Vietnamese; and destabilizing downward trends in per capita availability of rice and overall inadequate investment in foodgrain production.

66. Among the areas that had managed to keep the schedule were Hai Hung, Hoang Lien Son, Quang Nam-Da Nang and Minh Hai Provinces and Ho Chi Minh City. See Hanoi Domestic Service in Vietnamese, 0500 GMT, 3 February 1988, *FBIS-EAS*, 88-025, 8 February 1988, pp. 55–56.
67. *Nhan Dan*, 5 February 1988, pp. 1, 4.
68. On Ha Bac Province's programme, see Hanoi Domestic Service in Vietnamese, 0500 GMT, 12 April 1988, *FBIS-EAS*, 88-071, 13 February

1988, p. 55. On Minh Hai Provinces programme, see Hanoi Domestic Service in Vietnamese, 1100 GMT, 12 May 1988, *FBIS-EAS*, 88-095, 17 May 1988, p. 55. On Dac Lac Provinces programme, see Hanoi Domestic Service in Vietnamese, 0500 GMT, 12 May 1988, *FBIS-EAS*, 88-097, 19 May 1988, pp. 53–54. On Phu Khanh Province's programme, see Hanoi Domestic Service in Vietnamese, 0500 GMT, 31 May 1988, *FBIS-EAS*, 88-105, 1 June 1988, p. 61.

69. Hanoi Domestic Service in Vietnamese, 1100 GMT, 23 March 1988, *FBIS-EAS*, 88-057, 24 March 1988, pp. 45–46; Hanoi Domestic Service in Vietnamese, 0500 GMT, 8 June 1988, *FBIS-EAS*, 88-112, 10 June 1988, pp. 39–40; *Dai Doan Ket*, 2 April 1988, p. 5.
70. *Nhan Dan*, 5 June 1988; *Nhan Dan*, 25 March 1988, p. 3; *Nhan Dan*, 26 March 1988, p. 1; *Nhan Dan*, 3 February 1988, pp. 1, 4; Hanoi Domestic Service in Vietnamese, 2300 GMT, 7 April 1988, *FBIS-EAS*, 88-068, 8 April 1988, p. 54.
71. *Tap Chi Cong San*, July 1988, pp. 22–26.
72. Hanoi Domestic Service in Vietnamese, 1100 GMT, 11 September 1988, *FBIS-EAS*, 88-180, 16 September 1988, pp. 72–73; *Dai Doan Ket*, 18 June 1988, pp. 1, 5, 8; *Nhan Dan*, 21 June 1988, p. 3; Hanoi Domestic Service in Vietnamese, 1430 GMT, 27 May 1988, *FBIS-EAS*, 88-106, 2 June 1988, pp. 71–72.
73. "Thanh Uy Thanh Pho Ho Chi Minh Thong Qua Tu Phe Binh Va Phe Binh, Dua Vao Quan Chung De Kiem Tra Chat Luong Dang Vien", *Nhan Dan*, 5 February 1989, pp. 1, 4.
74. Hanoi Domestic Service in Vietnamese, 0500 GMT, 2 February 1988, *FBIS-EAS*, 88-023, 4 February 1988, p. 61.
75. Hanoi Domestic Service in Vietnamese, 0500 GMT, 12 April 1988, *FBIS-EAS*, 88-071, 13 April 1988, p. 35.
76. Hanoi Domestic Service in Vietnamese, 0500 GMT, 12 May 1988, *FBIS-EAS*, 88-095, 17 May 1988, p. 59; Hanoi Domestic Service in Vietnamese, 2300 GMT, 21 April 1988, *FBIS-EAS*, 88-080, 26 April 1988, p. 71; Hanoi Domestic Service in Vietnamese, 0500 GMT, 17 May 1988, *FBIS-EAS*, 88-097, 19 May 1988, pp. 51–54.
77. Hanoi Domestic Service in Vietnamese, 0500 GMT, 2 June 1988, *FBIS-EAS*, 88-131, 8 July 1988, pp. 71–72; Hanoi Domestic Service in Vietnamese, 0500 GMT, 8 July 1988, *FBIS-EAS*, 88-112, 10 July 1988, p. 39.
78. Hanoi Domestic Service in Vietnamese, 0500 GMT, 8 June 1988, *FBIS-EAS*, 88-112, 10 June 1988, pp. 39–40.

79. Hanoi Domestic Service in Vietnamese, 0500 GMT, 24 August 1988, *FBIS-EAS*, 88-169, 31 August 1988, p. 75; Hanoi Domestic Service in Vietnamese, 0500 GMT, 18 August 1988, *FBIS-EAS*, 88-162, 22 August 1988, pp. 69–70; *Nhan Dan*, 31 July 1988, pp. 1, 4; Hanoi Domestic Service in Vietnamese, 2300 GMT, 11 August 1988, *FBIS-EAS*, 88-155, 22 August 1988, p. 65.
80. Hanoi Domestic Service in Vietnamese, 0500 GMT, 1 November 1988, *FBIS-EAS*, 88-214, 4 November 1988, p. 40.
81. *Nhan Dan*, 13 September 1988, pp. 1, 4; Hanoi Domestic Service in Vietnamese, 2300 GMT, 23 October 1988, *FBIS-EAS*, 88-209, 28 October 1988, pp. 59–60; Hanoi Domestic Service in Vietnamese, 1100 GMT, 31 October 1988, *FBIS-EAS*, 88-211, 1 November 1988, p. 54.
82. *Saigon Giai Phong*, 30 August 1988, pp. 1, 2; Hanoi Domestic Service in Vietnamese, 1100 GMT, 31 October 1988, *FBIS-EAS*, 88-211, 1 November 1988, p. 54.
83. *Nhan Dan*, 13 June 1988, p. 1.
84. Dang Cong San Viet Nam, *Dieu Le* (Hanoi: Nha Xuat Ban Su That, 1987), article 14, p. 40.
85. *Nhan Dan*, 4 August 1988, pp. 1, 4; Hanoi Domestic Service in Vietnamese, 2300 GMT, 7 August 1988, *FBIS-EAS*, 88-155, 11 August 1988, p. 65.
86. *Saigon Giai Phong*, 30 July 1988, pp. 1, 3; Hanoi Domestic Service in Vietnamese, 0500 GMT, 12 August 1988, *FBIS-EAS*, 88-158, 16 August 1988, p. 64; *Saigon Giai Phong*, 30 July 1988, pp. 1, 3.
87. Hanoi Domestic Service in Vietnamese, 2300 GMT, 8 September 1988, *FBIS-EAS*, 88-176, 12 September 1988, pp. 71–72.
88. *Nhan Dan*, 13 September 1988, pp. 1, 4.
89. Hanoi Domestic Service in Vietnamese, 2300 GMT, 23 October 1988, *FBIS-EAS*, 88-209, 28 October 1988, pp. 59–60.
90. For all references to the plenary communiqué, pp. 35–40 above, see Hanoi Domestic Service in Vietnamese, 1100 GMT, 21 June 1988, *FBIS-EAS*, 88-119, 21 June 1988, pp. 57–59.
91. For all quotations from Linh's speech, pp. 40–44 above, see Hanoi Domestic Service in Vietnamese, 1100 GMT, 22 June 1988, *FBIS-EAS*, 88-122, 24 June 1988, pp. 35–42.
92. Hanoi Domestic Service in Vietnamese, 1100 GMT, 21 June 1988, *FBIS-EAS*, 88-120, 22 June 1988, pp. 44–46.
93. Hanoi Domestic Service in Vietnamese, 1100 GMT, 21 June 1988,

FBIS-EAS, 88-120, 22 June 1988, pp. 41–42; Hanoi Domestic Service in Vietnamese, 1100 GMT, 22 June 1988, *FBIS-EAS*, 88-120, 22 June 1988, pp. 43–46.
94. *Who's Who in North Vietnam* (Washington, D.C.: U.S. Government, November 1972), p. 19.
95. *Thanh Nien*, January 1988, pp. 12–14; *Thanh Nien*, April 1988, pp. 1–3, 18.
96. Hanoi Domestic Service in Vietnamese, 2300 GMT, 15 August 1988, *FBIS-EAS*, 88-161, 19 August 1988, p. 52; Hanoi Domestic Service in Vietnamese, 0500 GMT, 18 October 1988, *FBIS-EAS*, 88-203, 20 October 1988, p. 65.
97. Hanoi Domestic Service in Vietnamese, 0500 GMT, 18 October 1988, *FBIS-EAS*, 88-203, 20 October 1988, p. 65.
98. Hanoi Domestic Service in Vietnamese, 1100 GMT, 17 October 1988, *FBIS-EAS*, 88-203, 20 October 1988, p. 61.
99. In April and May, incidents of protest took place in Ngai Dang and An Dinh communes. In August, farmers from Cuu Long organized by a Co-ordination Action Committee travelled to Ho Chi Minh City to demonstrate against land policies. In early November, Mekong Delta peasants marched to Ho Chi Minh City to dramatize their grievances. See Le Thien Tung, "The Land Issue: The Internal Debate", *Vietnam Commentary*, January–February 1989, p. 2.
100. *Nhan Dan*, 12 April 1988, pp. 1–3; Tetsusaburo Kimura, "The Socialist Economy in Vietnam: A Complete Failure", *Vietnam Commentary*, January–February 1989, p. 11.
101. Hanoi Domestic Service in Vietnamese, 0500 GMT, 8 May 1989, *FBIS-EAS*, 88-094, 16 May 1988, p. 59.
102. Le Thien Tung, "The Land Issue", p. 2.
103. *Nhan Dan*, 26 May 1988, p. 2.
104. *Nhan Dan*, 8 August 1988, p. 1.
105. Hanoi Domestic Service in Vietnamese, 1430 GMT, 22 August 1988, *FBIS-EAS*, 88-163, 23 August 1988, pp. 70–71.
106. Hanoi Domestic Service in Vietnamese, 2300 GMT, 9 September 1988, *FBIS-EAS*, 88-179, 15 September 1988, pp. 72–76.
107. Ibid.
108. Hanoi Domestic Service in Vietnamese, 2300 GMT, 18 September 1988, *FBIS-EAS*, 88-182, 20 September 1988, p. 56.
109. *Saigon Giai Phong*, 17 August 1988, pp. 1–2.

110. *Nhan Dan*, 12 September 1988, pp. 1, 4.
111. Hanoi Domestic Service in Vietnamese, 1100 GMT, 18 November 1988, *FBIS-EAS*, 88-227, 25 November 1988, p. 65.
112. Hanoi Domestic Service in Vietnamese, 1100 GMT, 18 November 1988, *FBIS-EAS*, 88-227, 15 September 1988, p. 65.
113. Hong Ha, head of the Office of the Central Committee, Pham Bai, Central Committee member and Chairman of the Peasants Association, and Huynh Chau So, Chairman of the State Inspection Committee, headed the remaining three teams.
114. Hanoi Domestic Service in Vietnamese, 1100 GMT, 7 November 1988, *FBIS-EAS*, 88-220, 15 November 1988, pp. 73–74.
115. Hanoi Domestic Service in Vietnamese, 0500 GMT, 15 November 1988, *FBIS-EAS*, 88-220, 15 November 1988, pp. 73–74.
116. Hanoi Domestic Service in Vietnamese, 2300 GMT, 26 November 1988, *FBIS-EAS*, 88-234, 6 December 1988, p. 57.
117. *Nhan Dan*, 29 November 1988, pp. 2, 4.
118. Hanoi Domestic Service in Vietnamese, 2300 GMT, 8 December 1988, *FBIS-EAS*, 88-237, 9 December 1988, pp. 60–61.
119. *Nong Nghiep Viet Nam*, 28 July 1988, p. 5.
120. Hong Kong AFP in English, 1224 GMT, 12 December 1988, *FBIS-EAS*, 88-239, 13 December 1988, p. 62.
121. Hanoi Vietnamese News Agency in English, 1500 GMT, 23 December 1988, *FBIS-EAS*, 88-248, 27 December 1988, pp. 74–75. On 12 December, Vu Mao, Chairman of the Office of the Council of Ministers, stated at a news conference that the party would not intervene "to any great extent" in the Assembly's proceedings. Hong Kong AFP in English, 1224 GMT, 12 December 1988, *FBIS-EAS*, 88-239, 13 December 1988, pp. 62–63.
122. Hanoi Domestic Service in Vietnamese, 0500 GMT, 8 December 1988, *FBIS-EAS*, 88-236, 8 December 1988, p. 52; Hanoi Domestic Service in Vietnamese, 1100 GMT, 8 December 1988, *FBIS-EAS*, 88-237, 9 December 1988, p. 62.
123. *Dai Doan Ket*, 2 and 9 July 1988, pp. 1, 3.
124. Hanoi Domestic Service in Vietnamese, 2300 GMT, 15 December 1988, *FBIS-EAS*, 88-242, 16 December 1988, pp. 50–51.
125. In the aftermath of the eighth plenary session municipal services, in co-ordination with both the district party committee and the district administrative committee, were required to request the permission

of the municipal party and people's committees prior to the experimental sale of rice at a particular price. The district party committee appears to have exerted a major influence over the attempts of echelons subordinate to the district to conduct "experiments" regarding the new compensation policy. However, the ultimate shape of such "experiments" seems to have been determined by local "guidance committees" (Truong Ban Chi Dao), apparently constituted by a membership drawn from both local party and administrative committees. Linh seems to have endorsed this kind of evolution in the system. These experiments underscored the regime's commitment to co-ordination between party and local administrative committee authority. See "Thu Duc Bu Gia Vao Luong", *Nhan Dan*, 8 May 1985, pp. 1, 4; *Haiphong*, 1 June 1985, pp. 1, 4; *Nhan Dan*, 23 September 1985, p. 4.

126. Hanoi Domestic Service in Vietnamese, 1430 GMT, 24 January 1989, *FBIS-EAS*, 89-016, 26 January 1989, pp. 74–75; Hanoi Domestic Service in Vietnamese, 1100 GMT, 25 January 1989, *FBIS-EAS*, 89-016, 26 January 1989, p. 75; Hanoi Domestic Service in Vietnamese, 1100 GMT, 3 January 1989, *Joint Publications Research Service-Southeast Asia* 89–004, 26 January 1989, p. 16; Hanoi Domestic Service in Vietnamese, 1100 GMT, 30 January 1989, Hanoi Domestic Service in Vietnamese, 1000 GMT, 31 January 1989, *FBIS-EAS*, 89-016, 2 February 1989, p. 70.

127. Hanoi Domestic Service in Vietnamese, 1430 GMT, 24 January 1989, *FBIS-EAS*, 89-016, 26 January 1989, p. 75, discussing Hung Ha districts delegates to its Ninth Congress of party organization delegates.

128. Hanoi Domestic Service in Vietnamese, 1000 GMT, 31 January 1989, *FBIS-EAS*, 89-021, 2 February 1989, p. 70.

129. Hanoi Domestic Service in Vietnamese, 0500 GMT, 2 February 1989, *FBIS-EAS*, 89-033, 2 February 1989, p. 73.

130. Hanoi Vietnamese News Agency in English, 0713 GMT, 14 April 1989, *FBIS-EAS*, 89-073, 18 April 1989, p. 83; Hanoi Domestic Service in Vietnamese, 2300 GMT, 18 April 1989, *FBIS-EAS*, 89-075, 20 April 1989, p. 57.

131. *Saigon Giai Phong*, 15 March 1989, p. 2.

132. *Saigon Giai Phong*, 23 May 1989, p. 3.

133. Hanoi Domestic Service in Vietnamese, 2300 GMT, 8 June 1989, *FBIS-EAS*, 89-111, 13 June 1989, p. 58.

134. Hanoi Domestic Service in Vietnamese, 1100 GMT, 23 May 1989, *FBIS-EAS*, 89-101, 26 May 1989, p. 56.
135. "Bai Phat Bieu Cua Dong Chi Tong Bi Thu Nguyen Van Linh, Be Mac Hoi Nghi Trung Uong Sau (Ngay 29 Thang 3 Nam 1989", *Nhan Dan*, 31 March 1989, pp. 1, 4.
136. Translated passages from the General Secretary's closing speech concerning foreign trade, cited on pp. 59–60 above, are from Hanoi Domestic Service in Vietnamese, 1430 GMT, 30 March 1989, *FBIS-EAS*, 89-061, 31 March 1989, pp. 64–71. Translated passages from the plenary session communiqué concerning foreign trade are from Hanoi Domestic Service in Vietnamese, 1430 GMT, 30 March 1989, *FBIS-EAS*, 89-061, 31 March 1989, p. 72.
137. References concerning the role of the market quoted from Linh's closing speech, pp. 60–61 above, are from Hanoi Domestic Service in Vietnamese, 1430 GMT, 30 March 1989, *FBIS-EAS*, 89-061, 31 March 1989, p. 67.
138. References concerning socialist transformation in the plenary session communiqué and the General Secretary's closing speech, cited on pp. 61–64 above, are from Hanoi Domestic Service in Vietnamese, 1100 GMT, 30 March 1989, *FBIS-EAS*, 89-061, 31 March 1989, p. 72, and Hanoi Domestic Service in Vietnamese, 1430 GMT, 30 March 1989, *FBIS-EAS*, 89-061, 31 March 1989, pp. 64–71.
139. References concerning the role of the party in the plenary session communiqué and the General Secretary's closing speech, cited on pp. 64–65 above, are from Hanoi Domestic Service in Vietnamese, 1100 GMT, 30 March 1989, *FBIS-EAS*, 89-061, 31 March 1989, p. 72, and Hanoi Domestic Service in Vietnamese, 1430 GMT, 30 March 1989, *FBIS-EAS*, 89-061, 31 March 1989, pp. 64–71.
140. Hanoi Domestic Service in Vietnamese, 1430 GMT, 30 March 1989, *FBIS-EAS*, 89-061, 31 March 1989, p. 72.
141. *Far Eastern Economic Review*, 13 April 1989, p. 34; Hong Kong AFP in English 0534 GMT, 23 March 1989, *FBIS-EAS*, 89-05, 23 March 1989, p. 71. Jacques Bekaert, writing in the *Bangkok Post*, 18 January 1989, p. 4, suggested that an extraordinary Politburo session, convened during the first week of January in Ho Chi Minh City, heard a review of foreign policy and prepared for the March plenum. Thach reportedly insisted that it was time to think about the "Post Kampuchea" period.

142. *Tap Chi Cong San*, April 1989, editorial, p. 1.
143. *Nhan Dan*, 1 April 1989, editorial, p. 1.
144. For instance, an early April conference sponsored by the Central Committee's Propaganda and Training Department concluded with the acknowledgement that "practical and epistemological issues" required a re-evaluation of the "fundamental spirit" of Resolution Ten — a basic document laying the groundwork for the renovation of the mechanism of economic management in agriculture. The conference also recognized the need to re-examine the various decisions adopted by the party's Secretariat and the Council of Ministers in the service of Resolution Ten's provisions on signing contracts with the state, taxation, and the entitlement to dispose of production at the discretion of the individual agricultural producer. Hanoi Domestic Service in Vietnamese, 1430 GMT, 2 April 1989, *FBIS-EAS*, 89-064, 5 April 1989, p. 60.
145. *Dai Doan Ket*, 18 June 1988, pp. 1, 5, 8. *Nhan Dan*, 21 June 1988, p. 3. Participants in the conference, including party luminaries and editors, supported the utility of public debate, the active flow of information and the use of the press to initiate "dialogue". Importantly, Tran Cong Man, general editor of *Quan Doi Nhan Dan*, urged an independent role for the party's press, echoing Linh's call for a press that "searches for causes". Also see L.M. Stern, "Nguyen Van Linh's Leadership: A New Operational Code", *Indochina Report*, no. 16, January–March 1989.
146. Hanoi Domestic Service in Vietnamese, 1100 GMT, 15 April 1989, *FBIS-EAS*, 89-074, 19 April 1989, pp. 74–75.
147. Hanoi Domestic Service in Vietnamese, 1000 GMT, 10 June 1989, *FBIS-EAS*, 89-111, 12 June 1989, pp. 43–44; Hanoi Domestic Service in Vietnamese, 1100 GMT, 27 June 1989, *FBIS-EAS*, 89-132, 12 July 1989, pp. 65–66; *Quan Doi Nhan Dan*, 12 July 1989, pp. 1, 4.
148. Hanoi Domestic Service in Vietnamese, 1100 GMT, 27 June 1989, *FBIS-EAS*, 89-132, 12 July 1989, p. 18.
149. Hanoi Domestic Service in Vietnamese, 2300 GMT, 25 July 1989, *FBIS-EAS*, 89-143, 27 July 1989, p. 55; *Nhan Dan*, 28 November 1989, p. 4.
150. Hanoi Domestic Service in Vietnamese, 2330 GMT, 17 October 1989, *FBIS-EAS*, 89-202, 20 October 1989, p. 58.

151. Hanoi Domestic Service in Vietnamese, 2300 GMT, 27 October 1989, *FBIS-EAS*, 89-208, 30 October 1989, pp. 57–58; Hanoi Domestic Service in Vietnamese, 1100 GMT, 28 October 1989, Hanoi Domestic Service in Vietnamese, 2300 GMT, 28 October 1989, and Hanoi Domestic Service in Vietnamese, 1100 GMT, 29 October 1989, *FBIS-EAS*, 89-208, 30 October 1989, pp. 57–58.
152. Hanoi Vietnamese News Agency in English, 1420 GMT, 30 December 1989, *FBIS-EAS*, 90-001, 2 January 1990, p. 70.
153. Hanoi Domestic Service in Vietnamese 0515 GMT, 27 December 1989, *FBIS-EAS*, 89-247, 27 December 1989, p. 71.
154. Hanoi Domestic Service in Vietnamese, 1100 GMT, 27 December 1989, *FBIS-EAS*, 89-248, 28 December 1989, p. 70.
155. *Quan Doi Nhan Dan*, 7 August 1989, p. 4.
156. *Nhan Dan*, 18 August 1989, p. 1, editorial.
157. *Nhan Dan*, 9 August 1989, p. 3.
158. Hanoi Domestic Service in Vietnamese, 2300 GMT, 8 June 1989, *FBIS-EAS*, 89-111, 12 June 1989, p. 43; Hanoi Domestic Service in Vietnamese, 2300 GMT, 27 June 1989, *FBIS-EAS*, 89-133, 13 June 1989, pp. 54–55.
159. Hanoi Domestic Service in Vietnamese 1100 GMT, 18 December 1989, *FBIS-EAS*, 89-241, 18 December 1989, pp. 65–67.
160. Hanoi Domestic Service in Vietnamese 1430 GMT, 19 December 1989, *FBIS-EAS*, 89-245, 22 December 1989, p. 64.
161. Hanoi Vietnamese News Agency in English, 1420 GMT, 30 December 1989, *FBIS-EAS*, 90-001, 2 January 1990, p. 70; Hanoi Domestic Service in Vietnamese 1430 GMT, 30 December 1989, *FBIS-EAS*, 89-247, 27 December 1989, p. 71.
162. Vo Chi Cong summarized the party's preoccupation with the convulsive course of change in communist systems world-wide, and emphasized the cost of failing to reform. Communist parties had allowed non-antagonistic contradictions to become antagonistic, in Cong's formula, by failing to address issues such as internal corruption that could have been solved by means that would have preserved systems instead of ensuring their disaggregation. Hanoi Domestic Service in Vietnamese 1400 GMT, 26 December 1989, *FBIS-EAS*, 89-248, 28 December 1989, pp. 67–68; Hanoi Domestic Service in Vietnamese 1400 GMT, 20 December 1989, *FBIS-EAS*, 89-247, 27 December 1989, pp. 65–66; Hanoi Domestic Service

in Vietnamese 1100 GMT, 19 December 1989, *FBIS-EAS*, 89-245, 22 December 1989, p. 64.
163. *Saigon Giai Phong*, 16 August 1989, pp. 1, 2; *Nhan Dan*, 18 July 1989, p. 3; *Saigon Giai Phong*, 16 August 1989, pp. 1, 2; Hanoi Vietnamese News Agency in English, 0453 GMT, 18 June 1989, *FBIS-EAS*, 89-116, 19 June 1989, p. 52.
164. Le Khac Thanh, "Can Cai Cach Thuc Su He Thong Chinh Tri", *Quan Doi Nhan Dan*, 19 January 1989, pp. 1, 4.
165. *Dai Doan Ket*, 18–24 March 1989, p. 2.
166. *Hanoi Moi*, 17 March 1989, p. 2; *Saigon Giai Phong*, 15 March 1989, p. 1.
167. Hanoi Domestic Service in Vietnamese 2300 GMT, 5 December 1989, *FBIS-EAS*, 89-236, 11 December 1989, p. 59.
168. *Nhan Dan*, 31 July 1989, p. 2.
169. Nayan Chanda, "Force for Change", *Far Eastern Economic Review*, 5 October 1989, pp. 24–26; Barry Wain, "Old Revolutionaries in Vietnam Launch One Last Offensive", *Wall Street Journal*, 4 May 1989, pp. 1, 11.
170. Hanoi Domestic Service in Vietnamese, 1430 GMT, 28 August 1989, *FBIS-EAS*, 89-166, 29 August 1989, pp. 66–72.
171. *Quan Doi Nhan Dan*, 19 January 1989, pp. 1, 4.
172. Quotations from Nguyen Dang Quang's article, cited on pp. 82–85 above, are from *Tap Chi Cong San*, January 1989, pp. 18–22.
173. Quotations from Nguyen Huy's article, cited on pp. 85–86 above, are from *Tap Chi Cong San*, February 1989, pp. 19–25.
174. *Nhan Dan*, 23 January 1989, pp. 3–4.
175. References to Linh's closing speech to the sixth plenary session, cited on p. 88 above, are from Hanoi Domestic Service in Vietnamese, 1430 GMT, 30 March 1989, *FBIS-EAS*, 89-061, 31 March 1989, p. 70. The quotation from Linh's National Day speech, cited on p. 88 above, is from Hanoi Vietnamese News Agency in English, 0831 GMT, 2 September 1989, *FBIS-EAS*, 89-173, 8 September 1989, p. 68.
176. *Tap Chi Cong San*, January 1990, pp. 81–84; March 1990, pp. 75–77.
177. *Quan Doi Nhan Dan*, 23 May 1990.
178. See "Ong Thieu O Hoa Thinh Don De Nghi Xoa Bai Lam Lai, Trong Khi O Cali Ong Ky Noi San Sang Ve Nuoc Neu Cong San Noi Long Chinh Tri", *Tu Do*, 7 April 1990, pp. 1, 2; "Xuat Hien

Truoc 500 Nguoi Thuoc Thanh Phan Do Ban To Chuc, Chon Loc, Cuu Thong Tong Nguyen Van Thieu Chinh Thuc Nhan Lanh Trach Nhiem Lam Mat Nuoc Va Doi Xoa Bai Lam Lai", *Hoa Thinh Don Viet Bao*, 7 April 1990, pp. 1, 2. Also see Susuma Awanohara, "Reconciling the Past", *Far Eastern Economic Review*, 16 August 1990, pp. 21–22.

179. *Quan Doi Nhan Dan*, 23 May 1990.
180. Hanoi Domestic Service in Vietnamese, 2300 GMT, 14 April 1990, *FBIS-EAS*, 90-074, 17 April 1990, p. 73.
181. Hanoi Domestic Service in Vietnamese, 1430 GMT, 16 April 1990, *FBIS-EAS*, 90-075, 18 April 1990, p. 55.
182. Murray Hiebert, "Jailhouse Open Door", *Far Eastern Economic Review*, 31 May 1990, p. 22; Hanoi Domestic Service in Vietnamese, 1430 GMT, 7 June 1990, *FBIS-EAS*, 90-111, 8 June 1990, p. 8.
183. *Quan Doi Nhan Dan*, 30 May 1990, pp. 1,4; Hanoi Domestic Service in Vietnamese, 1100 GMT, 12 July 1990, *FBIS-EAS*, 90-138, 18 July 1990, pp. 57–58.
184. Hanoi Domestic Service in Vietnamese, 1430 GMT, 16 January 1990, *FBIS-EAS*, 90-013, 19 January 1990, p. 57.
185. Hanoi Domestic Service in Vietnamese, 2330 GMT, 14 January 1990, *FBIS-EAS*, 90-014, 22 January 1990, p. 59.
186. *Nhan Dan*, 16 November 1989, p. 3.
187. Hanoi Vietnamese News Agency in English, 0716 GMT, 7 March 1990, *FBIS-EAS*, 90-045, 7 March 1990, pp. 71–72; Hanoi Vietnamese News Agency in English, 0704 GMT, 25 February 1990, *FBIS-EAS*, 90-041, 1 March 1990, pp. 67–68; Hanoi Domestic Service in Vietnamese, 1100 GMT, 23 February 1989, *FBIS-EAS*, 90-044, 6 March 1990, pp. 70–71. Also see *Far Eastern Economic Review*, 29 March 1990, p. 18; *Saigon Giai Phong*, 6 March 1990, p. 2. Hanoi Domestic Service in Vietnamese, 1400 GMT, 9 April 1990, *FBIS-EAS*, 90-071, 12 April 1990, p. 44; Hanoi Domestic Service in Vietnamese, 1400 GMT, 15 March 1990, *FBIS-EAS*, 90-054, 20 March 1990, p. 54; Hanoi Domestic Service in Vietnamese, 1100 GMT, 22 March 1990, *FBIS-EAS*, 90-058, 26 March 1990, pp. 84–85; Hanoi Vietnamese News Agency in English, 1525 GMT, 19 October 1990, *FBIS-EAS*, 90-204, 22 October 1990, pp. 74–75; Hanoi Domestic Service in Vietnamese, 2330 GMT, 5 December 1990, *FBIS-EAS*, 90-244, 19 December 1990, p. 55.

188. Hanoi Vietnamese News Agency in English, 0716 GMT, 7 March 1990, *FBIS-EAS*, 90-045, 7 March 1990, pp. 71–72.
189. Hanoi Domestic Service in Vietnamese, 1100 GMT, 5 February 1990, *FBIS-EAS*, 90-028, 9 February 1990, p. 54.
190. Hanoi Vietnamese News Agency in English, 0716 GMT, 7 March 1990, *FBIS-EAS*, 90-045, 7 March 1990, pp. 71–72; Hanoi Vietnamese News Agency in English, 0704 GMT, 25 February 1990, *FBIS-EAS*, 90-041, 1 March 1990, pp. 67–68; Hanoi Domestic Service in Vietnamese, 1100 GMT, 23 February 1989, *FBIS-EAS*, 90-044, 6 March 1990, pp. 70–71.
191. Hanoi Domestic Service in Vietnamese, 1100 GMT, 5 March 1990, *FBIS-EAS*, 90-051, 15 March 1990, p. 54.
192. Hanoi Domestic Service in Vietnamese, 1000 GMT, 2 March 1989, *FBIS-EAS*, 90-044, 5 March 1990, p. 90; Hanoi Domestic Service in Vietnamese, 2300 GMT, 25 February 1990, *FBIS-EAS* 90-044, 1 March 1990, p. 68.
193. Hanoi Vietnamese News Agency in English, 0716 GMT, 7 March 1990, *FBIS-EAS*, 90-045, 7 March 1990, p. 72.
194. Hanoi Domestic Service in Vietnamese, 1400 GMT, 27 February 1990, *FBIS-EAS*, 90-046, 8 March 1990, p. 65.
195. Hanoi International Service in English, 1000 GMT, 29 March 1990, *FBIS-EAS*, 90-062, 30 March 1990, p. 71.
196. Hanoi Domestic Service in Vietnamese, 1100 GMT, 11 March 1990, *FBIS-EAS*, 90-053, 19 March 1990, p. 56.
197. Murray Hiebert, "Against the Wind", *Far Eastern Economic Review*, 12 April 1990, p. 13; Gareth Porter, "The Politics of 'Renovation' in Vietnam", *Problems of Communism* (May–June 1990), p. 87; Keith Richburg, "Vietnam's Communists Demote Leading Proponent of Political Change", *Washington Post*, 29 March 1989, pp. 29–30.
198. Hiebert, "Against The Wind", p. 13; Tran Xuan Bach, "Mot Doi Dieu Suy Nghi Tren Duong Loi Moi", *Tap Chi Cong San*, January 1990, p. 47.
199. Hanoi Domestic Service in Vietnamese, 1100 GMT, 5 January 1990, *FBIS-EAS*, 90-005, 8 January 1990, pp. 67–70.
200. Hanoi Domestic Service in Vietnamese, 1100 GMT, 5 January 1990, *FBIS-EAS*, 90-016, 24 January 1990, p. 75.
201. Hanoi Domestic Service in Vietnamese, 1100 GMT, 5 January 1990, *FBIS-EAS*, 90-005, 8 January 1990, pp. 68–69.

202. References to the plenary communiqué, cited on pp. 105–07 above, are from Hanoi Domestic Service in Vietnamese, 1100 GMT, 28 March 1990, *FBIS-EAS*, 90-060, 28 March 1990.
203. References to the party resolution cited on pp. 107–109 above are from "Nghi Quyet Hoi Nghi Lan Thu 8, BCHTUD (Khoai VI), Doi Moi Cong Tac Quan Chung Cua Dang, Tang Cuong Moi Quan He Giai Dang Va Nhan Dan", *Tap Chi Cong San*, May 1990, pp. 1–8.
204. Hanoi Domestic Service in Vietnamese, 1100 GMT, 29 August 1990, *FBIS-EAS*, 90-169, 30 August 1990, pp. 70–71 (communiqué); Hanoi Domestic Service in Vietnamese, 1100 GMT, 29 August 1990, *FBIS-EAS*, 90-169, 30 August 1990, pp. 69–70 (resolution).
205. *Nhan Dan*, 12 January 1990, pp. 3, 4; *Tap Chi Cong San*, February 1990, pp. 15–19, 32.
206. *Nhan Dan*, 12 January 1990, pp. 3, 4; Hanoi Domestic Service in Vietnamese, 0500 GMT, 10 October 1990, *FBIS-EAS*, 90-196, 10 October 1990, p. 59; Hanoi Domestic Service in Vietnamese, 2300 GMT, 13 November 1990, *FBIS-EAS*, 90-220, 14 November 1990, p. 68. Also see Hanoi Domestic Service in Vietnamese, 2300 GMT, 3 October 1990, *FBIS-EAS*, 90-193, 4 October 1990, p. 70; Hanoi Domestic Service in Vietnamese, 1430 GMT, 17 September 1990, *FBIS-EAS*, 90-184, 21 September 1990, p. 73; Hanoi Domestic Service in Vietnamese, 1430 GMT, 27 October 1990, *FBIS-EAS*, 90-210, 30 October 1990, p. 81; Hanoi Domestic Service in Vietnamese, 1430 GMT, 27 October 1990, *FBIS-EAS*, 90-210, 30 October 1990, p. 81.
207. *Nhan Dan*, 7 September 1990, p. 3; *Tap Chi Cong San*, February 1990, pp. 15–19, 32.
208. A January 1990 *Tap Chi Cong San* article suggested that of the 2,149,000 party members, 11.47 per cent had worked at enterprise work sites and state farms. A February 1990 *Tap Cong San* article noted that 8.8 per cent were workers participating directly in production. See *Tap Chi Cong San*, February 1990, pp. 15–19, 32; *Nhan Dan*, 29 August 1990, p. 3.
209. *Tap Chi Cong San*, February 1990, pp. 15–19, 32.
210. *Nhan Dan*, 12 January 1990, pp. 3, 4.
211. *Nhan Dan*, 29 August 1990, p. 3.
212. *Saigon Giai Phong*, 26 May 1990, p. 2.

213. *Nhan Dan*, 12 January 1990, pp. 3–4; *Tap Chi Cong San*, February 1990, pp. 15–19. According to a late August article about Hau Giang Province's basic party organizations, "In the rural area, the reorganization of party chapters by hamlet in place of production units and the formation of a number of chapters not directly engaged in production leadership (comprised largely of retired party members) have overcome a situation of party chapters 'meeting without decision or making decisions without achievement' and of 'those working not speaking or those speaking not working'". See *Nhan Dan*, 29 August 1990, p. 3.
214. *Nhan Dan*, 7 September 1990, p. 3.
215. *Nhan Dan*, 5 February 1990, pp. 3–4.
216. *Tap Chi Cong San*, February 1990, pp. 52–54.
217. Hanoi Vietnamese News Agency in English, 1414 GMT, 2 February 1990, *FBIS-EAS*, 90-024, 5 February 1990, p. 53.
218. Hanoi Vietnamese News Agency in English, 1528 GMT, 2 December 1990, *FBIS-EAS*, 90-232, 3 December 1990, pp. 71–72.
219. Hanoi Domestic Service in Vietnamese, 0500 GMT, 1 December 1990, *FBIS-EAS*, 90-233, 4 December 1990, pp. 54–55.
220. Hanoi Domestic Service in Vietnamese, 1100 GMT, 14 November 1990, *FBIS-EAS*, 14 November 1990.
221. Hanoi Domestic Service in Vietnamese, 1100 GMT, 14 November 1990, *FBIS-EAS*, 90-222, 16 November 1990, p. 70. For broadcasts following the plenary session, referenced on p. 120 above, see Hanoi Vietnamese News Agency in English, 1528 GMT, 2 December 1990, *FBIS-EAS*, 90-232, 3 December 1990, p. 71.
222. Hanoi Domestic Service in Vietnamese, 1100 GMT, 27 November 1990, *FBIS-EAS* 90-229, 28 November 1990, pp. 66–68.
223. All references to the Draft Platform, cited on pp. 122–23 above, are from Hanoi Domestic Service in Vietnamese, 1100 GMT, 30 November 1990; Hanoi Domestic Service in Vietnamese, 1430 GMT, 30 November 1990; and Hanoi Domestic Service in Vietnamese, 2300 GMT, 30 November 1990, *FBIS-EAS*, 90-229, 28 November 1990, pp. 66–68.
224. In a conversation during January 1991 with a senior Ministry of Foreign Affairs official, the official suggested that he and most of his colleagues, certainly all of those who knew Bui Tin, regarded his indiscretion as the result of a mental weakening or sickness, and as

such were not concerned with the political impact of Tin's act. Also see *Asian Wall Street Journal*, 3 December 1990, p. 15; *Asian Wall Street Journal*, 11 March 1991, pp. 1, 19; "Duong Thu Huong", *Xay Dung*, (published in California), 1991, pp. 59-62.

225. Author's interview with senior Ministry of Foreign Affairs official, April 1991, and with Vietnamese News Agency official, October 1990.

226. Hanoi Domestic Service in Vietnamese, 1100 GMT, 5 February 1990, *FBIS-EAS*, 90-026, 7 February 1990, p. 71; Hanoi Domestic Service in Vietnamese, 2300 GMT, 1 September 1990, *FBIS-EAS*, 90-173, 6 September 1990, p. 58. Vo Van Kiet and Le Duc Anh's positions were unchanged from the Sixth Party Congress line-up to the October death of Le Duc Tho when a listing of the funeral committee ranked Kiet and Anh after Linh, Vo Chi Cong and Do Muoi. However, Nguyen Thanh Binh climbed ahead of Nguyen Duc Tam, Nguyen Co Thach and Dong Sy Nguyen. Mai Chi Tho rose by several spots, displacing Doan Khue by one notch. Hanoi Domestic Service in Vietnamese, 2300 GMT, 13 October 1990, *FBIS-EAS*, 90-199, 15 October 1990, p. 78.

227. Hanoi International Service in English, 1000 GMT, 29 March 1990, *FBIS-EAS*, 90-062, 30 March 1990, pp. 67–68; Hanoi Vietnamese News Agency in English, 0721 GMT, 30 March 1990, *FBIS-EAS*, 90-063, 2 April 1990, pp. 50–55; *Ho Chi Minh Anh Hung Giai Phong Dan Toc Danh Nhan Van Hoa* (Hanoi: Uy Ban Khoa Hoc Xa Hoi Viet Nam, Nha Xuat Ban Khoa Hoc Xa Hoi, 1990).

228. Hanoi Domestic Service in Vietnamese, 1430 GMT, 5 September 1990, *FBIS-EAS*, 90-174, 7 September 1990, pp. 71–75.

229. Hanoi Vietnamese News Agency in English, 0721 GMT, 30 March 1990, *FBIS-EAS*, 90-063, 2 April 1990, p. 53.

230. Hanoi Domestic Service in Vietnamese, 2300 GMT, 14 February 1990, *FBIS-EAS*, 90-035, 21 February 1990, pp. 73–74. Also see Hanoi Domestic Service in Vietnamese, 1430 GMT, 9 March 1990, *FBIS-EAS*, 90-9052, 16 March 1990, p. 59 about the trial of the *Tien Phong* correspondent, Nguyen Minh Vien. Vien was convicted of libel for an article published on the 1989 crack-down on "decadent video cassettes" in mid-1989, and retried and found guilty of a lesser violation of the criminal code involving libel – by the High-Level Military Appellate Tribunal in Ho Chi Minh City during early March

1990; Hanoi Vietnamese News Agency in English, 1552 GMT, 6 April 1990, *FBIS-EAS*, 90-068, 9 April 1990, p. 74; *Nhan Dan*, 21 June 1990, p. 3; *Nhan Dan*, 24 June 1990 editorial.
231. Hanoi Domestic Service in Vietnamese, 1100 GMT, 13 June 1990, *FBIS-EAS*, 90-117, 18 June 1990, pp. 72–73.
232. Hanoi Domestic Service in Vietnamese, 1430 GMT, 13 June 1990, *FBIS-EAS*, 90-117, 18 June 1990, pp. 72–73.
233. Hanoi Domestic Service in Vietnamese, 1100 GMT, 30 July 1990, *FBIS-EAS*, 90-152, 7 August 1990, pp. 55–56; Hanoi Domestic Service in Vietnamese, 1100 GMT, 27 July 1990, *FBIS-EAS*, 90-153, 8 August 1990, pp. 56–59 for a text of the Secretariat's Directive on the Management of Literature and the Arts.
234. Hanoi Domestic Service in Vietnamese, 2300 GMT, 7 September 1990, *FBIS-EAS*, 90-176, 11 September 1990, p. 70.
235. Hanoi Domestic Service in Vietnamese, 1100 GMT, 1 October 1990, *FBIS-EAS*, 90-192, 3 October 1990, p. 53; Hanoi Domestic Service in Vietnamese, 1100 GMT, 19 October 1990, *FBIS-EAS*, 90-204, 22 October 1990, pp. 71–73.
236. Hanoi Domestic Service in Vietnamese, 1100 GMT, 9 November 1990, *FBIS-EAS*, 90-220, 14 November 1990, pp. 70–72.
237. Hanoi Domestic Service in Vietnamese, 1100 GMT, 24 September 1990, *FBIS-EAS*, 90-189, 28 September 1990, p. 56; Hanoi International Service in English, 25 September 1990, *FBIS-EAS*, 90-187, 26 September 1990, p. 72; Hanoi Domestic Service in Vietnamese, 2300 GMT, 13 September 1990, *FBIS-EAS*, 90-179, 14 September 1990, p. 68; Hanoi Domestic Service in Vietnamese, 1100 GMT, 11 September 1990, *FBIS-EAS*, 90-177, 12 September 1990, p. 56.
238. Hanoi Domestic Service in Vietnamese, 1100 GMT, 13 March 1990, *FBIS-EAS*, 90-052, 16 March 1990, pp. 58–59.
239. *Saigon Giai Phong*, 7 March 1990, pp. 1,3.
240. Hanoi Domestic Service in Vietnamese, 1430 GMT, 16 April 1990, *FBIS-EAS*, 90-075, 18 April 1990, p. 55–56.
241. Hong Kong AFP in English, 0833 GMT, 16 April 1990, *FBIS-EAS*, 90-073, 16 April 1990, p. 58; *Bangkok Post*, 14 May 1990, p. 6; *Saigon Giai Phong*, 19 June 1990, pp. 1,2; *Far Eastern Economic Review*, 31 May 1990, p. 22.
242. Hanoi Domestic Service in Vietnamese, 1100 GMT, 10 June 1990, *FBIS-EAS*, 90-118, 19 June 1990, p. 60.

243. Hanoi Domestic Service in Vietnamese, 1100 GMT, 8 June 1990, *FBIS-EAS*, 90-114, 13 June 1990, pp. 57–58.
244. Hanoi Domestic Service in Vietnamese, 1100 GMT, 4 June 1990, *FBIS-EAS*, 90-112, 11 June 1990, pp. 57–58.
245. Hanoi Vietnamese News Agency in English, 0711 GMT, 3 July 1990, *FBIS-EAS*, 90-129, 5 July 1990, pp. 72–73; *Nhan Dan*, 12 July 1990, pp. 3–4.
246. Hanoi Vietnamese News Agency in English, 0500 GMT, 25 August 1990, *FBIS-EAS*, 90-129, 28 August 1990, p. 59.
247. Hanoi Vietnamese News Agency in English, 2300 GMT, 13 September 1990, *FBIS-EAS*, 90-179, 14 September 1990, pp. 68–69; Hanoi Vietnamese News Agency in English, 1100 GMT, 24 September 1990, *FBIS-EAS*, 90-189, 24 September 1990, p. 56.
248. *Saigon Giai Phong*, 17 August 1990, p. 1; Hanoi Vietnamese News Agency in English, 1430 GMT, 23 September 1990, *FBIS-EAS*, 90-185, 24 September 1990, p. 65; Hong Kong AFP in English, 1020 GMT, 19 September 1990, *FBIS-EAS*, 90-182, 19 September 1990, p. 72; Hanoi Vietnamese News Agency in English, 1430 GMT, 15 September 1990, *FBIS-EAS*, 90-182, 19 September 1990, pp. 72–73; Hong Kong AFP in English, 0907 GMT, 7 October 1990, *FBIS-EAS*, 90-195, 9 October 1990, pp. 66–67; Hanoi Vietnamese News Agency in English, 1430 GMT, 7 October 1990, *FBIS-EAS*, 90-196, 10 October 1990, p. 59; Hanoi Vietnamese News Agency in English, 1100 GMT, 16 October 1990, *FBIS-EAS*, 90-201, 17 October 1990, pp. 67–68; William Branigan, "Hanoi Tries 38 Accused of Trying to Invade Vietnam", *Washington Post*, 11 October 1990, p. A. 32.
249. *Nhan Dan*, 7 January 1991, pp. 1, 4.
250. *Nhan Dan*, 12 January 1991, pp. 1, 4.
251. Hanoi Domestic Service in Vietnamese, 1430 GMT, 24 February 1991, *FBIS-EAS*, 91-038, 26 February 1991, pp. 39–40.
252. *Nhan Dan*, 7 January 1991, pp. 1, 4.
253. Hanoi Domestic Service in Vietnamese, 1100 GMT, 4 March 1991, and Hanoi Vietnam Television Network in Vietnamese, 1200 GMT, 3 March 1991, *FBIS-EAS*, 6 March 1991, p. 59.
254. Hanoi Domestic Service in Vietnamese, 2300 GMT, 4 March 1991, *FBIS-EAS*, 91-044, 6 March 1991, p. 58.
255. Hong Kong AFP in English, 1943 GMT, 28 February 1991, *FBIS-EAS*,

91-041, 1 March 1991, pp. 54–55; Interview with Ministry of Foreign Affairs official, April 1991; Hanoi Domestic Service in Vietnamese, 1100 GMT, 4 March 1991, *FBIS-EAS*, 91-044, 6 March 1991, p. 59, for example, which reports that for the first round of congresses, Vinh Phu had collected 48,000 suggestions to the Draft Platform for Building the Nation in the Period of the Transition to Socialism and 26,000 suggestions regarding the Draft Strategy for Socio-economic Stabilization and Development.

256. Hanoi Domestic Service in Vietnamese, 1430 GMT, 12 March 1991, *FBIS-EAS*, 91-050, 14 March 1991, p. 57. Hanoi Domestic Service in Vietnamese, 1400 GMT, 11 March 1991, *FBIS-EAS*, 91-050, 14 March 1991, p. 56 recounts the process in Song Be Province.
257. Hanoi Domestic Service in Vietnamese, 2300 GMT, 12 March 1991, *FBIS-EAS*, 91-050, 14 March 1991, pp. 56–57; Hanoi Domestic Service in Vietnamese, 0500 GMT, 14 March 1991, *FBIS-EAS*, 92-051, 15 March 1991, p. 68.
258. Hanoi Domestic Service in Vietnamese, 1400 GMT, 11 March 1991, *FBIS-EAS*, 91-050, 14 March 1991, p. 56; Hanoi Domestic Service in Vietnamese, 1000 GMT, 18 March 1991, *FBIS-EAS*, 91-053, 19 March 1991, pp. 72–73.
259. Hanoi Vietnam Television Network in Vietnamese, 1200 GMT, 17 March 1991, *FBIS-EAS*, 91-055, 21 March 1991, p. 70; Hanoi Domestic Service in Vietnamese, 2300 GMT, 28 March 1991, *FBIS-EAS*, 91-062, 1 April 1991, p. 45.
260. Hanoi Domestic Service in Vietnamese, 1100 GMT, 10 April 1991, *FBIS-EAS*, 91-073, 16 April 1991, p. 53; Hanoi Vietnamese Television Network in Vietnamese, 1200 GMT, 20 March 1991, *FBIS-EAS*, 91-073, 16 April 1991, pp. 53–54; Hanoi Domestic Service in Vietnamese, 1400 GMT, 1 April 1991, *FBIS-EAS*, 91-074, 17 April 1991, pp. 71–72.
261. Hanoi Domestic Service in Vietnamese, 2300 GMT, 4 May 1991, *FBIS-EAS*, 91-091, 10 May 1991, p. 63.
262. Hanoi Voice of Vietnam Network in Vietnamese, 2300 GMT, 28 April 1991, *FBIS-EAS*, 91-099, 22 May 1991, p. 52.
263. Hanoi Voice of Vietnam Network in Vietnamese, 2300 GMT, 22 April 1991, *FBIS-EAS*, 91-098, 21 May 1991, p. 64.
264. Hanoi Voice of Vietnam Network in Vietnamese, 2300 GMT, 1 May 1991, *FBIS-EAS*, 91-100, 23 May 1991, p. 58.

Notes

265. Hanoi Voice of Vietnam Network in Vietnamese, 2300 GMT, 22 April 1991, *FBIS-EAS*, 91-098, 21 May 1991, p. 64.
266. Hanoi Vietnamese Television Network in Vietnamese, 1200 GMT, 2 May 1991, *FBIS-EAS*, 91-091, 10 May 1991, p. 64.
267. Hanoi Voice of Vietnam Network in Vietnamese, 2300 GMT, 28 April 1991, *FBIS-EAS*, 91-099, 22 May 1991, p. 52.
268. Hanoi Voice of Vietnam Network in Vietnamese, 2300 GMT, 1 May 1991, *FBIS-EAS*, 91-100, 23 May 1991, p. 58.
269. Hanoi Domestic Service in Vietnamese, 1430 GMT, 29 April 1991, *FBIS-EAS*, 91-091, 10 May 1991, p. 65.
270. Hanoi Vietnamese Television Network in Vietnamese, 1200 GMT, 7 May 1991, *FBIS-EAS*, 91-091, 10 May 1991, p. 65; Hanoi Voice of Vietnam Network in Vietnamese, 1200 GMT, 3 May 1991, *FBIS-EAS*, 91-091, 10 May 1991, p. 64.
271. Hanoi Voice of Vietnam Network in Vietnamese, 2300 GMT, 1 May 1991, *FBIS-EAS*, 91-100, 23 May 1991, p. 58; Hanoi Domestic Service in Vietnamese, 1100 GMT, 29 April 1991, *FBIS-EAS*, 91-091, 10 May 1991, p. 65.
272. Hanoi Domestic Service in Vietnamese, 1100 GMT, 29 April 1991, *FBIS-EAS*, 91-091, 10 May 1991, p. 65; Hanoi Voice of Vietnam Network in Vietnamese, 2300 GMT, 24 April 1991, *FBIS-EAS*, 91-099, 22 May 1991, p. 53.
273. For example, see Hanoi Domestic Service in Vietnamese, 2330 GMT, 31 March 1991, *FBIS-EAS*, 91-078, 23 April 1991, p. 65.
274. *Saigon Giai Phong*, 3 March 1991.
275. Hanoi Domestic Service in Vietnamese, 1100 GMT, 29 April 1991, *FBIS-EAS*, 91-085, 2 May 1991, p. 62.
276. See "Vietnam: Draft Political Report", Daily Report Supplement, *FBIS-EAS*, 91-080-S, 25 April 1991, pp. 1–24.
277. *Tap Chi Cong San*, June 1991, pp. 2–4; Hanoi Voice of Vietnam Network in Vietnamese, 0228 GMT, 26 June 1991, *FBIS-EAS*, 91-123-S, 26 June 1991, pp. 15–18.
278. Hanoi Domestic Service in Vietnamese, 2300 GMT, 13 January 1991, *FBIS-EAS*, 91-009, 14 January 1991, pp. 56–57.
279. Hanoi Voice of Vietnam Network in Vietnamese, 1100 GMT, 29 May 1991, *FBIS-EAS*, 91-104, 30 May 1991, pp. 67–68.
280. Hanoi Voice of Vietnam Network in Vietnamese, 0228 GMT, 24 June 1991, *FBIS-EAS*, 91-123-S, 26 June 1991, p. 19.

281. *Nhan Dan*, 30 May 1991 editorial, p. 1.
282. Hanoi Domestic Service in Vietnamese, 1100 GMT, 6 April 1991, *FBIS-EAS*, 91-080-S, 25 April 1991, pp. 21–22.
283. See, for example, Hanoi Vietnamese News Agency in English, 0735 GMT, 22 January 1991, *FBIS-EAS*, 91-014, 22 January 1991, p. 55.
284. Hanoi Domestic Service in Vietnamese, 1100 GMT, 6 April 1991, *FBIS-EAS*, 91-080-S, 25 April 1991, p. 22; *Nhan Dan*, 29 January 1991, pp. 1,4, *FBIS-EAS*, 91-033, 19 February 1991, pp. 53–54; Hanoi Domestic Service in Vietnamese, 1100 GMT, 6 April 1990, *FBIS-EAS*, 90-080-S, 25 April 1991, pp. 21–22.
285. Hanoi Domestic Service in Vietnamese, 1100 GMT, 6 April 1991, *FBIS-EAS*, 90-080-S, 25 April 1991, pp. 21–22.
286. Hanoi Voice of Vietnam Network in Vietnamese, 1430 GMT, 23 June 1991, *FBIS-EAS*, 91-123-S, 26 June 1991, p. 6; Murray Hiebert, "More of the Same", *Far Eastern Economic Review*, 11 July 1991, p. 11.
287. Hanoi Vietnamese News Agency in English, 1514 GMT, 27 June 1991, *FBIS-EAS*, 91-027-S, 2 July 1991, p. 19.
288. Hanoi Voice of Vietnam Network in Vietnamese, 1100 GMT, 24 June 1991, *FBIS-EAS*, 91-123-S, 26 June 1991, p. 11. Also see Hanoi Voice of Vietnam Network in Vietnamese, 1100 GMT, 24 June 1991, *FBIS-EAS*, 91-123-S, 26 June 1991, p. 3, and Hong Kong AFP in English, 1420 GMT, 23 June 1991, *FBIS-EAS*, 91-123-S, 26 June 1991, p. 7.
289. Hanoi Voice of Vietnam Network in Vietnamese, 0205 GMT, 24 June 1991, *FBIS-EAS*, 91-123-S, 26 June 1991, p. 15.
290. Hanoi Voice of Vietnam Network in Vietnamese, 1400 GMT, 25 June 1991, *FBIS-EAS*, 91-127-S, 2 July 1991, pp. 3–5.
291. Hanoi Voice of Vietnam Network in Vietnamese, 1100 GMT, 28 June 1991, *FBIS-EAS*, 91-133-S, 11 July 1991, p. 10.
292. Hanoi Voice of Vietnam Network in Vietnamese, 1100 GMT, 27 June 1991, *FBIS-EAS*, 91-127-S, 2 July 1991, p. 27.
293. Murray Hiebert, "More of the Same", pp. 10–11.
294. Hanoi Vietnam Television Network in Vietnamese, 0228 GMT, 24 June 1991, *FBIS-EAS*, 91-123-S, 26 June 1991, p. 1.
295. Hanoi Vietnam Television Network in Vietnamese, 1430 GMT, 24 June 1991, *FBIS-EAS*, 91-127-S, 2 July 1991, p. 1.

296. Hanoi Voice of Vietnam Network in Vietnamese, 1100 GMT, 26 June 1991, *FBIS-EAS*, 91-133-S, 11 July 1991, p. 4.
297. Hanoi Voice of Vietnam Network in Vietnamese, 1100 GMT, 1 July 1991, *FBIS-EAS*, 91-129, 5 July 1991, p. 53.
298. *Saigon Giai Phong*, 26 June 1991, pp. 1, 3.
299. Hanoi Voice of Vietnam Network in Vietnamese, 1100 GMT, 3 July 1991, *FBIS-EAS*, 91-133, 11 July 1991, p. 55.
300. Hanoi Voice of Vietnam Network in Vietnamese, 0500 GMT, 28 June 1991, *FBIS-EAS*, 91-133-S, 11 July 1991, p. 9.
301. Hanoi Voice of Vietnam Network in Vietnamese, 1100 GMT, 26 June 1991, *FBIS-EAS*, 91-133-S, 11 July 1991, pp. 4, 6; and Hanoi Voice of Vietnam Network in Vietnamese, 1100 GMT, 1 July 1991, *FBIS-EAS*, 91-129, 5 July 1991, p. 53.
302. Hanoi Voice of Vietnam in English, 1000 GMT, 25 July 1991, *FBIS-EAS*, 91-127-S, 2 July 1991; *Nhan Dan*, 1 July 1991, p. 2.
303. Hanoi Vietnamese News Agency in English, 1445 GMT, 26 June 1991, *FBIS-EAS*, 91-127-S, 2 July 1991, p. 10.
304. Hanoi Voice of Vietnam Network in Vietnamese, 0500 GMT, 27 June 1991, *FBIS-EAS*, 91-133-S, 11 July 1991, pp. 6–8; Hanoi Voice of Vietnam Network in Vietnamese, 0500 GMT, 28 June 1991, *FBIS-EAS*, 91-133-S, 11 July 1991, pp. 8–9, 9–10.
305. Hanoi Voice of Vietnam Network in Vietnamese, 1430 GMT, 23 June 1991, *FBIS-EAS*, 91-123-S, 11 July 1991, p. 6.
306. References to Linh's speech, cited on pp. 161–68 above, are from Hanoi Vietnam Television Network in Vietnamese, 0228 GMT, 24 June 1991, *FBIS-EAS*, 91-123-S, 26 June 1991, pp. 15–28.

Note on Terminology

Article 24, Chapter Five, of the Party Statutes, revised in 1991, defines the basic units, or the foundations of the party, in the following manner:

> The basic party chapters and basic party organizations (generally known as basic organizations of the party) form the foundation of the party. Each basic unit (village, ward, town, organ, co-operative, enterprise, corporation, school, hospital, scientific research institute, and each of the basic units in the armed forces and other basic units) with three or more regular party members can establish a party chapter. If a basic unit has less than three regular party members, a higher party committee echelon can introduce these party members directly to a nearby basic party organization to carry out party activities.
>
> A basic unit or a component of a basic unit (a workship of an enterprise, a hamlet in a village, a department of a school, and so forth) with 30 or more party members can establish several party chapters to be directly subordinate to a basic party committee.
>
> A basic party committee must inform and seek approval from the next higher party committee echelon when it wants to:
> - Organize several party chapters on one basic unit or in a component of a basic unit have less than 30 party members;

- establish only one party chapter in a basic unit or in a component of a basic unit having more than 50 party members;
- establish a component party organization in a basic party organization.

This book uses the terms "basic party organizations", "local party organizations", and "sectoral party organizations" to draw distinctions between the types of fundamental party entities, and employs the terminology used by the party itself to distinguish between basic units (sometimes referred to as primary cells), basic party organizations (sometimes referred to as primary party organizations), party chapters, and party committees. See *Tap Chi Cong San*, July 1991, pp. 40–49 for the Statutes of the Vietnamese Communist Party adopted by the Seventh National Congress of Party Delegates on 27 June 1991. Also see Dang Lao Dong Viet Nam, *Dieu Le*, (Hanoi: Ban Chap Hanh Trung Uong, 1968), p. 43; *Nhan Dan*, 3 February 1977, pp. 2–5; Dang Cong San Viet Nam, *Dieu Le*, (Hanoi: Nha Xuat Ban Su That, 1987); Charles N. Spinks, John C. Durr, and Stephen Peters, *The North Vietnamese Regime: Institutions and Problems*, (Washington, D.C.: The American University Center for Research and Social Systems, April 1969), pp. 4–9; Dang Cong San Viet Nam, *Cac To Chuc Tien Than Cua Dang*, (Hanoi: Ban Nghien Cuu Lich Su Dang Trung Uong Xuat Ban, 1977), pp. 345–52; Robert F. Turner, *Vietnamese Communism: Its Origins and Development*, (Stanford, California: Hoover Institution Press, 1975), pp. 115, 117.

Lewis M. Stern, Ph.D., is Director for Indochina, Thailand and Burma in the Office of the Assistant Secretary of Defense for Regional Security Affairs, United States Government.